Paulo Freire in the 21st Century

Interventions: Education, Philosophy & Culture
Michael A. Peters & Colin Lankshear, Series Editors

Education, Globalization, and the State in the Age of Terrorism
edited by Michael A. Peters (2005)

Beyond Learning: Democratic Education for a Human Future
by Gert J. J. Biesta (2006)

Toward an Imperfect Education: Facing Humanity, Rethinking Cosmopolitanism
by Sharon Todd (2009)

*Good Education in an Age of Measurement:
Ethics, Politics, Democracy*
by Gert J. J. Biesta (2010)

*Paulo Freire in the 21st Century:
Education, Dialogue, and Transformation*
by Peter Roberts (2010)

Paulo Freire in the 21st Century

Education, Dialogue, and Transformation

Peter Roberts

Paradigm Publishers
Boulder • London

All rights reserved. No part of this publication may be transmitted or reproduced in any media or form, including electronic, mechanical, photocopy, recording, or informational storage and retrieval systems, without the express written consent of the publisher.

Copyright © 2013 by Paradigm Publishers

Published in the United States by Paradigm Publishers, 5589 Arapahoe Avenue, Boulder, CO 80303 USA.

Paradigm Publishers is the trade name of Birkenkamp & Company, LLC, Dean Birkenkamp, President and Publisher.

Library of Congress Cataloging-in-Publication Data

Roberts, Peter, 1963–
  Paulo Freire in the 21st century : education, dialogue, and transformation / Peter Roberts.
    p. cm. — (Interventions. Education, philosophy & culture)
  Includes bibliographical references and index.
  978-1-54951-681-8 (paperback : alk paper) 1. Freire, Paulo, 1921–1997. 2. Education—Philosophy. 3. Education—Political aspects. 4. Education—Aims and objectives. 5. Critical pedagogy. 6. Literacy. I. Title.
  LB880.F732R623 2010
  370.1—dc22
                                                                        2009036341

Printed and bound in the United States of America on acid-free paper that meets the standards of the American National Standard for Permanence of Paper for Printed Library Materials.

Designed and Typeset by Straight Creek Bookmakers.

17 16 15 14 13   5 4 3 2 1

Contents

Preface and Acknowledgments		*vii*
Introduction		1
1	Pedagogy, Politics, and Intellectual Life: Freire in the Twenty-First Century	13
2	Reason and Emotion in Freire's Work	31
3	Freire and the Problem of Defining Literacy	51
4	Freire and Political Correctness	65
5	Critical Literacy, Breadth of Perspective, and the University Curriculum: A Freirean Perspective	83
6	Freire and Dostoevsky: Uncertainty, Dialogue, and Transformation	105
7	Conscientization in Castalia: A Freirean Reading of Hermann Hesse's *The Glass Bead Game*	121
8	Bridging East and West: Freire and the *Tao Te Ching*	141
References		*161*
Index		*179*
Credits		*189*
About the Author		*191*

Preface and Acknowledgments

Paulo Freire is a complex pedagogical thinker, and his work demands ongoing reflection and discussion. Although the years following Freire's death in 1997 have brought new problems and challenges, Freirean ideas appear to be as relevant today as they ever have been. Over the past twelve years, numerous books and papers on Freire's theory and practice have been published, and this interest shows no signs of waning in the foreseeable future. Freire's written words have continued to live on long after his death, with a number of books being released posthumously.

This book is intended to complement an earlier volume, *Education, Literacy, and Humanization* (Roberts, 2000), in which I attempted to provide a comprehensive, critical examination of Freire's philosophy and pedagogy. The present text continues the theoretical work undertaken in *Education, Literacy, and Humanization,* but in a more selective way and with a more applied focus. Here, Freire's ideas are put into conversation with other thinkers and with some of the educational questions, issues, and debates that have shaped our age.

I first encountered Freire's ideas more than a quarter of a century ago. At that time, I found his educational philosophy engaging and thought provoking. I continue to find surprises in his writings today. Freire's work has its weaknesses, and these must be acknowledged, but no one theorist can provide all the answers to pedagogical questions. Freire is, then, just one part of a larger educational journey.

Among the many people who have helped me on my way, I would especially like to thank the colleagues and students with whom I have worked at the University of Waikato, the University of Auckland, and the University of Canterbury over the past twenty-two years. I am grateful to Dean Birkenkamp for supporting the publication of this book with Paradigm. Ann Hopman's assistance has also been invaluable. Finally, I wish to acknowledge the love and encouragement of my wife, Linda, and our children, Ben and Emma, without whom this book would not have been possible.

Introduction

When Paulo Freire died in May 1997, he was arguably in his intellectual prime. Having first gained international recognition for his work in adult literacy programs in Brazil and Chile in the 1960s and for the publication of his classic text *Pedagogy of the Oppressed* (Freire, 1972a), Freire had, in the last decade of his life, enjoyed a strong "second wind" of publishing activity. He averaged more than a book a year in this period. In his sixties, Freire had also become active in Brazilian politics again. His work has continued to generate interest and debate in the years following his death. Since 1997, Freire has provided the focus for a considerable number of authored books and edited collections (e.g., Coben, 1998; O'Cadiz, Wong, and Torres, 1998; Mayo, 1999, 2004; Roberts, 1999, ed., 2000; McLaren, 2000; Dallaire, 2001; Darder, 2002; Morrow and Torres, 2002; Slater, Fain, and Rossatto, 2002; Bowers and Apffel-Marglin, 2005; Rossatto, 2005; Torres and Noguera, 2008), along with numerous conference papers and journal articles.

As was already apparent from earlier edited collections (e.g., Shor, 1987; McLaren and Leonard, 1993; McLaren and Lankshear, 1994), Freire's work provides fertile territory for reflection and investigation from a variety of perspectives and disciplines. Over the last twelve years, Freirean ideas have continued to be engaged and applied in a wide range of different scholarly and practical domains. These have included science education (dos Santos, 2008), participatory action research (Guishard, 2009), systems research and behavioral science (Mejía, 2004; Mejía and Espinosa, 2007), applied psychology (Burton and Kagan, 2005), educational gerontology (Findsen, 2007), autophotography (Armstrong, 2005), ecological education (Gruenewald,

2003; Kahn, 2006a), spirituality and education (Dallaire, 2001), prison education (Baird, 1999), and health education (Rindner, 2004), among other areas of inquiry.

This book aims to make a distinctive contribution to the ever expanding literature on Freire's work. It addresses a number of themes, questions, and issues that have received relatively little attention to date, including Freire's conception of the critical intellectual, Freire and the problem of defining literacy, and the possibility of a Freirean response to debates over political correctness. The book also puts Freire's ideas into conversation with writers seldom considered by other Freirean scholars: Israel Scheffler, Fyodor Dostoevsky, and Hermann Hesse, among others. The book explores some of the implications of Freirean theory for educational practice (e.g., in relation to university reading requirements), compares aspects of his educational thought with elements of Taoism, and shows how Freire can be helpful in crossing literary and philosophical genres of writing. Although some commentators continue to concentrate on classic earlier works such as *Pedagogy of the Oppressed* (Freire, 1972a), this book makes extensive reference to Freire's later (post-1986) publications.

Freire's Life and Work

Most educationists have some familiarity with Freire's biography. Freire was born in 1921 in Recife, Brazil, to a middle-class family. After struggling through the years of the Great Depression, he later excelled in his studies and was able to assist other secondary school students with their learning of Portuguese grammar. After leaving school, Freire enrolled at the University of Recife as a law student but became increasingly interested in educational and philosophical questions. He married Elza Oliveira in his twenties and spent a decade working for the Social Service of Industry in Pernambuco. In this position, Freire began to formulate his pedagogical ideas, working with impoverished adults in popular education programs. Freire's success in adult literacy initiatives in the early 1960s led to his appointment as director of the Cultural Extension Service at the University of Recife and later to his role as director of a national literacy program. The military coup in 1964 brought the campaign to a halt, and Freire was arrested as a subversive.

INTRODUCTION

The next fifteen years were spent in exile, principally in Chile (where Freire became involved with the Chilean Agrarian Reform Corporation) and Geneva (where he served with the World Council of Churches). Freire wrote *Education: The Practice of Freedom* (1976), also published under the title *Education for Critical Consciousness*, in the 1960s, but it was the release of *Pedagogy of the Oppressed* (1972a) in English in 1970 that brought Freire into international prominence. Freire's experience in Chile had an important bearing on the shift from the liberal framework evident in the former work to the more radical political orientation of *Pedagogy of the Oppressed* (Holst, 2006). Freire's other book from this early period, *Cultural Action for Freedom* (1972b), emerged from a year he spent at Harvard University. In the 1970s Freire also published *Pedagogy in Process* (1978), based on his work in Guinea Bissau. Freire played a consultative role in adult literacy initiatives in São Tomé and Príncipe, Grenada, and Nicaragua, among other countries. He returned to Brazil in 1980 and later became an important figure in the Brazilian Workers Party. He served as secretary of education in the São Paulo Municipal Bureau of Education from 1989 to 1991 (see Torres, 1994a; O'Cadiz, Wong, and Torres, 1998; Weiner, 2003). Following the death of his first wife, Elza, Freire married Ana Maria Araújo, a friend from childhood.

After a relatively quiet period as a writer from the mid-1970s to the mid-1980s, the publication of two coauthored "talking" books in 1987—one, *A Pedagogy for Liberation*, with Ira Shor (Freire and Shor, 1987), the other, *Literacy: Reading the Word and the World*, with Donaldo Macedo (Freire and Macedo, 1987)—marked the beginning of a new phase of intense intellectual activity. Freire went on to publish other dialogical volumes with Antonio Faundez (Freire and Faundez, 1989) and Myles Horton (Horton and Freire, 1990), among others. Other books from the 1990s, some of which were published posthumously, included *Pedagogy of the City* (Freire, 1993), *Pedagogy of Hope* (Freire, 1994), *Paulo Freire on Higher Education* (Escobar, Fernandez, Guevara-Niebla, and Freire, 1994), *Letters to Cristina* (Freire, 1996), *Pedagogy of the Heart* (Freire, 1997a), *Teachers as Cultural Workers* (Freire, 1998a), *Pedagogy of Freedom* (Freire, 1998b), *Politics and Education* (Freire, 1998c), and *Critical Education in the New Information Age* (Castells, Flecha, Freire, Giroux, Macedo, and Willis, 1999). Further works—notably, *Pedagogy of Indignation* (Freire, 2004) and *Daring to Dream* (Freire, 2007)—have appeared in more recent years.

Key Educational Ideas

Freire's educational theory grew out of his practical experiences as an adult educator in a number of Third World countries. Although Freire lectured all over the world, he always saw himself as a man of the Third World, with a particular concern for the deep social problems in his native Brazil (Roberts, 1996a). As Ira Shor (1998) points out, Freire might have been known as a world philosopher whose influence extended across the globe, but it was only in Brazil that he felt fully at home. There, his work had a concreteness that could not be fully attained elsewhere. Freire's effectiveness as an adult literacy educator was attributable not just to his technical competence but also to his recognition that teaching and learning are political processes (Mayo, 1997; Roberts, 2008a). The political nature of education is evident in the views both teachers and students bring with them to a learning situation, in the *way* teaching and learning occur, in the forms of assessment and evaluation conducted, in the funding arrangements for an educational process, in the physical layout of a teaching and learning environment, in what appears and does not appear in the curriculum, in the justifications provided for education, in the reading and writing completed or recommended, in the value (or lack of it) placed on credentials and qualifications, in the language of instruction, and in the government policies that frame the learning process, among other ways. Indeed, in the latter part of his career, Freire came to believe that education *is* politics (Freire and Shor, 1987; Shor, 1993). Social and economic structures never completely *determine* what occurs in individual sites of educational activity, but they set limits on what becomes possible—indeed, on what is even *envisaged* as legitimate and worthwhile—in teaching and learning.

Freire learned, partly through his own mistakes, the importance of connecting education with lived experience. He encouraged illiterate adults in poor urban and rural communities to reflect on themselves and their social world. The words that formed the basis of his literacy programs were intimately connected with the existential reality of the participants (see Freire, 1972b, 1976). Thus, terms such as *tijolo* (brick) or *favela* (slum) might serve as the first words in working with a group of urban adult learners. Freire fostered a spirit of dialogue among participants, prompting educational conversations with "generative" (charged, connotative) words and pictorial representations of everyday Brazilian life. Experience provided the starting point for learning, but as participants moved through an educational program, initial readings of reality would be increasingly problematized and reinterpreted. Freire himself was to undertake a similar process throughout his career, deepening and extending his ideas as he gained more practical experience and published additional books. His dialogues with the coauthors of his "talking" books were pivotal in pushing him to consider new theoretical questions, problems, and perspectives. Freire remained, by his own account, "constantly curious" and never stopped asking questions of himself, his areas of study, and those with whom he worked.

As discussed more fully elsewhere (e.g., Roberts, 1998, 2000), Freire's educational ideas are inseparable from his ontology, epistemology, and ethic. Freire's understanding of the nature of reality owes much to the work of Marx and, to a lesser extent, Hegel (Torres, 1994b; Allman, 1999). Freire's educational philosophy also draws on liberalism (in his earlier work), existentialism, phenomenology, critical theory, radical Catholicism, and, in his later publications, aspects of postmodernism (Mackie, 1980; Mayo, 1999; Morrow and Torres, 2002). Freire stresses the dialectical relationship between "consciousness" and "world." Humans, as conscious beings, are capable of reflecting on their world, of imagining that it might be otherwise, and of changing it. But the world we create through conscious practical activity also "acts back on us," influencing the way we think, feel, and respond to others. Reality—the physical world, the social world, and the *inner* world of thought, emotion, and experience—is in constant motion. The ontological core of Freire's philosophy is the ideal of humanization, or becoming more fully human (Freire, 1972a). We humanize ourselves when we engage in critical, dialogical praxis; we *de*humanize others (and ourselves) when we actively impede the pursuit of this vocation. Humanization is a necessarily incomplete process. *Knowing*, similarly, is never complete. For Freire, knowing involves striving to come closer to the essence that explains the object of study, while nonetheless accepting that as reality changes, further reflection, investigation, and relearning will need to occur. Knowledge, on the Freirean view, arises not from isolated, individual, abstract, purely theoretical activity but through dialogue, human practice, and engagement with the messy realities of everyday life.

Freire saw oppression, in its myriad forms across the globe, as a defining theme of the twentieth century. Oppression represents the concrete manifestation of dehumanization. It is possible to speak of oppressive structures, policies, ideologies, and actions. Liberation, for Freire, consists not in reaching some contented end point; rather, it involves, in part, a constant process of *struggle* against conditions of oppression. Education, Freire maintained, can play a role in both perpetuating and resisting oppressive practices and ideas. In *Pedagogy of the Oppressed* (Freire, 1972a) and other early works, Freire distinguished between "banking education" and "problem-posing education." The former is oppressive in character and involves a narrating subject (the teacher) depositing information into docile, obedient objects (students). Banking education suppresses criticism and questioning, denies the value of experience in the learning process, treats reality and knowledge as static, and hinders the consideration of alternative ways of understanding the world. Problem-posing education, by contrast, is a dialogical, critical, liberating approach to education. It begins with the posing of problems rather than the issuing of answers; it builds on, but does not celebrate uncritically, the existing knowledge of learners; and it welcomes questions, discussion, and constructive debate.

In later writings, Freire deepened and extended these ideas, stressing the importance of structure, direction, and rigor in educational dialogue, and delineating in greater detail some of the distinguishing features of a critical mode of being (see further, Freire, 1996, 1997a, 1997b, 1998a, 1998b, 1998c, 2004, 2007; Freire and Shor, 1987; Freire and Faundez, 1989; Horton and Freire, 1990). Freire evolved as a writer and thinker, while also striving for consistency and coherence (cf. Schugurensky, 1998). He sought to clarify his views on teacher-student relations, making it very clear, for example, that he saw himself as a teacher and not merely a facilitator (Freire and Macedo, 1995; cf. also, Bartlett, 2005). He showed that he supported neither an "anything goes" nor an authoritarian approach to education (Freire and Shor, 1987). He stressed that he did not have a "method," or even a set of methods, that could be transported without change from one educational situation to the next. Instead, Freire noted repeatedly, attention must be paid to the specificities of pedagogical contexts; the methods that will be appropriate in one context will differ from those that might be best in another. (On the "methods fetish," see also Aronowitz, 1993; Bartolome, 1994; Macedo, 1997.) From the later publications, a more complex view of liberation also emerged: one tied not just to the struggle against oppression but to the development of key virtues (see Roberts, 2008b). Some of these virtues will be identified and discussed at length in the chapters that follow.

The Purpose and Structure of this Book

As noted in the Preface and Acknowledgments, this book builds on and extends the work undertaken for an earlier volume: *Education, Literacy, and Humanization: Exploring the Work of Paulo Freire* (Roberts, 2000). My intention in *Education, Literacy, and Humanization* had been to provide a detailed analysis of Freire's ontology, ethic, epistemology, and educational theory. Attention was paid to Freire's approach to adult literacy education in Brazil, and a number of critiques of Freire's work were outlined and assessed. Here the focus is more applied, and the range of themes addressed has been broadened.

Ira Shor has been an international leader in applying Freirean ideas to practical educational problems (Shor, 1980, 1987, 1992, 1996). Shor must be acknowledged not just for his work *on* Freire but also for his work *with* Freire. His influence on the development of Freire's thought is readily apparent in *A Pedagogy for Liberation* (Freire and Shor, 1987). It was in that text that many of the pedagogical issues Freire was to address over the last decade of his life are first confronted. *A Pedagogy for Liberation* is, in many respects, a model of carefully structured applied analysis. The present volume owes much to Shor, even if the approach taken is somewhat different. In several chapters, a comparative methodology has been adopted. The value of critical comparative work has been demonstrated by a number of other scholars in the years following Freire's death (e.g., Mayo, 1999, 2007; Malcolm, 1999; Ng, 2000; Ledwith, 2001; Morrow and Torres, 2002; Kahn and Kellner, 2007; Shim, 2007). This book, in part, represents an attempt to develop this tradition further, by bridging different genres and bodies of scholarly work in ways that have hitherto remained underdeveloped.

Some of the limits of the inquiry undertaken in the chapters that follow should be noted. First, to avoid unnecessary overlap with my earlier work (particularly, but not exclusively, Roberts, 2000), this book will not provide an in-depth, systematic account of Freire's philosophy and pedagogy. Brief comments on Freire's key educational ideas have been made previously in this introduction, but these are intended to serve only as a preliminary orientation to his thought.

Insightful book-length critical discussions of Freire's educational theory can be found elsewhere (among more recent texts, see, for example, Mayo, 1999, 2004; McLaren, 2000; Morrow and Torres, 2002; Darder, 2002; Rossatto, 2005). Second, the book will not be concerned with elaborating and defending a particular methodology in studying Freire's work; anything the book has to offer in this regard will be implied rather than explained. Third, I have not set out to consider or address, in an extended way, major critiques of Freire's work. I have made a start on this task in earlier publications (e.g., Roberts, 1996b, 1996c, 1999, ed., 2000, 2003a, 2003b, 2008b), and there is plenty of scope for ongoing reflection on strengths and weaknesses in both Freire's arguments and those of his critics. Freire welcomed constructive criticism and sought to regard this as an opportunity to strengthen his understanding of the philosophical, political, and pedagogical issues raised by his work. Rigorous, respectful *engagement* with the ideas is the key (or one of the keys) to a meaningful encounter with Freire's educational philosophy, and this can take many forms. Applying Freirean ideas to a range of theoretical and practical problems and issues, and putting Freire into conversation with other thinkers, while also drawing attention to some of the limitations of his work, is one of those forms. This is the approach undertaken in the present volume.

A brief comment on the spirit in which this book is written is in order. As we shall see in later chapters, Freire placed great importance on virtues such as humility, tolerance, open-mindedness, care for those with whom we work, an investigative and searching frame of mind, and political commitment. Above all, he stressed the need for love in education: love of the students being taught, of the subject being studied, and of life itself. This included the whole of life, not just a love for one's fellow human beings, but for all other living creatures and for the wider natural environment of which we are a part. There is anger, of a kind, in some of Freire's publications (e.g., Freire, 2004), but there is also a certain intellectual gentleness, built on an ethic of love, that can be detected throughout his writing career. This quality has sometimes been lacking in debates over his ideas. Freire's concept of educational dialogue is complex, multilayered, and not without its problems (cf. Walker, 1980; Ellsworth, 1989; Weiler, 1991; Freedman, 2007), but on one point we can be reasonably certain: Mean-spirited, vitriolic responses from one scholar to another's work are at odds with the ideal Freire had in mind. To write or speak to another scholar with an underlying attitude of hostility and aggression is, from a Freirean perspective, a moment of sadness (Freire would not have been afraid to stress the emotional content of such situations) and a difficult starting point for productive intellectual discussion. Dialogue of the kind Freire envisaged presupposes a willingness to listen, to enter into an educational conversation not in a dogmatic or reactionary manner but with humble respect for the Other.

There is such a rich body of academic work on Freirean themes, that anyone encountering scholarship in this area might at first not know where to begin. Freire provides some signposts for an attitude that might underpin that journey, without prescribing in precise existential detail the end that must be reached. This hints at one way of characterizing a relationship to Freire as a thinker. Freirean commentators have sometimes been cast, in effect, as either enemies or disciples, in a fashion that would seem unusual when considering those who engage the writings of, say, Michel Foucault or Jacques Derrida. Neither uncritical acceptance nor wholesale rejection are adequate responses to Freire's philosophy and pedagogy. I have never regarded myself as a "follower" of Freire but rather as a fellow traveler: one who finds agreement with him in some areas, disagreement in others, and a need for theoretical and practical sustenance from other sources in addressing some educational questions. Freire is just one of the many teachers from whom we might learn something worthwhile, and this book is but a small contribution to the ongoing conversation on his work.

Chapter 1 addresses Freire's stance on the roles and responsibilities of the critical intellectual. The chapter concentrates on key questions and issues raised in one of the more recent books to appear under Freire's name: *Pedagogy of Indignation* (2004). Freire's ideal is considered in the light of wider critiques of universalism and vanguardism in Marxist and Maoist portraits of the intellectual. A comparison is drawn with Foucault's notion of the specific intellectual. The chapter attempts to demonstrate the significance of the links among education, politics, and intellectual activity in Freire's work. I argue that Freire's approach to intellectual life, for all of its shortcomings and flaws, remains relevant and important in a twenty-first century policy environment dominated by neoliberal and "Third Way" agendas.

It has sometimes been claimed that there is a strong rationalist thrust in Freire's epistemology and ethic. Freire has, at times, been portrayed as a thinker who did not give emotion and feeling their due in his pedagogical theory and practice. In Chapter 2, I suggest that these views are mistaken. I argue that Freire's project, which remained incomplete at the time of his death in 1997, was to develop a critical ideal in which reason, emotion, and political commitment would be dynamically intertwined. The chapter explores key elements of this ideal (paying particular attention to the themes of solidarity and love) and considers some of its strengths and limitations.

Over the years, dozens of different definitions of literacy have been advanced by policy makers, politicians, academics, teachers, and others. It is not always easy, however, to know how one definition might relate to another or differ from it. Chapter 3 offers a framework, based on the work of the educational philosopher Israel Scheffler, for identifying and distinguishing between different types of definition. Modified to have particular relevance to statements about literacy, the three types of definition are: stipulative, essentialist, and prescriptive. The chapter shows how this modified framework can be helpful in understanding and addressing apparent tensions in statements about literacy by Paulo Freire. Possibilities for further study are signaled briefly at the end of the chapter.

Chapter 4 tackles the thorny issue of political correctness from a Freirean point of view. An identification of the range of areas to which the label *political correctness* has been applied reveals a confusingly multifaceted term. I concentrate on the key characteristics of intolerance, conformity, the impeding of questioning and criticism, the stifling of debate, and the denial of alternatives. Thus defined, I argue, political correctness has no place in Freirean education.

Chapter 5 considers one feature of debates over core curricula and canons in higher education—the problem of finding the right balance between breadth and depth in reading—from a Freirean point of view. The chapter falls into two major parts: The first explores the Freirean notion of critical literacy; the second applies Freire's ideas to the questions of what, how, and why students in universities ought to read. Freire promotes a dynamic linking of "word" with "world." Critical reading, for Freire, demands a restless, curious, probing stance toward both texts and contexts. Although Freire advocates a slow, careful, in-depth approach to the study of texts, he also stresses the importance of encountering and addressing a broad range of theoretical perspectives. Noting the importance of time in planning reading requirements, I sketch three levels at which a core course based on Freirean principles might proceed. At each level, the aim is to enhance breadth of perspective through critical reading. Freirean critical literacy is seen as both an ideal on which core courses might be founded and the means through which students might go beyond such courses to other worthwhile forms of learning.

An underdeveloped area of Freirean scholarship is the relationship between Freire's educational philosophy and literary works. Chapters 6 and 7 make a beginning in addressing this domain of inquiry. These chapters form part of a wider project concerned with demonstrating the value of literature for educationists (see further, Roberts, 2008c, 2008d, 2008e, 2008f, 2009a, 2009b). Chapter 6 undertakes a critical comparative analysis of key themes in the work of Freire and the great Russian novelist Fyodor Dostoevsky. It is suggested that, despite their apparent differences, Freire and Dostoevsky share much in common. I argue that a careful reading of both Dostoevsky's novels and Freire's pedagogical texts can deepen our understanding of the significance of uncertainty, dialogue, love, and struggle in transformative education.

Chapter 7 considers Hermann Hesse's classic novel *The Glass Bead Game*, in the light of Freire's theory of education. *The Glass Bead Game* is set in Castalia, a "pedagogical province" of the twenty-third century. It is argued that the central character in the book, Joseph Knecht, undergoes a complex process of conscientization. Knecht develops an increasingly critical understanding of Castalian society, questioning some of its most cherished assumptions while nonetheless deepening his appreciation of the beauty of the Glass Bead Game. He becomes less certain of his certainties as he grows older, and he eventually decides to give away his prestigious post as Magister Ludi (Master of the Glass Bead Game) to pursue a quiet life as a tutor. Dialogue plays a key role in the development of Knecht's critical consciousness. Freirean theory is seen to provide a robust framework for the analysis of key themes in Hesse's novel. At the same time, *The Glass Bead Game* is helpful in demonstrating the meaning and significance of conscientization and dialogue for educational lives.

The book concludes, in Chapter 8, with a discussion of key differences and similarities between Freirean and Taoist ideals. I limit my focus to the *Tao Te Ching*, paying brief attention to the origins of this classic work of Chinese philosophy before concentrating on several themes of relevance to Freire's work. An essay by James Fraser (1997), who makes three references to the *Tao Te Ching* in his discussion of love and history in Freire's pedagogy, provides a helpful starting point for this investigation. My analysis suggests that although the differences between these two systems of thought are significant and must be acknowledged, reflection on these differences has the potential to be educationally productive. There are also some surprising points of convergence, and these merit further exploration.

Chapter 1

Pedagogy, Politics, and Intellectual Life

Freire in the Twenty-First Century

Freire's posthumous publications have played a significant role in stimulating ongoing international interest in his work. This chapter addresses some of the key questions raised in *Pedagogy of Indignation*, a collection of previously unpublished letters and other writings released in 2004. Particular attention is paid to a somewhat neglected theme in Freirean scholarship: the characteristics and responsibilities of the critical intellectual. It is argued that Freire's approach to intellectual life, although not without its weaknesses, remains relevant and important in the twenty-first century. Freire's work provides a clear critique of, and alternative to, a neoliberal orientation to the world—an orientation still dominant in many countries across the globe.

A Pedagogy of Indignation

Freire's *Pedagogy of Indignation* (2004) needs to be read and understood against this broader context of his life and work. The book was published by Paradigm as part of the Series in Critical Narrative edited by Donaldo Macedo, Freire's close friend, coauthor, and translator. A further book by Freire, *Daring to Dream* (2007), was published in the same series some years later. *Pedagogy of Indignation* comprises three letters and several other short pieces by Freire, together with a foreword by Macedo, a prologue by Ana Maria Araújo Freire (Freire's second wife and widow), and a letter by Balduino A. Andreola (another friend, invited to respond with a reply to Freire's letters). Freire's letters were composed in the last months of his life, whereas the majority of the other essays were written in 1996. The titles of the letters—"On the Spirit of This Book," "On the Right and the Duty to Change the World," and "On the Murder of Galdino Jesus Dos Santos—Pataxó Indian"—are broadly indicative of their content, although Freire ranges widely over a number of philosophical, political, and educational themes throughout. Two of the other writings ("Challenges to Adult Education Posed by the New Technological Restructuring" and "Television Literacy") ostensibly deal with the theme of technology and education; again, though, the focus is considerably broader than this. One of the other pieces included in the book—"The Discovery of America"—was written in 1992 but has not previously been published. There is a chapter on "Literacy and Destitution." The remaining two chapters—"Education and Hope" and "Denouncing, Announcing, Prophecy, Utopia, and Dreams"—had both been intended for publication in other books (see A. M. A. Freire, 2004, p. xxx). In a novel touch, there is also (prior to the Contents page) a poem by Freire, "Obvious Song," written in 1971.

Many of the key themes in *Pedagogy of Indignation* are familiar ones for readers of Freire's work. Freire discusses the political nature of education, the question of change, the relationship between theory and practice, the inadequacies of technicist and scientific approaches to education, the idea of reading and writing the word and the world, the process of knowing, and the ongoing importance of love, hope, and social justice. There is renewed emphasis on the significance of emotion as well as reason in education and human life. Freire also reinforces his opposition to neoliberalism and the ethics of the market. Questions of spirituality surface briefly, as they have from time to time in previous publications, and there are fresh thoughts on the new information technologies. In addition, however, Freire comments in some detail on the crucial role played by the *will* in meeting personal and pedagogical goals. He employs a revealing personal example—his overcoming of a heavy smoking habit—in illustrating key theoretical points about the power of willing. Freire also pays more direct and extended attention here to families—to the responsibilities of parents and their relationships with their children. Finally, Freire stresses, in more than one place, his strong commitment to ecological issues. It would be deplorable, Freire suggests, to engage in progressive, revolutionary discourse "while embracing a practice that negates life—that pollutes the air, the waters, the fields, and devastates forests, destroys the trees and threatens the animals" (Freire, 2004, p. 120). Freire continues to embrace the dream of creating a better world. This, he says, is a process of struggle against, among other things, discrimination, lies, impunity, and all forms of violence—including "violence against the life of trees, of rivers, of fish, of mountains, of cities, against the physical marks of historic and cultural memories" (p. 121). Without this struggle, he believes, life could become "something to play with only for a time, determined by fate, in which one winds up living only while not dead and able to sustain life" (p. 121).

Balduino Andreola, near the end of his letter, situates Freire's work within a constellation of thinkers, spiritual leaders, and activists who collectively contribute to a "pedagogy of great convergences" (Andreola, 2004, p. xliii). He places Freire in the company of other "great masters of humanity" from the twentieth century who "fought for and devoted their lives to a more human, fraternal, and solidarity-based vision for the world" (p. xliii). This group includes "Gandhi, Pope John XXIII, Martin Luther King Jr., Simone Weil, Lebret, Frantz Fanon, Che Guevara, Teresa of Calcutta, Don Helder, Mounier, Teilhard de Chardin, Nelson Mandela, Roger Garaudy, the Dalai Lama, Teovedjre, Betinho, Paramahansa Yogananda, Michel Duclerq, Fritjof Capra, Pierre Weil, Leonardo Boff, Paul Ricoeur, and others" (pp. xliii–xliv). Andreola detects in Freire's later writings a movement "away from the West toward the East and the South" (p. xliii): "Reading your letters has confirmed this impression that, while not renouncing the rigor of science and philosophy, you are much closer to the thinking and the vision for the world of the great Eastern masters, as well as to the cosmic, mystical, and welcoming spirit of the African peoples" (p. xliii).

This, in my view, is an accurate assessment of where Freire's thinking was heading in the later years of his life. Care needs to be taken, however, in the way Andreola's comments are interpreted. Freire said very little *directly* about Eastern philosophy or spiritual traditions in his published work. Readers seeking a substantial discussion of mysticism or meditation and their significance for education will search in vain in Freire's books. Yet, there is, as Andreola recognizes, an important sense in which Freire's work is closer to the "spirit," intentions, and commitments of many Eastern thinkers than it is to dominant currents of Western thought. There is, of course, no one way of thinking, no one mode of being, in either the East or the West (cf. Roberts, 1996b). It is, moreover, easy to exaggerate the differences between diverse Eastern and Western traditions, ignoring important points of compatibility. For Freire, it is not a case of moving away from *all* Western ways of thinking but from those he regarded as most destructive. There is no doubt that Freire regarded one of the most powerful ideologies of the last two decades of the twentieth century—neoliberalism—as deeply flawed. As Peter Lownds (2005) puts it, Freire "growled the word *neoliberal* like a lion in pain" (p. 177). In *Pedagogy of Indignation* and other later books, Freire rails repeatedly against the rise of marketization policies across the planet. Yet, he remained true to some of the fundamental ideals promoted by other Western thinkers over the centuries. He continued, until his death, to place a premium on the value of critical thought, dialogue, tolerance, and democracy (see Freire and Shor, 1987; Horton and Freire, 1990; Freire, 1994, 1996, 1997a, 1998a, 1998b, 1998c, 2007). These ideals, he would have stressed, are by no means exclusively Western, and they have been understood and enacted in myriad different ways in the West and East, within both the "Third World" and the "First World," in recent decades. Freire's kinship with the "great Eastern Masters" and the "cosmic, mystical, and welcoming spirit of the African peoples" is perhaps most evident in his unswerving commitment to love as a human virtue, his holistic approach to pedagogical and political questions, and his respect for life in all of its forms. In these ways, among others, his work stands opposed to the thinking underlying policy reform agendas in many countries of the Western world in the 1980s, 1990s, and early years of the present century.

Ana Maria Araújo Freire notes in her prologue that it was she who gave the book its title. At first glance, the reference to "indignation" seems somewhat misplaced. Indignation is sometimes taken to imply an insistent—perhaps reactionary or possibly hostile—response to a problem or issue. Indignation seems to lack the reflectiveness and the gentleness that were hallmarks of Freire's theory and practice as an educator. Yet, as is explained in the prologue, "We cannot forget something Paulo always said—that all truly ethical and genuinely human actions are born from two contradictory feelings, and only from those two: love and anger. This book, perhaps more than others, is 'drenched,' as he might say, in his humanistic love and his political anger or indignation, which translated into his entire body of work, as he lived those feelings through his very existence" (A. M. A. Freire, 2001, pp. xxx–xxxi). Indeed, it becomes clear when reading the book that Freire retained a certain anger toward what he saw as utterly intolerable human injustices right up to his death in May 1997. He reserved much of this anger for the politics of late capitalism under neoliberalism and globalization, drawing attention to the extraordinarily destructive impact of corporate greed and market inequities on his fellow Brazilians and others across the globe.

Freire's style of writing here and in many of his other later works has both strengths and weaknesses. Conveying ideas in the form of letters is a stylistic technique employed to good effect by Freire in *Letters to Cristina* (1996) and *Teachers as Cultural Workers: Letters to Those Who Dare Teach* (1998a). In those works, as in *Pedagogy of Indignation*, the letters become self-contained chapters, each with a distinct theme, written in a relatively informal register. In some ways, the structure provided by the form of the letter has allowed for a tighter presentation of ideas than has been the case with some of Freire's other later works employing more traditional chapter formats (e.g., 1994). In most of his later books, Freire speaks more directly to readers, reveals more of himself as an author, teacher, and person, and allows his work to become more "readable" than earlier texts such as *Pedagogy of the Oppressed* (1972a). Yet, Freire's informal style also has its limits. Freire wrote a great deal in the last decade of his life, while also carrying very significant other responsibilities (including the enormous challenges he faced as secretary of education in the municipality of São Paulo from 1989 to 1991). It is clear that he continued to value not only the act of writing but also the process of reading in these years, and, as has been noted earlier, he extended and deepened many ideas from his earlier work during this energetic period of publishing activity (see further, Mayo, 2001). He came to rely rather heavily, however, on anecdotal and personal examples in illustrating theoretical points, drawing only infrequently on other published studies and empirical research findings to support his key claims. This lack of scholarly "clutter," with relatively few citations of other studies, allowed for a more relaxed and accessible style, but it also left some gaps.

For example, Freire developed a perceptive *feeling* for aspects of the postmodern turn in social theory, but he never undertook a systematic review or critique of the work of key thinkers associated with this turn. Carlos Torres (1994c) argues, correctly in my view, that Freire's view of the critical intellectual combines traditional, modernist, and postmodernist elements. Of the three broad elements, the postmodern component is perhaps the weakest. The beginnings of a distinctive approach to postmodernism and education are present in Freire's later writings. Mention might be made here of Freire's emphasis on not being too certain of his certainties, his revival and reworking of modernist concepts such as tolerance in the face of postmodern notions of difference, his attempt to sustain ideals such as solidarity and collectivity while shedding some of the doctrinaire baggage associated with their earlier use, his critique of sectarianism among intellectuals on both the Right and the Left, his distinction between conservative and progressive approaches to postmodernism, and his identification of convergences between some strands of postmodernism and neoliberalism. Yet, nowhere in his corpus of later published writings does Freire pay sustained and detailed attention to theoretical work on postmodernism and postmodernity. Freire does engage some of the criticisms of his theory of oppression and liberation made by postmodern feminist writers in education (see, for example, Freire, 1997b; Freire and Macedo, 1993, 1995), but his response to many of the other issues raised by postmodernists remains underdeveloped. Freire has even less to say about the related scholarly domains of postcolonial theory and poststructuralism. (For a thoughtful discussion of the former, in relation to Freire's work, see Giroux, 1993.) Freire's position on postmodernism emerges, for the most part, in "pieces" across various writings (cf. Peters, 1999). It is possible to put these pieces together to make a coherent whole, but the lack of in-depth theorizing in any one publication leaves too many unanswered questions.

Feelings were important to Freire, as will be evident to any reader of his later publications. (See also Ana Maria Araújo Freire's comments in Borg and Mayo, 2000.) The relationship between reason and emotion is discussed in depth in Chapter 2 of this book, but a few brief points can be made here. Reading, writing, studying, teaching, and political activism were all, for Freire, deeply emotional experiences. Freire was not afraid to describe his experiences as "joyous," or to speak of the beauty of writing and books, or to assert the overriding necessity for love in learning and life. Yet, in many ways, his account of emotion—and its relationship to reason—remains underdeveloped. He made little overt reference to work in areas such as the philosophy of emotion, the ethics of care, and virtue ethics, all of which could have been helpful in constructing a robust philosophical framework for his views on the significance of emotion in educational life. His pedagogical theory and practice might also have been enriched had he engaged other published work on feminism and education, education and the ecological crisis, neoliberalism and educational policy, spirituality and education, and indigenous education in greater depth and detail.

At the same time, it must be acknowledged that one theorist can only do so much. Freire himself was aware that he could not be all things to all people, and he urged others to take up some of the questions and issues addressed only briefly in his own writings. In that spirit, the remainder of this chapter will be devoted to a discussion of a somewhat neglected theme in Freire's work: his position on the roles and responsibilities of the intellectual. Freire touched on this theme in a number of publications over the years, but he never paid book-length attention to it. A number of Freirean scholars have commented on this issue (e.g., Torres, 1994c; Mayo, 1999), but, overall, there has been less interest in Freire's stance on the nature of intellectual life than might reasonably have been expected, given its relevance to contemporary debates in education. I want to suggest that Freire's approach to critical intellectual activity, although not without its problems, remains especially important in an educational age dominated by market imperatives.

Freire on the Role of the Intellectual

Freire's position on the role of the intellectual is intimately connected with his ontology and ethic, his educational theory, and his political practice. Freire's principal concern is with the development of what might be called the *critical* intellectual. What does this mean? Freire encourages those undertaking intellectual work to adopt a curious, investigative, probing, searching, restless attitude toward the world (Freire, 1985). In *Pedagogy of Indignation*, Freire captures the importance of curiosity in these words: "Curiosity, intrinsic to the vital experience, deepens and improves in the world of human existence. Disquieted by the world outside of the self, startled by the unknown, by mystery, driven by a desire to know, to unveil what is hidden, to seek an explanation for the facts, to verify, to investigate in order to apprehend—curiosity is the engine for the discovery process" (Freire, 2004, p. 87). As curious beings, we ask questions. The critical intellectual, for Freire, enjoys asking, pondering, and addressing questions, but, and this is a point often forgotten, this does not mean all ideas need to be questioned all the time. A questioning frame of mind also demands a certain form of acceptance. We must take *some* things as given if we are to ask a thoughtful question or develop a coherent line of critique or pose a well-conceived problem. Questioning, if it is to lead to genuine knowledge, cannot be merely an intellectual "game." Critical intellectual life, for Freire, involves striving to know through a constant process of interaction with others and an ever-changing world. The quest to know is simultaneously a commitment to a certain mode of acting and *being*. This, as Chapter 2 will show, is not merely a "rational" process.

Specific intellectual dispositions such as a questioning frame of mind are, from a Freirean perspective, inseparable from broader human virtues. These include humility, commitment, openness, hope, tolerance, and love (see Freire, 1972a, 1998a, 1998c, 2004, 2007; Escobar et al., 1994). The last two of these have special significance in the present context and will also be discussed in more detail in subsequent chapters.

The importance of love as a key theme in Freire's view of education and intellectual life cannot be overemphasized (see Fraser, 1997; McLaren, 2000; Darder, 2002, 2003). Freire saw love as a *revolutionary* virtue. "Love" takes on multiple meanings in Freire's work. Freire once said that after he met Marx he continued to meet Christ at the corner of the street, and this claim hints at the way he built the concept of love into a theory of social action. Freire never wavered in his support for Christ's call to "love one's neighbor as oneself." He was, however, much more willing than some of his intellectual contemporaries to see this principle as a call, in some circumstances, for radical, perhaps even revolutionary, social change. Love, Freire shows in *Pedagogy of Indignation,* is often connected with anger. Both anger and love can provide motivation to struggle for change (Freire, 2004, pp. 58–59). Freire also regarded love as central to the process of dialogue. Indeed, in *Pedagogy of the Oppressed* he maintains that love is "at the same time the foundation of dialogue and dialogue itself." "No matter where the oppressed are found," Freire says, "the act of love is commitment to their cause—the cause of liberation.

And this commitment, because it is loving, is dialogical." Freire is adamant about the importance of love as a condition for dialogue: "If I do not love the world—if I do not love life—if I do not love men [and women]—I cannot enter into dialogue" (Freire, 1972a, p. 62). Freire sees love of the students with whom one works as an essential requirement for liberating pedagogy, and he also speaks of the need to love the processes of reading, writing, and study (see, among other sources, Freire, 1985, 1996, 1998a; Freire and Shor, 1987; Horton and Freire, 1990).

With love comes *tolerance*. Freire regards tolerance as an intellectual virtue of profound importance, particularly within university settings (see Freire, 1998c; Escobar et al., 1994). He argues that critical intellectuals have a responsibility not merely to *allow* alternative points of view but to *actively stimulate* serious consideration of them. *Disclosing* one's political views, where and when appropriate, is not the same as *imposing* them. Protecting the right to differ is vital. For Freire, critical intellectuals in the university environment have a duty to foster discussion and debate and to assist in providing the theoretical resources necessary for this (see further, Chapter 4 of this book). Tolerance does not mean the abandonment of one's own views or ideals, or the passive acceptance of other positions. From a Freirean point of view, one of the best ways to demonstrate respect for another intellectual is to *engage* his or her ideas, taking them seriously, reflecting on them, considering both strengths and weaknesses. Freire argued against the reactionary responses of those on the political Right to changes in education and social life. He was equally critical, however, of the dogmatism he observed among some intellectuals on the Left (see, for example, Freire, 1997a). Both dogmatic and reactionary stances have authoritarian tendencies: They are characterized by antidialogue, by an unwillingness to listen—to see the world from another point of view, to consider the position of the "Other" (as far as this is ever possible).

Freire was not an epistemological or ethical relativist. It is clear that he always regarded some ideas, some ways of living one's life, and some forms of social organization as better than others. In later works, Freire emphasized the need for what he called "unity in diversity" (Freire, 1994) in the face of growing fragmentation among groups on the Left. Freire saw a need for solidarity and new forms of collective political activity in resisting the dominance of neoliberal policy agendas, the rise of multinational capitalism, and the relentless marketization of everyday life in the latter part of the twentieth century. Unlike some of his former intellectual colleagues, he also never disowned the label "socialist." He remained a staunch advocate for democratic socialism as a genuine alternative to what he called the "intrinsically evil" system of capitalism (Freire, 1998b, p. 114). Freire urged critical intellectuals to become involved in the struggle to build a better social world. Freire was, as Andreola notes in *Pedagogy of Indignation,* not one of the "intellectuals in retreat" identified by James Petras; rather, he was, as Ernani Fiori put it, someone who *hadn't quit* (Andreola, 2004, p. xxxvii). Freire makes it clear, however, that there are multiple ways of participating in the process of social transformation, and sometimes the most effective approaches, *in the long term,* are the quiet, unnoticed forms of gentle intellectual "subversion" practiced by educationists and others as they go about their daily work. In other cases, protest demonstrations, union activities, letters to members of parliament, or critical journalism might be appropriate. Freire's point is that *whatever* we do, we cannot remain neutral: As intellectuals and educationists, we are always political beings. Intellectuals are *always* taking a stand, even this is an implied one, whether they acknowledge it or not.

Freire's willingness, as an intellectual, an activist, and a teacher, to take a stand on questions of politics and social change has opened him up to plenty of criticism over the years. At different points in his life, Freire appeared to set up a problematic dichotomy between intellectuals and "the masses" (or "the people" or "the popular classes"). For critics such as Peter Berger (1974) and James Walker (1980), Freire is seen to promote an elitist, antidialogical, paternalistic relationship between a knowing group of higher-class intellectuals and an ignorant, lower-class group of educational participants. C. A. Bowers (1983), in a related line of argument, maintains that Freirean pedagogy, with its commitment to intellectual qualities such as critical reflection, questioning, and problematization, would in some contexts become culturally invasive. Frank Margonis (2003), similarly, identifies elements of colonialist thought in Freire's work. Freire's appeal to universal propositions in discussing issues of oppression and liberation has also attracted critical comment (Ellsworth, 1989; Weiler, 1991). These critics argue that Freire does not deal adequately with the multiple, often contradictory positions educators and students occupy as both oppressors and the oppressed. They also claim that Freire fails to interrogate his own position of privilege and authority as a teacher. I have addressed these criticisms at length elsewhere (e.g., Roberts, 1996b, 1996c, 2000, 2003a, 2003b, 2008b).

The focus on universalist thought has a parallel in wider debates over the role of the intellectual. Thinkers such as Antonio Gramsci (1971), Mao Tse-Tung (1968), and Jean-Paul Sartre (1973), building on the work of Marx, assumed that intellectuals had a key role to play in systematizing and elucidating a universal proletarian consciousness. The idea of a "universal" intellectual—someone who is supposed to speak the truth on behalf of others—has, however, been called into question by Michel Foucault (1980), Gilles Deleuze (Foucault and Deleuze, 1977), Julia Kristeva (1986), Jean-François Lyotard (1993), and Zygmunt Bauman (1988, 1993), among others. It is not difficult to see how some of Freire's earlier publications—especially *Pedagogy in Process: The Letters to Guinea-Bissau* (1978) and, to a lesser extent, *Pedagogy of the Oppressed* (1972a) and *Cultural Action for Freedom* (1972b)—invite comparison with Marx, Gramsci, and Mao. Marx, as has already been noted, was a major influence on Freire's thought, not just in the development of his political theory but, perhaps more importantly, on his ontology and epistemology. In his introduction to *Pedagogy in Process,* Freire cites, with approval, Mao's call to teach the masses with precision what they already know confusedly (1978, p. 25), and there is, as Peter Mayo's work shows, a close intellectual kinship between Freire and Gramsci on many key educational and political questions (see Mayo, 1994, 1996, 1999).

Some of Freire's comments in *Pedagogy of Indignation* appear, at first glance, to reinforce the notion of an intellectual vanguard lifting the masses up from their confusion. Freire argues that as an educator he needs to "constantly 'read,' better and better, the reading of the world that the oppressed populations I work with make of their immediate context" (2004, p. 63). He is critical of political militants who adopt a messianic, authoritarian approach in their work with oppressed groups, *imposing* rather than *proposing* their ideas. He cautions that he must not, under any circumstances, fail to consider the "experience-built knowing" of the "popular" groups with whom he works. Yet, he also stresses the need to go further than this:

> If on the one hand I cannot adapt or become "converted" to the innocent knowing of oppressed groups, on the other, I must not, if truly progressive, arrogantly impose my knowing upon them as the only *true knowing*. The dialogue within which one gradually challenges

oppressed groups to think through their social history as the equally social experience of their members reveals, little by little, the need to overcome certain portions of their knowing, as they begin to show their "incompetence" to explain the facts. (p. 64)

It is not difficult to see how some of the terms employed here could be off-putting. References to *innocent knowing* and *incompetence* in explaining facts seem to suggest a stance of paternalistic intellectual superiority. Such comments must, however, not be taken out of context. Freire is happy to defend the position that some people will have a deeper understanding of some social issues or areas of study or domains of technical expertise than others. But he also stresses, in *Pedagogy of Indignation* and in many of his other published writings, that knowledge is incomplete for *all of us*. No one is all-knowing, just as no one is completely ignorant. Here as well as elsewhere, Freire points out that our understanding of the world does not develop in a vacuum. We are often *encouraged*, sometimes directly but usually indirectly, to limit our knowledge of political realities. Arguing that ideas are socially constructed and that some groups exert a more powerful influence than others in shaping worldviews is, of course, nothing new. From a Freirean perspective, however, such claims bear repeating in a world so heavily dominated by neoliberal structures, practices, and policies. Educationists and intellectuals have an important role to play in encouraging others to reflect critically on how ideas—including those relating to globalization, so-called free trade, and the market—come to be formed.

Freire's emphasis on dialogue, critical consciousness, and education distinguished him from a number of other Left intellectuals. Indeed, he was criticized by some Maoists and Marxists for his faith in dialogue as a revolutionary virtue and for an allegedly weak model of political economy and class consciousness. Somewhat ironically, in later years, Freire was to attract criticism for paying *too much* attention to questions of class, at the expense of gender and ethnicity, in his analysis of oppression (see Freire and Macedo, 1993). Some of Freire's readers have found his work helpful in addressing the politics of difference (e.g., McLaren, 1997), and in developing indigenous, critical Africanist, and feminist pedagogies (e.g., Smith, 1999; Murrell, 1997; Stefanos, 1997; Hughes, 1998). Others in, for example, feminist educational theory, have seen some merit in Freirean ideas while also emphasizing their shortcomings (e.g., Weiler, 1991; Jackson, 1997; Boler, 1999b).

It is instructive to recall the contexts in which Freire worked (see further, Mayo, 1993). Much of Freire's practical experience as an adult educator was in highly volatile political situations. The language of some of his books—predominantly but not exclusively his earlier texts—has a revolutionary flavor, and this seems to be a stumbling block for some critics. Given the language he employs to describe education, conscientization, and social change in these earlier works, Freire *appears* to support the "universal intellectual" position. Talk of educators undergoing "Easter experiences," and even committing *class suicide* (a term Freire took from Amilcar Cabral), in working with "the people" for a "utopian dream" is, for many contemporary readers, vague, irritating, and riddled with philosophical problems. But this sort of language might be understandable and appropriate when employed in a country immediately prior to, or following, a nationwide political uprising—especially if the text is one comprising letters to leaders in a revolutionary process. It need not, and in Freire's case arguably *does* not, imply a commitment to the view that revolutionary leaders—or educators—believe themselves to be vehicles for a *universal* proletarian or oppressed consciousness.

It is possible to detect in Freire's writings a nascent view of what Foucault (1980) termed, in opposition to the "universal" intellectual, the "specific" intellectual. Specific intellectuals, Foucault said, need not be writers; they might, for example, be social workers, doctors, laboratory technicians, or magistrates. To this list, we might conceivably add teachers, librarians, journalists, and others. For Foucault, the contemporary polymorphous university, as a key site for scientific and technological activity, becomes crucial in the formation of specific intellectuals. Freire's view is not too far removed from this. What distinguishes Freire from Foucault is the emphasis Freire places on *education*. I believe Freire regarded *all* participants in a genuinely educational process—not just the teachers or coordinators or revolutionary leaders but the students as well—as intellectuals (cf. Giroux, 1988). Freire stressed, long before this became fashionable in educational circles, that no one is ignorant of everything, just as no one knows everything (see Freire, 1972a, 1976). Education, Freire would often say, should be seen as a permanent process of formation. Different groups and individuals have distinctive intellectual roles to play in a teaching and learning setting, but all are engaged in a process that is necessarily incomplete. Thus, although Freire made it clear, particularly in his later writings (e.g., Freire and Shor, 1987;

Horton and Freire, 1990; Freire, 1998a), that teachers are not the same as students, this does not mean that he saw students as the only learners in an educational situation. Teachers have a responsibility to prepare thoroughly, to know their subject, to provide structure and direction to the learning process, and to intervene where this proves necessary to allow respectful, critical dialogue to proceed (Roberts, 1996d). But teachers, as intellectuals, also relearn their material and extend their pedagogical knowledge as they teach.

For Freire, intellectuals might work in universities, schools, informal adult education classes, families, prisons, or any number of other settings. Anyone seeking to *know*, with others, might be regarded as a specific intellectual. To this extent, I believe Freire would have been supportive of attempts to locate and explore intellectual life in a range of learning environments. Roger Boshier (2002), for example, has argued that some of the most successful intellectuals in the New Zealand context—he names Edmund Hillary, Kiri te Kanawa, Arthur Lydiard, and Tom Schnackenberg as examples—have been of the "farm gate," rather than university trained, variety. Boshier notes that universities, adult educators, and leaders in industry could all benefit from understanding "how and why farm-gate intellectuals go about learning" (p. 5). Of course, care needs to be taken in such analyses to avoid the sort of fawning, uncritical admiration Boshier has found objectionable elsewhere (1999). Freire's principal concern was with critical intellectuals in educational situations—particularly those in university and revolutionary settings—but he would have welcomed studies of intellectual life and learning in other professions and fields of human endeavor.

Although there is much in Freire's work that is compatible with Foucault's notion of specific intellectuals, there remains, it must be said, a certain kind of *ethical* universalism that some critics find unacceptable. Freire was quite happy, in his last years, to talk about a universal human ethic, contrasting this with the ethics of the market. The latter, he says in *Pedagogy of Indignation*, is "solely the ethic of profit" (2004, p. 104) and is indifferent toward the suffering of the dispossessed. The former can be seen as a reworking of the concept of humanization, first advanced by Freire several decades ago (most notably, in Freire, 1972a), and stands opposed to oppression in all its forms. Neoliberalism, Freire argued, is a deeply fatalistic discourse. The acceptance of widespread destitution, exploitation, and unemployment at this moment in human history is a triumph for the ideology and politics of neoliberalism, but these realities, Freire stresses, are not inevitable (see also, Dunn, 1998; Apple, 1999). In the last interview he gave before his death, Freire had this to say about the emerging hegemony of neoliberal globalization:

> You see, from a third world perspective, when one reads texts about globalization, newspaper articles, documents from conferences and symposia on the subject, all originating from first world countries, one gets the impression that globalization is its own creator—a metaphysical entity, something spontaneously natural and historical, something that emerged because it had to. I don't believe any of that. I believe in history, history made by us, history that molds us as we move forward in the process of making it. Globalization is a specific point in time in the process of the capitalist economic development. Globalization from the point of view of the United States, then, cannot be the same globalization as seen from Brazil's point of view. (Freire and Rossatto, 2005, p. 17)

Neoliberalism, from a Freirean point of view, denies one of the defining attributes of humankind: the capacity to imagine the world otherwise. Neoliberalism "speaks about the death of dreams and utopia and deproblematizes the future" (Freire, 2004, p. 110). One of the key roles of the critical intellectuals is to *re*problematize the social reality of the present.

In countries driven by neoliberal policy agendas over the past three decades, a reliance on markets has often been portrayed as the only realistic and desirable way forward. The "Third Way" approaches adopted in the United Kingdom, New Zealand, and other countries in the second half of the 1990s and first few years of the new century witnessed a decline in the recitation of the "more market" mantra, with stronger appeals to social inclusion, but in many respects the Third Way remained a neoliberal way. There was a continuing emphasis on international economic competitiveness, so-called free trade agreements were sought, and globalization was cast in a largely positive light. (See further, Roberts and Peters, 2008.) "Third Way" ideas have also exerted an influence on Brazilian politics in the years following Freire's death, with negative consequences for agrarian reform policies, employment and wages, retirement allowances, and economic growth (Petras and Veltmeyer, 2003). Freire reminds us that multiple social and economic futures are possible and that intellectuals, particularly in higher education settings, have a duty to foster critical awareness of alternatives (cf. Freire, 2004, pp. 58–60). For Freire, "the future does not make us"; rather, "we make ourselves in the struggle to make it" (p. 34).

Concluding Comments

Freire's work has been engaged by scholars and practitioners in a very wide range of fields and disciplines. Whatever we might say about Freire's shortcomings as a theorist, a teacher, an administrator, or a person, there is clearly something in his work that encourages intellectual bridge-building—that crosses traditional boundaries and allows apparently disparate groups to address themes in common. What can we learn from Freire that might be worth knowing in the contemporary world? Zygmunt Bauman (1988, 1993) has argued that in the age of the market, intellectuals have been rendered largely *irrelevant*. This has created a crisis of legitimation, with intellectuals struggling to establish a role for themselves in a world where all that counts is that which *sells*. From a Freirean perspective, intellectuals are needed, in part, *precisely because* they are told, directly or implicitly, that they no longer matter. Freire teaches us that the shutting down or "dumbing" down of contemporary intellectual debate in many corners of the world is no accident: This is a political process, and intellectuals have a key role to play in showing how and why this is so.

At this moment in history, life for many people moves at a relentless pace. The world has, in Freire's words, become "shortened" and time has become "diluted" (2004, p. 94). Freire encourages us to make spaces for genuine reflection and debate amid the hustle and bustle of everyday activities. Against the current obsession with measurement in schools, teachers colleges, universities, and other educational institutions, Freire has demonstrated, through both his writings and his work as an adult educator, that much of what really matters in education *cannot* be measured. A good intellectual life, for Freire, is messy, complicated, and difficult: We learn, in attempting to make intellectual activity matter, that educational questions and problems seldom have neat, tidy answers or easy, quick-fix solutions.

In the face of increasing divisiveness across the globe, Freire reasserts the importance of community and communication. In *Pedagogy of Indignation* and other later books, Freire argues consistently against the ethos of self-interested competitive individualism that underpins neoliberal thinking. In a world where intellectuals, at least in a university environment, are encouraged to "market" not only their work but *themselves*, one of the most important contributions Freire makes is to remind us of the importance of humility. Exercising humility requires courage (Freire, 1995, p. 19). Recognizing our own limits as scholars, teachers, and activists is often the first step—and sometimes the hardest one to take—in seeking more productive dialogue with others, a stronger sense of intellectual fulfillment, and a deeper understanding of the world around us.

Chapter 2

Reason and Emotion in Freire's Work

> Teachers must not be afraid of tenderness, must not close themselves to the affective neediness of beings who are indeed kept from being. Only the poorly loved ones can understand teaching as a trade for the insensitive, so filled with *rationalism* that they become empty of life or feeling. (Freire, 1998a, p. 50)

Over the past two decades, considerable attention has been paid to the nature, role, and significance of emotions in education (see, among many other sources, Morgan, 1994; Zigler, 1994; Beck and Kosnik, 1995; Nias, 1996; Boler, 1997, 1999a; Hargreaves, 1998; Zembylas, 2002). Freire has sometimes been accused of prioritizing reason and rational processes over emotion and feelings. I hope to show in this chapter that such a view is misguided and that the importance of emotion for Freire can be seen not only in his ideas on teaching, learning, dialogue, and reading, but in his style of writing and the way he lived his life.

In considering Freire's position on emotions, an article published by Ann Sherman in 1980 provides a helpful starting point. Sherman draws our attention to some important tensions and weaknesses in Freire's early references to the role of emotions in education, dialogue, and political transformation. This chapter assesses the extent to which Freire addressed the concerns raised by Sherman in his later work. I suggest that Freire's project, which remained incomplete at the time of his death in 1997, was to develop a critical ideal in which reason, emotion, and political commitment would be dynamically intertwined.

The chapter falls into three major parts. The first section summarizes Sherman's argument and considers the interconnectedness of reason and emotion in Freire's language (written and spoken), ontology, epistemology, and educational theory. The second part comments in more detail on the *political* significance of these ideas, focusing on the pivotal themes of solidarity and love. The final section assesses some of the strengths and weaknesses in Freire's critical ideal.

Reason and Emotion in Freire's Work

In 1980, Ann Sherman published a concise critique of Freire's position on the relationship between emotion, education, and social change. Sherman identifies a tension between Freire's valuing of certain emotions (love, hope, faith, and trust) for critical educative dialogue and his rejection of "emotionality." In discussing the movement from "closed" to more open forms of social organization in Brazil, Freire warned against the dangers of highly emotive, irrational responses to oppressive structures, practices, and relationships. Freire also felt that the critical character of the communicative process could be compromised if strongly emotive individuals exerted undue influence on others within a group. Sherman points out that motivating students to learn was an important part of adult literacy education for Freire and that emotions were pivotal in this process; yet, emotions are seen as inadequate for understanding causal relationships in the social world. Sherman argues that Freire provides only a vague and superficially developed account of the emotions necessary for educative dialogue. This, she maintains, is no accident, for "if Freire has a lingering conception of emotions as totally uncritical forces it would not make much sense to discuss critical methods for developing them." She continues: "Since the methods of development are part of what the end product is, to advocate critical methods for developing emotions would entail that emotions were, at least in part, critical" (p. 38). Having identified the shortcomings and apparent contradictions in Freire's work, Sherman suggests that further research will be needed if we are to develop a more meaningful and substantial account of the role of emotion in educational dialogue.

When Sherman published her article, there were only four major texts by Freire available in English: *Pedagogy of the Oppressed* (1972a), *Cultural Action for Freedom* (1972b), *Education: The Practice of Freedom* (1976), and *Pedagogy in Process: The Letters to Guinea-Bissau* (1978). In subsequent years, Freire was to publish more than a dozen additional books. He was particularly productive in the last decade of his life. Freire collaborated with a number of other scholars in coauthoring a series of "talking" books, written in the form of structured dialogues around key educational themes (Freire and Shor, 1987; Freire and Macedo, 1987; Freire and Faundez, 1989; Horton and Freire, 1990). Several of his books had a semiautobiographical flavor (1994, 1996): one reflected on his experiences as secretary of education for the municipality of Sao Paulo (1993), one addressed issues in higher education (Escobar et al., 1994), one focused on the process of teaching (1998a), and several paid particular attention to questions of politics (1997a, 1998b, 1998c, 2004, 2007).

Freire never addressed the nature of emotion, or its relationship to reason, in a systematic and extended way. He did not, for example, devote an entire book, or even a substantial portion of a book, to this theme. This does not mean, however, that these issues were unimportant to him or that he ignored them in his written and practical work. I want to suggest that although there are limits to what Freire has to offer in addressing the challenge posed by Sherman in 1980, he nonetheless saw emotions as of vital significance for his educational work. This, I believe, has been evident to some degree in all of his writing but has come into sharper focus in his later publications. Emotions and feelings (I shall use the two terms interchangeably in this chapter) were significant for Freire at multiple levels: in relation to teaching, learning, studying, reading, writing, speaking, and knowing.

Those who knew Freire, or experienced his work as a teacher, or witnessed him speaking at conferences and seminars, almost always attest to his highly passionate nature (see, for example, *Taboo*, 1997; *Convergence*, 1998; Boshier, 1999; McLaren, 2000; A. M. A. Freire, 2001; Darder, 2002, 2003). Freire expressed himself with feeling and conviction, but also with reason. He would apply himself to reading and studying with concentrated enthusiasm, and he was an engaging, often animated, participant in educational conversations. Although it is important not to "heroize" Freire (Coben, 1998; Boler, 1999b), it seems clear that as a person, he generally *lived* what he talked about

33

in his books. Donaldo Macedo, who worked closely with Freire for years and translated several of his books into English, observes that there was "a great coherence between his [Freire's] words, deeds, and ideas" (Macedo, 2001, p. 3).

Freire's philosophy became, in Pierre Hadot's (1995) terms, *a way of life*, rather than mere intellectualizing. In philosophy as the practice of theorizing, the aim is, in Alexander Nehamas's words, to "deface the particular personality that offers answers to philosophical questions, since all that matters is the quality of the answers and not the nature of the character who offers them" (cited in Neiman, 2000, p. 576). Philosophy as a way of life, by contrast, requires style, idiosyncrasy, and a sustained effort—not just to understand the world more deeply, but to *be* in and with it in a new way. The character and lived experience of the person become central. As Alven Neiman puts it, the "entire rationale has to do with the life of a particular person" (p. 576). Freire's lived philosophy was one in which feelings played a central role. For Freire—as a person, and a writer, and a teacher—these feelings could not be disentangled from reason and from action. There was, to employ the categories developed by Rudolf Steiner (1995) among others, a strong connection between thinking, feeling, and willing in Freire's work. Freire *felt* distress and pain and frustration and anger (and many other emotions) when he worked with severely impoverished adults in Brazil in the 1950s and early 1960s; he *thought* deeply about the nature of the social system that produced such oppression (and went on to convey those thoughts in books such as *Pedagogy of the Oppressed*); and he *willed* himself to action through his efforts in major literacy campaigns and other educational initiatives.

The integration of emotion and reason in Freire's work is evident in the style he used to construct his later books. A book such as *Pedagogy of Hope* (1994), for example, might be criticized for its somewhat rambling character. This book lacks the tight structure often demanded of academic writers. Freire does not provide extensive footnotes or references for his ideas in this text or other later books. In fact, he seldom makes direct reference to the work of other scholars. In some of his later published writings, Freire's second wife, Ana Maria Araújo Freire, has added detailed endnotes elaborating on points made in the text. Freire does not employ a "stream of consciousness" style, but he does allow his feelings to exert greater influence on the direction and nature of his prose than many of his international academic peers. Many of Freire's later books address a very wide range of philosophical, pedagogical, and political themes, and considerable work is left to the reader in creating a coherent overall picture of his views. Freire must be read *holistically* if we are to gain a full appreciation of what he has to offer educational theory and practice (see further, Roberts, 2000; Mayo, 1997, 1999, 2001). There is more of "Freire himself" in the later books. Freire shares his feelings with readers, reveals more of his biography, acknowledges his failures and shortcomings more openly, confesses his discomforts and frustrations more readily, and allows moments of anger and joy to find their way more directly into his writing. In these works, Freire does not attempt to "remove himself" from the text: The ideas he expresses are, in an open and obvious way, *his* ideas.

Yet, the faculty of reason is never absent in these writings. There *is* logic, coherence, and sound argumentation in Freire's later books, but the reader must assume a certain kind of relationship with these texts if the deeper reasoning behind many of Freire's ideas is to be found. The reader needs, among other things, to adopt a critical posture, to put the different books into conversation with each other, to consider them in the light of Freire's practical commitments in the last ten years of his life (particularly his role in the Brazilian Workers' Party and his responsibilities as secretary of education), and to make a definite effort to disentangle particulars (e.g., references to Freire's personal experience) from universals (e.g., the notion of humanization underlying Freire's work).

Freire argued, from his earliest writings, that humans are "unfinished" or incomplete beings. In *Pedagogy of the Oppressed* (1972a), he advanced an ethical ideal of humanization, which he saw as a process of becoming more fully human (not *fully* human) through critical, dialogical praxis. Freire posited humanization as an ontological and historical vocation for all human beings. He saw *de*humanization as a distortion of this vocation. Dehumanization is manifested, in concrete terms, by structures, practices, policies, and relations of oppression. As noted in the Introduction to this book, it is through struggling against oppression—in a reflective, dialogical, active manner—that humans pursue their liberation. Freire depicts liberation as an ongoing *process* of struggle, not as an endpoint to be reached. There will *always* be a need for further reflection, action, and social transformation.

Freire's account of oppression and liberation was later to draw criticism from postmodernists who found fault with his appeal to universal propositions, his failure to theorize adequately his own position of privilege, and the somewhat abstract manner in which he articulated his ideas (compare, Ellsworth, 1989; Weiler, 1991; Freire and Macedo, 1993). In later works, Freire engaged postmodern ideas and made an attempt to address, in a more explicit and extended way, questions of diversity and difference. Arguably, however, the philosophical core of his ontology remained the same throughout his writing career. In some books, Freire uses different terms to describe the same ideal. In *Pedagogy of Freedom* (1998b), for instance, he argues for a "universal human ethic." Despite the shift in terminology, the essential features of his ideal remain the same: All humans, he maintained, are "called" to think, feel, act, and communicate with others in certain ways in pursuit of a shared vocation. This way of understanding human beings runs counter to some strands of postmodern thought, but Freire was deliberate in his political choice here. As Claudia Rozas (2007) puts it in her eloquent phrase, there is no need to "rescue Freire from modernity" (p. 569).

In *Pedagogy of the Heart* (1997a), Freire takes up the theme of human unfinishedness as the basis for educational life. Freire points out that not only are we unfinished, we are capable of *knowing* ourselves as such. This provides the ground for the permanent process of searching, which Freire regards as a distinguishing characteristic of all human beings. It is consciousness of our inconclusiveness that makes us educable. Engaging in this process of constant searching, which provides an important motivating force for the process of education, cannot be a purely rationalistic process:

> *Consciousness of*, an intentionality of consciousness does not end with rationality. Consciousness about the world, which implies consciousness about myself in the world, with it and with others, which also implies our ability to realize the world, to understand it, is not limited to a rationalistic experience. This consciousness is a totality—reason, feelings, emotions, desires; my body, conscious of the world and myself, seizes the world toward which it has an intention. (p. 94)

In later writings, Freire makes it plain that knowing is a multifaceted process, incorporating physical, emotional, and intellectual elements: "I know," Freire says, "with my entire body, with feelings, with passion, and also with reason" (1997a, p. 30). Ana Maria Araújo Freire, in conversation with Carmel Borg and Peter Mayo, extends these ideas. Paulo, she says, was "never ashamed to say that everything he knew came from his curiosity, awakened by his feelings, by what his skin said, his intuition aroused, his emotion dictated" (Borg and Mayo, 2000, p. 112). Her husband's language, she argues, was richly emotional in character: "Paulo was a radically coherent man: what he said contained what he felt and thought and this is not always easy to translate. There are emotions whose meanings can only be well perceived, understood, and felt inside a certain culture. And we Brazilians are unique in this way" (p. 112). Translators of Paulo's work would sometimes err too much on the side of form, ignoring other words that might be perceived as "too full of feelings." In doing so, they would unwittingly lose something of the imaginative quality of his work. Studying the Portuguese language, Ana Maria suggests, is not the same as *living* it within Brazilian culture. For Paulo, language—whether in written or spoken form—was a way of expressing his love of knowledge and humanity. Ana Maria recalls an incident shortly after Paulo's death in which cultural differences on the relationship between reason, emotion, and language came into sharp focus:

> First World intellectuals said to me: "Don't cry, don't become emotional! You are giving a scientific speech, an academic work in surroundings where there is no place for emotions!" Can you imagine? I was in Hamburg, at an Adult Education congress where everything, or almost everything, turned around Paulo. The conference paid great homage to him. His ideas and his name filled the atmosphere of the meeting. And I had lost Paulo less than three months before! The terrible sense of loss was strongly reflected in the form of working I had learnt exactly from him: to say what one felt when thinking. Why would it be wrong to think, crying? Can it be true that when we cry we lose our reason? I felt I could not even control myself to stop crying, but I knew I was thinking. And so, why control myself? That is the question! (p. 111)

Ana Maria makes it clear that Freire would not work *just* with feelings or intuition but rather subjected what arose from them to deep, critical, reflective thought. For Freire, intuition and emotion were an important *part* of the process of knowing, but without serious questioning and thinking they could lead to distortions and misunderstandings. Equally, and this is a point that is often forgotten, Freire believed that an exclusive or dominant focus on the intellect will yield an incomplete and inadequate understanding of human beings and the world. Freire "never maintained the emotion should subjugate reason. But he also vehemently rejected the opposite 'academicist' view" (p. 112). Freire's stance is captured effectively in this passage from *Teachers as Cultural Workers*:

> The problems of teaching imply educating and, furthermore, educating involves a passion to know that should engage us in a loving search for knowledge that is—to say the least—not an easy task. It is for this reason that I stress that those wanting to teach must be able to dare, that is, to have the predisposition to fight for justice and to be lucid in defense of the need to create conditions conducive to pedagogy in schools; though this may be a joyful task, it must also be intellectually rigorous. The two should never be viewed as mutually exclusive. (Freire, 1998a, p. 4)

In his later books, Freire stresses repeatedly that educational dialogue should be structured, with a clear sense of purpose and direction (see Freire and Shor, 1987; Roberts, 1996d). Freire argues against both authoritarian and "anything goes" learning environments. Students and teachers have both rights and responsibilities in an educational dialogue. Freire acknowledges the right for all students to speak, provided their actions do not impede others from doing so. Equally, participants should have the right to refrain from speaking. *Engagement* with the object of the study and the content and movement of the dialogue is the key; this need not always involve speaking. Indeed, a tendency to want to "thrust oneself forward" all the time, to insert oneself into the conversation, often betrays a certain egoism and inability to wait and to listen to what others have to say. (I return to this point later in the chapter.) The notion of discouraging "emotionality," detected by Sherman in Freire's earlier writings, continues here.

Freire's intentions must be considered carefully. Preventing or discouraging others from speaking by "shouting them down" in an emotional outburst represents a failure to live up to one's responsibilities in a dialogue and to recognize the rights and feelings of others. Allowing *some* emotions to exert undue influence on a dialogue could, Freire believed, be damaging to the educational process and dehumanizing for participants. Allowing one's excitement, anger, or frustration to boil over compromises the dialogical process not only for others but for oneself as well. What is needed is the moderating influence of reason and a certain kind of balance in the expression of one's feelings. This can involve striving to inculcate feelings of care, calmness, patience, and respect as well as enthusiasm, commitment, and courage. Acknowledging one's own limitations, retaining a sense of curiosity and wonder, and developing the ability to listen are also qualities of fundamental importance.

Solidarity, Hope, and Love

In his last books, several of which were published posthumously, Freire continued to stress the importance of getting involved in the process of political struggle. He saw this as an integral part of his intellectual life (see Escobar et al., 1994). This process, he recognized, was difficult, often slow, and seldom straightforward. Freire never gave up the view that capitalism was an inherently unjust mode of production, and he saw the marketization of social and economic life under neoliberalism as highly problematic. For Freire, the increasing dominance of a small class of corporate elites was further evidence of the need to resist the politics of capitalist expansion. Freire was appalled by the destruction of the natural environment and the growing gap between "haves" and "have-nots" within and among countries across the planet. As a further impediment to liberation, groups on the Left had developed deep divisions and had expended considerable emotional, intellectual, and political energy fighting among themselves. This fragmentation had hampered efforts to resist forms of oppression relevant to all groups and had allowed those on the economic and cultural Right to prevail.

Ladislau Dowbor (1997), in his preface to Freire's *Pedagogy of the Heart*, stresses the importance of solidarity in a world increasingly driven by division, functionality, and anonymity. Solidarity, for Freire, is forged not merely through words but through *action* (cf. Duarte, 2006). In contemporary capitalist societies built on a manufactured ethic of relentless consumption, people find themselves working harder than ever before. Yet, for all the technological advancements of recent years, we seem unable to build better lives. In many parts of the world, we have lost a strong sense of community. We have been encouraged to depersonalize suffering, to remove ourselves from it, and to build up our defenses against the shock of witnessing other human beings starving, desperately poor, or in pain. "With the global society of long distances and large numbers," Dowbor says, solidarity has become "no longer a matter of the heart, of feelings naturally generated before the known person; it has shifted over to the intellect, reason, which is satisfied with rationalization" (p. 27). For Dowbor, Freire offers an alternative approach: "In Paulo Freire's reasoning, rationality is rationally clamoring for the right to its emotional roots. This is the return to the shade of the mango tree, to the complete human being. And with the smells and tastes of childhood, it is much broader a concept than that of the right or the left, a deeply radical one: human solidarity" (p. 28).

In reflecting on the enormous challenges posed by neoliberal capitalism, Freire continued to stress the importance of hope. He believed, however, that developing and retaining the *feeling* of hope was not sufficient on its own. "Hope of liberation," he said, "does not mean liberation already. It is necessary to fight for it" (Freire, 1997a, p. 44). It is not a case of separating the feeling from the action, but rather of acknowledging how one might be informed and nourished by the other. Holding firm to the feeling of hope when everything around us suggests we should be lapsing into despair allows us to go on, to continue to find meaning in our existence. This feeling is made all the richer and more complex, however, when we communicate with others about our dreams and fears, and when we find ways (appropriate to the problems of our time, place, and social situation) to keep working for social change.

The concept of love is arguably even more significant than the notion of hope in Freire's later work. Indeed, it is possible, as Antonia Darder (2002, 2003) has shown, to view love as the foundation for Freire's entire pedagogy. The importance of love in Freire's work has also been addressed by a number of other theorists in recent years (compare, for example, Spring, 1994; Fraser, 1997; McLaren, 1999, 2000; Blumenfeld-Jones, 2004). Freire employed the concept of love in a number of different ways. At the broadest level, he speaks repeatedly of the need for a profound love of human beings and the world. He sees this as a defining characteristic of the vocation of humanization. The influence of both Marx and radical Catholicism can be detected here. In *Pedagogy of the Oppressed* Freire quotes, with approval, Che Guevara's famous statement about love as a revolutionary virtue (Freire, 1972a, p. 62), and he contrasts this with what he sees as the distortion of the word *love* in the capitalist world. Genuine revolutionaries, Freire argues, are motivated by a deep concern to address conditions of oppression, which are characterized by a dehumanizing *lack* of love and often a deliberate, sadistic desire to dominate others. Freire accepts the Christian imperative to "love your neighbor as yourself" (*The New English Bible: New Testament*, Matthew 22, 39), but he also takes from Marx the need to respond to conditions of exploitation and oppression. "No matter where the oppressed are found," Freire says, "the act of love is commitment to their cause—the cause of liberation" (p. 62).

Freire, like others in the tradition of liberation theology (where his work was influential: see Oldenski, 2002), reads the Gospels as a call for social action. From a Freirean point of view, to engage in humanizing praxis—critical, dialogical reflection and action for transformation—is to put into practice the ideal of love fostered by Christ (cf. Freire, 1997a, pp. 103–105; Lange, 1998). There is a deeper sense, however, in which the Christian imperative comes to life in Freire's work. For to love one's neighbor *as* oneself is to recognize that, in a very significant sense, one's neighbor *is* oneself. This point has, of course, been explored in great detail by theologians, philosophers, and others over the centuries. Freire was not a theologian, and he did not address this question directly or at length in his writings. Nevertheless, his position, when his work as a whole is surveyed, seems clear. We are, Freire argues, always *social* beings. Our thoughts, emotions, experiences, and actions are always shaped by—and to this extent *defined* by—our relationships with others. Others *live through* us. We are not isolated, autonomous selves; rather, we are always *connected*, often in ways we cannot recognize, with others. This is why, in *Pedagogy of the Oppressed* and other works, Freire speaks of oppression dehumanizing both the oppressed and the oppressor(s). Similarly, to *love* others, treating them as we would want to be treated, is also to love oneself. It is to live as one should in fulfilling the ontological vocation of humanization.

Freire also speaks, more specifically, of the importance of love for educational dialogue, for teaching, for the students with whom one works, for processes of reading, writing, and study, for knowledge, and for life itself. Love is both "the foundation of dialogue and dialogue itself" (Freire, 1972a, p. 62). Without loving respect for other participants in a dialogue, one cannot truly *listen* to, and hence learn from, what they have to say. Freire argues that listening is an activity that goes beyond mere hearing. Listening involves "being open to the word of the other, to the gesture of the other, to the differences of the other" (Freire, 1998b, p. 107). This does not mean one should be "reduced" to the other; this would, from Freire's point of view, not be listening but *self-annihilation*. Freire explains:

> True listening does not diminish in me the exercise of my right to disagree, to oppose, to take a position. On the contrary, it is in knowing how to listen well that I better prepare myself to speak or to situate myself vis-à-vis the ideas being discussed as a subject capable of presence, of listening "connectedly" and without prejudices to what the other is saying. In their turn, good listeners can speak engagedly and passionately about their own ideas and conditions precisely because they are able to listen. (p. 107)

With love, there must also be humility—a willingness to acknowledge one's weaknesses as well as strengths and to "step back," removing the focus from oneself and allowing others to show what they know. "To be humble," Freire observes, "implies understanding oneself in the process of being with all the abilities and all the faults; to accept oneself as one who is becoming" (Freire, 1995, p. 19). Humility is especially important in a *critical* dialogue, where ideas—including those we cherish most—are subject to rigorous questioning and debate. Humility "calms and pacifies what our vanity may have difficulty tolerating, even when the criticisms we receive are just" (Freire, 1998c, p. 57). Freire sees teaching as an act of love (see his comments in Leistyna, 1999, p. 57). Love sustains the teaching process in the face of what Freire sees as an utterly contemptuous attitude on the part of those responsible for the funding of schooling. Without the profound love many teachers have for their vocation, they would not be able to put up with such "shameful" wages, underresourcing, and poor working conditions (cf. Freire, 1998a, pp. 40–41). In later works, Freire refers often to reading, writing, and study as difficult, demanding processes. In reading a text we should, Freire suggests, be prepared to be challenged by it, but we should also be prepared to ask questions of it. Freire advocates a stance of loving the text while fighting with it (Freire and Shor, 1987, p. 11). This kind of critical reading involves the active linking of "word" and "world" (Freire and Macedo, 1987), where the reader attempts to relate the content of a text to contemporary contexts, to the issues and problems of the day, and to the struggles with which he or she is associated. Freire also encourages readers to set texts appropriately in the *author's* context: to try to understand something of the circumstances under which the author was writing.

If we are to love the process of study, we must come to appreciate that joy and rigor are not mutually exclusive. In *Letters to Cristina*, Freire recalls how he, as a young intellectual, would experience intense emotional pleasure as he watched boxes of books being opened in a bookstore in Recife, Brazil. He also notes that at that time he threw himself into the study of grammar and the Portuguese language. His interest was not in the merely technical study of grammar. "My passion," he says, "was always directed toward the mysteries of language in a never anguished but always restless search for its substantive beauty" (Freire, 1996, p. 79). The joy of study arises not just when we discover what we sought to know, but from the process of investigation itself; that is, from searching, asking questions, exploring beneath the surface—in short, from the attempt to engage the object of investigation critically (see Freire, 1985, pp. 1–4, 1998a, p. 4, 1998b, p. 125). If this process of reading, studying, and learning works well, we come to develop a deep love of knowledge and will continue to seek out opportunities to better understand the world over the course of our lives. Indeed, the process is crucial in shaping the degree to which we love life itself:

> What I want to say is that the sequence of learning in which we all participate inculcates the love of life or the love of death in us, shapes the way that we relate from a young age to animals, plants, flowers, toys, and people; the way that we think about the world; and the way that we act in the world. If we treat objects with meanness, destroying them or devaluing them, the testimony we give to our offspring is a lack of respect for the powerless and a disdain for life. We learn to either love life or to reject it. (Freire, 1996, p. 75)

The Limits of Freire's Critical Ideal

Freire's position on reason and emotion cannot be fully appreciated without considering the contexts within which he worked. His commitment to a critical educational ideal grew out of his experiences in Brazil and Chile, where the disparities between different social groups were readily apparent. Freire's concept of liberation is also linked to these experiences. As noted earlier, Freire sees liberation as a form of struggle against oppression. In defining liberation in this way, Freire has been able to make a distinctive and lasting contribution to the theory and practice of teaching and learning. He was one of the most important figures in twentieth century educational thought in bringing the *political* dimension of education to our attention (Mayo, 1999). Much of what Freire has to say about reason and emotion is tied to his political project. Freire saw liberation as "the most fundamental task" of the twentieth century (Freire, 1993, p. 84), and when he spoke about the significance of love and hope for educationists he was not concerned with romantic ideals but with the messy, difficult, complex realities of political transformation.

Seen in this light, it is perhaps not surprising that Freire placed such a heavy emphasis on the development of a *critical* mode of being. Freire's intellectual kinship with other theorists in the critical tradition is evident in his published work. The influence of Marxism, existentialism, and radical Catholicism has long been noted (see, for example, Mackie, 1980), but there are also important connections that can be drawn between Freirean ideas and the work of critical theorists such as Jürgen Habermas (see Morrow and Torres, 2002). Freire's integration of insights from these scholarly traditions had an overt political purpose: He saw critical reflection, dialogue, and action as essential in addressing the realities of oppression.

This should not, however, be seen as a commitment to a narrow form of rationalism: Freire saw emotions as a vital part of his critical ideal. It is not a case of supplanting emotion with the cold gaze of reason, but rather of understanding how thinking, feeling, and acting depend on each other for their intelligibility. For Freire, when we attempt to think in a disciplined way—to theorize, to argue, to reason—we simultaneously commit ourselves to an emotional process. Through critical reading, writing, and investigation, we experience a range of emotions—sometimes frustration, sometimes joy, often (in the longer run, if not immediately) a sense of fulfillment. The very process of struggling to make our reading critical, rather than passive or merely entertaining, is itself an indicator of its emotional character. Similarly, when we commit ourselves, with others, to social action, this commitment cannot be sustained without a deep, ongoing *feeling* that conditions of oppression can and ought to be resisted. In Freire's case, this feeling was first cultivated in childhood experiences (e.g., his observations of racism) and continued to grow and develop through his educational work in his adult life.

Yet, the very features that make Freire's approach distinctive also pose their own limits. Freire leaves us searching for more when we ask how we might develop ourselves as emotional and rational beings beyond the process of addressing—through critical, dialogical praxis—conditions of oppression. His repeated references in later books to the virtues of good teachers and learners go part of the way to addressing this concern, but if we are to understand the significance of his comments in this area it is helpful to look beyond Freire's work. A much fuller exploration of human virtues can be found in Aristotle's *Nichomachean Ethics* (Aristotle, 1976) and the contemporary philosophical literature on virtue ethics. Freire spoke about the importance of *caring* for students, but for an in-depth investigation of this theme we need to look elsewhere (e.g., Gilligan, 1982; Noddings, 1984). Freire pays scant attention to the wider literature on the philosophy of emotion within feminist theory (for an excellent overview of scholarship in this domain, see Boler, 1997, 1999b). Similarly, although Freire was supportive of efforts to enhance ecological awareness, he did not consider, in any detail, how such work might be helpful in rethinking human experience, modes of understanding, and forms of social life (cf. Mayo, 2002). Others, however, have seen value in making constructive connections between Freirean theory and ecological concerns (e.g., Gruenewald, 2003; Kahn, 2006a, 2006b). Freire also has little to say about the relationships among reason, emotion, and spirituality, a theme that has been addressed thoughtfully by others (e.g., Zigler, 1994). Freire does not comment, directly, on the ways in which our lives as thinking, feeling, and willing beings might be enhanced (or impeded) by contemplative or meditative activities. There is scope for extending Freire's ideas on liberation to include these dimensions (see, for example, Dallaire, 2001). Freire's view of the reading process also raises questions. Freire's emphasis on the importance of critical reading—which is, it must be remembered, both a rational and an emotional process—leaves us wondering what he might have said about other ways of approaching texts (cf. Endres, 2001). It might be argued that something is *lost* in promoting a critical approach to reading, and that there is value, at times, in attempting to read a book in a distinctly *non*critical way. I want to finish the chapter with a few remarks on this last issue: the limits of Freire's view of reading.

Freire has a great deal to say about reading, but his purposes in addressing this subject are primarily educational. In exploring the role of reading in developing a rich life of feeling, questions of aesthetics inevitably arise. Freire does not position himself self-consciously within any particular school of aesthetics. This is not to say that he ignores aesthetic questions altogether. Indeed, Tyson Lewis (2009) argues that the aesthetic dimension is central to Freire's pedagogy of the oppressed. Freire comments in places on the relationships among curiosity, a sense of wonder, and the spirit of investigation. He talks about the role of "aesthetic curiosity" in allowing one to become pleasurably immersed in a challenge, or lost in contemplation of a sunset or the clouds, or touched by a work of art (Freire, 1997a, pp. 95–96). Freire also stresses the importance of the aesthetic dimension of language, not just for artists but for all engaged in intellectual work. "It is the duty," Freire maintains, "of all those who write to write beautifully. It does not matter what one writes or writes about" (Freire, 1996, p. 80). And in *Pedagogy of Freedom* (1998b), he argues that ethical formation ("decency") and aesthetic appreciation ("beauty") need to proceed hand in hand.

Yet, Freire's account of aesthetic appreciation remains sketchy and incomplete. As readers, we have to develop a *feeling* for Freire's position on questions of aesthetics; he does not provide us with a well-developed, systematic theory. Moreover, as has been noted elsewhere (Roberts, 2000, p. 93), where Freire refers to the aesthetic moment in reading or the beauty of books, he tends to do so in relation to a broader *critical* ideal (see, for example, Horton and Freire, 1990, pp. 23–27, 31–32). This begs the question of whether and how books might be encountered and experienced in ways *other* than those tied to notions of critical consciousness or critical literacy. A number of theorists have spoken about the ways in which reading—particularly the reading of literary works—can educate the emotions (among many other examples, compare Hepburn, 1972; Gribble, 1983; Solomon, 1986; Nussbaum, 1990; Cunningham, 2001). Freire has little to say about this. When we consider the theme of reading, then, the problem is not, as Sherman (1980, p. 38) suggests, that Freire sees emotions as "totally uncritical forces" but rather that he pays adequate attention *only* to the ways in which emotions might become critical forces.

Freire talks about the need for humility (on the part of the reader) and a willingness to be challenged by the text. He warns us not to become "too certain of our certainties" (see Freire, 1994), fooling ourselves that we have all the answers already and have nothing to learn from the ideas conveyed by others in books and dialogues. But Freire also stresses that this is a reciprocal relationship: Readers can—

and *ought to*—ask questions of texts, just as texts can raise questions for readers. Freire promotes rational and emotional *engagement* with texts; he does not support a more passive approach in which readers attempt to *minimize* their critical capacities in the reading process. A case could be made, however, for exactly this sort of attitude—*in some contexts*, with some texts, for some purposes. There are some circumstances, it might be argued, when experiencing the process of reading a text, "absorbing" it, living with it, and letting it talk to us without subjecting it to systematic examination or critique or analysis could be worthwhile. Applying too firm a critical hand too early can sometimes dampen, hinder, or even destroy some of the benefits we might otherwise gain from reading a text.

Much depends here, I think, on the sorts of texts with which we are dealing. (It is also important to consider what we mean by "critique": see Ruitenberg, 2004.) Freire was concerned primarily with scholarly texts, and particularly with those that addressed philosophical, sociological, and educational themes. His notion of "fighting with the text while loving it" emerged from his own struggles with texts of this kind. When he spoke, in *A Pedagogy for Liberation* (Freire and Shor, 1987) and elsewhere, about the importance of reading classic texts, he was referring not to literary works but to the writings of theorists such as Marx or Gramsci. Freire has little to say about literary texts and the forms of reading he believes are appropriate for them. His scattered remarks about aesthetic appreciation provide some clues in determining what he *might* have said had he written in these areas. It is certainly clear, I believe, that he would have stressed the need to respond to literary works—and creative works more generally—not just in a "rational" way but also in an emotional way. Freire speaks fondly of his own *immersion* in books, of encountering new texts with great excitement and enthusiasm. We also know that he was moved by the power of language and the beauty of the written word. But he tells us virtually nothing about the way a literary text in particular might "work on us," shaping and building our emotions. Reading for Freire can play an important role in encouraging educationists to "side with the oppressed." There are links here with the work of moral philosophers who talk about the development of altruistic emotions—compassion, sympathy, empathy—through the reading of novels (see Boler, 1999a, pp. 158–160). Freire has in mind works of nonfiction: *theories* of oppression or factual accounts (historical or contemporary) of oppressive structures, policies, and practices.

He does not deal with the question of how literary works—or other artistic forms such as film or drama—might develop a "feeling" for oppression in a different way.

Freire's notion of fighting with a text while loving it does give us some purchase on an attitude that might be helpful in reading at least some literary works. I am thinking, especially but not exclusively, of those authors who confront searching philosophical questions, problems and issues in and through their work. A good example here would be Fyodor Dostoevsky, arguably one of the most deeply philosophical of all novelists. There is much to be gained, I believe, in both attempting to "just read" a book such as *The Brothers Karamazov* (Dostoevsky, 1991) and in self-consciously reflecting on it. This is where the interconnectedness of emotion and reason becomes apparent. If we are too eager to bring our own questions to the text, subjecting it to critical analysis prematurely, some of the emotional impact of the book could be lost. We need to allow Dostoevsky's narrative to unfold, working on us, forming an appreciation of the characters and the events in the novel. Yet, as this development of our "feeling" for the characters emerges, so, too, does our *thinking* about them. This is one of the marks of Dostoevsky's genius: His novels are so richly textured, so complex and multilayered, that it is difficult to avoid becoming reflective in reading them. We become entwined in the lives of Dostoevsky's characters—in their thoughts, emotions, dilemmas, challenges, tensions, contradictions, actions, and relationships—and in doing so, we are prompted to ponder questions of importance in our own lives.

We should not, from a Freirean point of view, set out to dissect the book—or to impose a rigid critical framework or to question Dostoevsky's motives—before hearing what he has to say. This is not to say that we start from a "neutral" position. Freire has long argued that this is impossible. Our prior experiences and our current understanding and circumstances will always have some bearing on how we read and what we gain from a literary work (or any other text). But these things do not *determine* our experience of a book. Coming to *love* the book is not possible without this experience. We might "fight" with the text, wrestling, as Dostoevsky's characters do, with competing ideas. We might also consider the possible influence of Dostoevsky's own experiences (e.g., his imprisonment in Siberia) on his writing. We might be critical of his Russian nationalism, his dislike of Poles, his anti-Semitic tendencies, or his positions on Catholicism and socialism. But none of this rational-critical activity need diminish our love of the book. Dostoevsky teaches us about the limits of reason and the power of feelings, but he does not encourage us to abandon reason altogether. A more detailed examination of Dostoevsky's work in the light of Freirean ideas is provided in Chapter 6.

Concluding Comments

Where, then, does the mature Freire rest in relation to Sherman's 1980 critique? Sherman criticized Freire for the rather vague and underdeveloped account of emotions in *Pedagogy of the Oppressed*. A holistic reading of Freire's later works yields a clearer, more robust account of the role of emotions in educational life. This is particularly true of emotions such as love and hope, both of which received extended attention in the last few years of Freire's life. Freire continued to be critical of "emotionality," conceived as an excessive, uncontrolled, and often violent expression of human passion. He could not sanction revolutionary action based entirely on the highly emotional and unreflective chanting of slogans. Similarly, he spoke at length about the need for tolerance, openness, and humility in educational dialogue. Any notion of Freire retaining a "lingering conception of emotions as totally uncritical forces" (Sherman, 1980, p. 38) had, I think, well and truly disappeared by the mid-1990s. I have suggested, to the contrary, that Freire saw emotions as an integral part of his critical ideal and that what is missing in his work is an extensive investigation of dimensions of emotional life *other* than those tied to a critical mode of being.

It seems certain that Freire would have said more about the nature and role of emotion had he lived for another ten years. When he died in 1997, he was still in his writing prime, and this theme, along with several others of importance to him (e.g., the impact of neoliberalism and globalization on education; reading and intellectual life; the relationship between faith, education, and social transformation), would undoubtedly have received ongoing attention. Of course, as was implied in the previous chapter, it is unreasonable to expect any one theorist to explore all dimensions of educational experience. There is merit, however, in considering possibilities for further research, where the contributions Freire has made might be combined with insights from other bodies of work to extend and deepen our understanding of reason, emotion, politics, and educational life.

Chapter 3

Freire and the Problem of Defining Literacy

Literacy figures prominently in many popular and academic discussions of education. References to literacy, and its associated terms (illiteracy, semiliteracy, functional literacy, computer literacy, and so on), appear frequently in books, journals, policy reports, political speeches, newspaper and magazine articles, television items, and conference programs. In some contexts, the importance of literacy for learning, social and economic advancement, and human fulfillment will be stressed; in others, emphasis might be placed on "reading problems," "literacy crises," or the "scourge" of illiteracy. From these myriad discussions, multiple definitions of literacy have emerged. Determining how one definition might relate to another, or differ from it, can be a difficult process. Literacy was a central theme for Freire, but he appears to have used the term in a number of different ways in his theory and practice.

This chapter offers a framework for distinguishing among three types of definition—stipulative, essentialist, and prescriptive—when examining statements about literacy. This framework is an adaptation of Israel Scheffler's (1960) groundbreaking work on definitions in education. The first section provides a concise account of Scheffler's three main types of definition; the second modifies and extends this framework for the purposes of analyzing definitions of literacy. The final part of the chapter shows how such a framework can be helpful in addressing apparent tensions in Freire's work.

Scheffler's Framework

Israel Scheffler is widely regarded as one of the most important figures in twentieth century philosophy of education. Among the many areas of his work that remain relevant to contemporary educational issues and problems is his discussion of different types of definition in his classic text, *The Language of Education* (1960). Scheffler's concern is to analyze "nonscientific discourses in which definitions of educational notions are offered, for example, in curriculum statements, in enunciations of program and objectives, in interpretations of education addressed to the general public, in debates over educational policy" (p. 12). He draws an initial distinction between "scientific" and "general" definitions, the former being those tied to professional research activity and requiring specialized technical knowledge, the latter representing the translation of scientific ideas into public or professional statements (pp. 12–13). Three types of "general" definition are delineated: stipulative, descriptive, and programmatic.

A stipulative definition "exhibits some term to be defined and gives notice that it is to be taken as equivalent to some other exhibited term or description, within a particular context" (p. 13). Such definitions do not attempt to comply with past or accepted usages; indeed, there might be no prior use to which the definer can turn. Where a term has a previous history of use, but a new use is promoted, the definition is of the "noninventive," stipulative variety. I might begin an essay, for example, by saying: "Although the term *teaching* has been employed in myriad different ways over the years, for the purposes of discussion here I shall define it as 'the process whereby one person enables another person to learn.'" Where a term is used for the first time, it is an "inventive" form of stipulative definition. Stipulative definitions, whether noninventive or inventive, reduce the need for laborious or repetitious description; they allow discussion to proceed where space may be limited and where lengthy digressions on the meaning or contestability of specific terms might impede the aim of presenting a coherent and concise overall argument. No appeal is made to the way a term is used in our "ordinary language" or to linguistic norms accepted by scholars within a given field of study. Instead, such definitions "legislate conventions that may be more or less helpful in discussion"; they "can neither be fairly justified nor rejected by consideration of the accuracy with which they mirror predefinitional usage" (p. 15).

"Descriptive" definitions, by contrast, explain terms by reference to their prior use. They are frequently evinced in response to the question, "What does this term *mean*?" (p. 15). There could be more than one meaning for a term, but each meaning is supposed to be "correct" within a particular context. Dictionary definitions, as Jonas Soltis (1978, p. 8) points out, are often of this kind. Descriptive definitions might endeavor to unpack the rules that govern the proper use of terms. Scheffler gives the example of a definition of "indoctrination" as "the presentation of issues as if they had but one side to them" to demonstrate the principle at work here (Scheffler, 1960, p. 15). Definitions of this type "are frequently presented in an attempt to clarify the term as it is ordinarily and most clearly applied. Such definitions aim at the distillation of a general rule out of the term's prior usage, a rule that may at once sum up such usage and clarify it by relating it to the usage of other familiar terms, a rule that may thus be employed to teach someone how the term is normally used" (p. 16).

Of course, it does not follow that because rules for the application of a term have been established in the past, adjudicating over the legitimacy of all *possible* applications of that term will always be straightforward. Scheffler claims that for any term prior use dictates clear cases where it can or cannot be properly applied, as well as instances where a certain ambiguity remains (p. 18). Hence, the assertion "X is a table" might confidently be judged correct if X is a piece of furniture with a wooden rectangular top and four legs around which people customarily seat themselves and upon which objects such as items of crockery are periodically placed. Comment on the use made of X (e.g., "people regularly eat their meals at the X") could strengthen the case here. It might be said that the term *table* would be inappropriately applied to Y, if Y swims in the sea, has gills and a tail, and eats shellfish. However, other cases—for example, a flat piece of rock from which a camper eats his or her meal—remain ambivalent. Scheffler argues that for a definition to be accurate, "it must accord with prior usage only in the sense of not violating clear instances of such usage. That is, where prior usage clearly applies a term to some object, the definition may not withhold it; where prior usage clearly withholds the term from some object, the definition may not apply it" (p. 18).

A "programmatic" definition, Soltis notes, "tells us overtly or implicitly that this is the way things *should* be." Definitions of education, he adds, "are frequently mixtures of the *is* and the *ought*, of the descriptive and the prescriptive" (Soltis, 1978, p. 9). Scheffler stresses the practical intent of such definitions: "some terms (e.g., the term 'profession') single out things toward which social practice is oriented in a certain way" (Scheffler, 1960, p. 19). If the term *profession*, for instance, implies the granting of some sort of privileged treatment, then assigning this term to something else (as in talking about, say, the "teaching profession") suggests that the activity of teaching ought to be accorded the same privileges as other professions. If, on the other hand, the term *profession* deliberately withheld in this case, the implication is that teachers ought not to expect to enjoy the same privileges as others in occupations designated "professions." Programmatic definitions raise moral and practical questions; they "call for evaluation of practice, for appraisal of commitments, for the making of extralinguistic decisions" (p. 21).

Scheffler summarizes the purpose of each type of definition thus: "The interest of stipulative definitions is *communicatory*, that is to say, they are offered in the hope of facilitating discourse; the interest of descriptive definitions is *explanatory*, that is, they purport to clarify the normal application of terms; the interest of programmatic definitions is *moral*, that is, they are intended to embody programs of action" (p. 22, emphasis added).

Adapting the Framework

When dealing with complex terms such as *education*, it is, as Soltis observes, hardly surprising that matters of morality arise. Education, by almost any definition, involves purposeful human activity and as such implies some form of commitment to certain values or ideals (cf. Soltis, 1978, p. 10). Discourses on literacy—including those where definitions are advanced—fall into a similar category. We often believe there is much at stake (for learners, teachers, and others) in programs of literacy instruction; and many definitions of literacy turn, implicitly or explicitly, on ethical questions. Soltis argues that "a search for *the* definition of education is most probably a quest for a statement of the *right* or the *best* program for education and, as such, is a prescription for certain valued means or ends to be sought in educating" (p. 11). Although it might be possible to come up with one definition of education that will suffice whatever the context (e.g., "education is learning"), this is likely to be so vague as to be of little use to anyone (pp. 10–11).

Soltis's view resonates with the position on literacy I want to adopt here. I would suggest that if our goal is to find a single definition of literacy that will satisfy all specific legitimate applications of the term, we will remain dissatisfied. The search for a satisfactory single descriptive definition of literacy is a journey without end; one can at best hope to specify "the" definition of literacy for particular purposes—either *speculatively* or *programmatically,* to use Scheffler's terms. Many statements of the kind "literacy *is* . . . ," where literacy is ostensibly being defined in unitary terms, are, in effect, propositions about what literacy *ought* to be. First, however, I wish—in light of issues canvassed in contemporary debates over reading and literacy—to propose a modification to Scheffler's terminology and an additional category of definition.

I believe the first type of definition can be retained largely in the form presented by Scheffler. Stipulative definitions take the form "X shall *for present purposes* be defined as A." To Scheffler's original description, I would simply add that such definitions perform not only a useful role in allowing discussion to proceed; they also serve a practical (if often unacknowledged) function in everyday life. In many of our daily activities we assume—in effect—that for particular purposes "X will be taken to mean A, and not B or C or D, etc." We *designate* meanings in negotiating our way in the world, frequently allowing X to mean A in the knowledge that it might also (alternatively or better) be defined as B or C or D. For example, when switching between drinking vessels in consuming tea or coffee at different times during the day, we seldom pause to draw distinctions between (say) mugs and cups when offering to "get a cup of tea." For the purposes of communication in daily life, the term *cup* suffices to cover both types of receptacle. The implied definition of a cup here might be something like this: "a vessel with a handle, used for holding hot beverages." If pressed to find a more exacting definition, however, we might distinguish cups from mugs by saying that the former usually have smaller handles than the latter, or that cups are designed to be placed on saucers, whereas mugs are not. These distinctions might be helpful in a philosophical analysis, or might be of importance for those who design and produce drinking vessels, but are of little practical consequence in day-to-day living.

In focusing on reading, writing, and literacy, there is merit in replacing Scheffler's notion of "descriptive" definitions with a more specific term: what I shall call *essentialist* definitions. These take the form "X *is* A, and *not* B, C, D, etc." The assumption here is that despite the many ways in which a term might be used in different contexts, there remains an essential, core meaning that sets this term apart from others. Thus, to return to an example discussed earlier, describing a flat piece of rock as a "table" would be legitimate if and only if it fell within the boundaries of the core definition. Hence, if a table was defined as "a piece of furniture with a flat top built upon a stand or several legs and around which people eat meals at regular intervals," the rock would not count as a table; if, however, the definition was "any reasonably flat surface upon which a meal can be eaten," it would (so, too, might any piece of flat earth, a bench, a box, and so on).

Why is the term *essentialist* helpful in examining definitions of reading, writing, and literacy? For more than two decades, there has been considerable debate over essentialism in constructs of "reading." (For a useful early overview of the issues at stake in the debate, see Luke, 1991.) Some theorists have claimed that reading is a unitary, individual, cognitive process, which is in essence the same no matter what the context. Others argue that there is no essence to reading but rather a multiplicity of different "readings" (i.e., specific social practices that are constructed as examples of "reading"). Those who adopt the former position use essentialist definitions of reading; those who subscribe to the latter view are explicitly antiessentialist in their approach. The essentialist group are happy to concede that reading is practiced in different ways in disparate situations (e.g., in reading a novel as compared with reading an academic text), but maintain that the underlying process is the same in each case. Reading, on this view, has an essential "nature," from which specific instances of reading in given contexts derive. Provided the definition of reading is sufficiently precise, the process of distinguishing "reading" from "not reading" should be relatively straightforward.

Antiessentialist theorists often adopt what I shall call "particularist" definitions. The term *definition* must, however, be used with caution in this context, and might better be replaced with the term *construct*. Particularist constructs can be represented thus: "X is A, and X is B, and X is C, ad infinitum." Or, to put it another way: "A is one form of X, B is another form of X, C is a further form of X, and so on." In discourses on literacy, those who directly or indirectly advance particularist constructs talk about *literacies* rather than "literacy" (cf. Street, 1984; Lankshear with Lawler, 1987; Lankshear, 1997). The singular form of the word is employed only with regard to a *specific* mode—sometimes termed a *form* or a *discourse*—of reading or writing (which is recognized as one among the multiplicity of actual and possible literacies) in a *particular* situation. Modes of literacy include "functional literacy," "critical literacy," "proper literacy," and so on. Literacies can be distinguished from each other by the assumptions and practices—ways of being in the world—that give them their distinctive form. There is, in this way of thinking, no single definition of literacy but rather multiple constructs that serve to describe particular examples of literacy X, literacy Y, and so on.

I wish finally to suggest a change in name and a slight change in focus for the last type of definition identified by Scheffler. When considering discussions of literacy, the term *prescriptive* is perhaps more helpful than the term *programmatic*. Programmatic definitions imply a moral dimension for Scheffler in the sense that they "are intended to embody programs of action" (Scheffler, 1960, p. 22). Yet, questions of ethics do not *necessarily* have to be tied to "programs" (of action or practice), although, of course, they might be in many cases. The ambiguity over the term *programmatic* is heightened in relation to literacy, for it is often *programs* of one kind or another (children's classroom reading programs, one-to-one programs of instruction for adults, national literacy programs, etc.) that are under examination. Prescriptive definitions take the form "X *should* be A," where "should" has two possible senses. First, in a general sense, to say X should be A is to suggest that A denotes some kind of ideal. In a second, more specific sense, the term *should* can mean X *ought* to be A. Definitions of this (more specific) kind are normative in character: That is, they imply that there are good *ethical* reasons for X being A. In either sense (the general or the normative), the range of possible definitions under consideration is considerably wider than Scheffler's original term suggests.

My modification to Scheffler's framework thus suggests three types of definition (stipulative, essentialist, and prescriptive), plus an additional category (particularist constructs), which might be applied when analyzing statements on literacy. Stipulative definitions facilitate discussion, allow everyday life and communication to proceed without unnecessary interruptions and lengthy analysis, and serve specific instrumental purposes in particular literacy policies and programs. Essentialist definitions attempt to pin down the "true" meaning of literacy and assume that there is an essential "nature" to literacy waiting to be uncovered. Prescriptive definitions seek to give grounds (especially of an ethical kind) for literacy being this way or that. Those who adopt particularist constructs abandon the notion of searching for a unitary essence or nature and focus on different modes or forms of literacy: Collectively, these constitute myriad *literacies*.

Applying the Framework

The modified framework described previously might be applied to any number of different contexts in which terms such as *literacy, reading, writing,* and *illiteracy* have been used. For present purposes, I shall address just one of these. Literacy was a key theme for Paulo Freire. Freire was involved with important literacy and adult education programs in Brazil, Chile, and Guinea Bissau, among other countries. He developed a distinctive approach to adult literacy education, stressing the relationships among reading, writing, and politics (see Freire, 1972a, 1972b, 1976; Taylor, 1993; Mayo, 1999; Roberts, 2000). For Freire, learning to read was seen as a potentially important part of the wider process of liberation from conditions of oppression. Freire also discussed reading at the university level (Freire and Shor, 1987), considered the importance of reading in his formative years (Freire, 1983), and commented on the aesthetic dimensions of written language (Freire, 1996). Freire's central theoretical construct in his discussions of literacy in the 1980s and 1990s was the notion of "reading the word and the world" (Freire and Macedo, 1987).

In these writings, an apparent tension in the way Freire understands literacy can be detected. When describing what it means to "read," Freire often links this with a critical, dialogical mode of knowing and being. He asserts, for example, that "reading *always* involves critical perception, interpretation" (Freire, 1983, p. 11, emphasis added). Yet, Freire also makes it clear that some practices that are usually described as examples of reading do *not* involve critical perception. In *A Pedagogy for Liberation* (Freire and Shor, 1987), for instance, he talks of the problems associated with trying to read too many books and failing to read any well. Elsewhere (e.g., Freire, 1972a), he shows how reading in the classroom can become an exercise in "banking education." Freire (1972b, 1976) also problematizes domesticating approaches to adult literacy instruction, where there is a radical disconnection between the world of the illiterates and the words at the heart of a literacy program.

How might we understand these seemingly divergent views of reading and literacy in Freire's work in the light of the framework advanced in the preceding section? For Freire, not everyone who might claim to be reading *is* reading—at least not in the sense in which he defines "reading." Mechanically repeating words without attempting to understand them or place them in some form of social context does not, in Freire's view, constitute "true" reading. In such instances, it might be said that there is something going on which *appears* to be reading, but which does not get to the heart of what reading involves. If someone is *really* reading, he or she will, according to Freire, be reading critically (Freire and Shor, 1987, p. 10). When Freire identifies and discusses noncritical forms of reading, then, he is referring to something that passes for reading, but which he would not recognize as "real" reading (cf. Freire, 1983, p. 9). The same logic applies to Freire's conception of "literacy." Many adult education programs and school-based reading systems might claim to be promoting "literacy," but Freire would argue that a person could not be characterized as "truly" literate unless he or she had learned something more than simply how to inscribe and interpret symbols on a piece of paper. Strictly speaking, a system for teaching people basic skills with print could not, for Freire, be described as a "literacy" program at all unless the learning of these skills was coupled with the development of some sort of critical reflection, through dialogue with others.

The distinction between essentialist and prescriptive definitions is helpful in assessing Freire's position here. If "real" reading, for Freire, is *critical* reading, and if a "truly" literate person is one who reads critically, is Freire adopting an essentialist or a prescriptive definition of literacy? I would argue that it is a mix of the two (as Soltis observed was often the case in the field of education) but more the latter than the former. When Freire says, "Literacy makes sense *only* in these terms" (Freire, 1976, p. 81, emphasis added), he can be seen to be making both a logical and a prescriptive or *normative* declaration about what literacy "really" means, and can *only* mean, if it is to make sense as part of his philosophical system.

There is neither space nor need here to elaborate in detail on Freire's ontology, epistemology, ethic, and pedagogy. (These aspects of Freire's work are examined in Roberts, 2000.) Briefly, however,

Freire sees humans as reflective, active, social beings, capable of knowing themselves and of transforming the world. Knowledge is constantly created and recreated through our interaction with an ever-changing world. "Knowing" demands an attempt to delve beneath surface-level explanations—with an investigative, curious, probing frame of mind—in search of a deeper understanding of the object of study. For Freire, as I have noted earlier in this book, the vocation of all human beings is humanization—the process of becoming more fully human—through critical, dialogical praxis. Education can play an important role in encouraging us to "see the world otherwise," but schools and other educational institutions can also *de*humanize students, inhibit dialogue and critical reflection, and contribute to a deepening of existing social inequalities.

These basic ideas underpin Freire's stance on reading and literacy. Freire would not deny that others have defined reading—whether explicitly through their theoretical work, or by implication through their practice—in terms quite different from his own; indeed, he would concede that his conception of what reading "really" is, or *ought* to be, is strictly a minority view. He would agree that reading—or what normally *passes* for reading—can certainly be practiced in passive, unreflective ways. Indeed, Freire has often noted that reading is frequently depicted as a neutral, contextless, largely "mechanical" process. But, *given* the philosophical assumptions with which Freire begins, this view must (in the logical as well as normative sense of *must*) be regarded as mistaken.

Freire recognizes that programs of instruction in reading and writing take different forms. To some extent, his work is compatible with those who speak of multiple literacies rather than "literacy" in the singular. He tends, however, to collapse the multiplicity of particular and localized literacies into opposing binary theoretical categories. The major contrasting forms, at least in Freire's early work, are "literacy as domestication" and "literacy for liberation," the former being dehumanizing and the latter humanizing. Freire argues that banking systems of education typically promote domesticating forms of reading and writing, whereas problem-posing approaches take as their starting point the liberation of the oppressed (see Freire, 1972a).

A number of literacy studies scholars have followed a similar pattern of analysis, recognizing that there are multiple specific literacies but dividing these, for evaluative purposes, into two broad categories. Colin Lankshear and Moira Lawler (1987), for example, distinguish between "proper" and "improper" forms of literacy. Modifying a distinction first drawn by Wayne O'Neil (1970), they suggest, "Proper literacy enhances people's control over their lives and their capacity for dealing rationally with decisions by enabling them to identify, understand, and to act to transform, social relations and practices in which power is structured unequally.... Improper literacy either fails to promote, or else actively impedes, such understanding and action" (1987, p. 74). These categories provide a framework for analyzing historical and contemporary practices of reading and writing. Thus we find, in Lankshear and Lawler's account, the following as examples of "proper" literacy: the activities of the London Corresponding Society in England in the nineteenth century, the pedagogy of Ira Shor at the City University of New York, the teaching practices of Chris Searle in working-class schools in London's East End in the early 1970s, the work of Paulo Freire, and the Nicaraguan literacy crusade.

Although this division into two primary opposing forms might be regarded by many postmodernists as problematic (in as much as it glosses over the heterogeneity and specificity of actual and possible literacies), it is important to examine the relationship between "universals" and "particulars" in this work. One way of addressing this is to think of levels of specificity in forms of literacy. Lankshear and Lawler advance opposing generic forms (proper and improper literacy), from which more specific forms or modes of literacy derive. Within any of these more specific forms there might be other even more specific and localized forms. As the level of specificity increases, one form, in effect, becomes "nested" within another. Hence, if we take "proper literacy" as the generic form, the Nicaraguan literacy crusade as a whole—as a "moment" in Nicaraguan and world history—can be taken as one example of proper literacy. Within the crusade a host of more specific forms of proper literacy emerged. One could focus, for instance, on the efforts of women confronting issues of patriarchy through organizations such as AMNLAE (the Association of Nicaraguan Women, named for Luisa Amanda Espinosa) (see Lankshear with Lawler, 1987, pp. 202–216). At a more specific level still, attention could be paid to the work of particular women in different communities. This process of analysis could continue to even greater levels of specificity, if need be, and attention could be paid to the way these women conduct themselves at different moments

CHAPTER 3

in time, or the way they interact with some students compared with others, and so on.

The same logic could apply to Freire's work. A case might be made for the view that Freire's adult literacy program in Brazil in the early 1960s constituted a form of liberating literacy. (There is not space to defend such a claim here, but see Roberts, 2000, for a more extended examination of Freire's literacy work.) If the program as a whole were to be regarded as the generic form, it becomes possible to identify a number of more localized forms of liberating literacy at work. Hence, liberating literacy in an urban culture circle (learning group) will have a different character than liberating literacy in a rural peasant community. Similarly, the practices that are necessary and effective in working with adults who might have had some prior encounter with the written word will differ from those required in situations where reading and writing are completely foreign activities for participants. Teachers in such a campaign, similarly, will have to work in different ways with students to make the most of their own knowledge and experience. Methods and practices might differ from one group or setting to another in a major campaign, yet all can remain true to an underlying set of philosophical and pedagogical principles. The forms reading and writing take in particular contexts within a campaign collectively give empirical substance to claims about the *overall* character of that campaign.

To summarize, Freire makes statements about reading and literacy that *appear* to be essentialist in character, but which, on closer analysis, might better be viewed as implied prescriptive definitions. This view is reinforced by the fact that Freire wants to distinguish between at least two broad forms of literacy, one liberating, the other oppressive. One of these—the liberating—is consistent with his prescriptive statements about reading and literacy; the other is not. Freire's work is thus not incompatible with those who favor particularist constructs of literacy, but the number of different literacies identified and analyzed by Freire is limited. A more subtle and complex account of literacy emerges in Freire's later publications, where reading and writing are considered in relation to wider debates over difference, unity, and the politics of transformation (see, for example, Freire, 1996, 1997b, 1998b). Throughout these writings, however, there remains an underlying concern with liberation and oppression as dominant themes in understanding the theory and practice of literacy education.

Concluding Comments

This chapter has provided a framework, based on the work of the educational philosopher Israel Scheffler, for analyzing definitions of literacy. This is, of course, just one of the many possible approaches to delineating, understanding, and comparing such definitions. I have applied the modified framework to the writings of just one important literacy theorist. There is scope, however, for further work in analyzing statements on literacy by educationists, policy makers, and others in a wide range of settings, both formal and informal. There is also value in undertaking metalevel analyses of the different approaches to the problem of defining literacy. Such analyses sharpen our grasp of some of the conceptual and practical issues at stake in attempts to characterize, categorize, interpret, critique, and apply definitions of literacy. Finally, ongoing theoretical and empirical work on differences in definitions across time, cultures, classes, and countries will continue to yield interesting results, particularly as we contemplate the bearing new technologies have had and will have on conceptions and practices of literacy. Projects in these areas, among others, could contribute significantly to the wider ongoing international dialogue on the nature, purpose, and value of literacy.

Chapter 4

Freire and Political Correctness

"Political correctness" was one of the most hotly contested educational topics of the 1990s. Following earlier battles in the United States over the nature and purpose of higher education—generated in the first instance by the publication of Allan Bloom's *The Closing of the American Mind* (1988), and later fueled by other conservative works, such as Roger Kimball's *Tenured Radicals* (1991) and Dinesh D'Souza's *Illiberal Education* (1991)—charges of political correctness in the academy became the subject of considerable scholarly and popular debate. During this period, "political correctness" came to serve as a referent for an extraordinary range of different policies, attitudes, and events. In the educational sphere alone, the term was used in relation to: the encroachment of politics into university classrooms (education, it was charged, had "become political"); "multiculturalism"; Marxist, feminist, deconstructionist, postmodernist, and other critical approaches to particular fields of study (especially literary criticism); moves to reform language use—particularly, though not exclusively, to make it "nonsexist"; affirmative action policies (e.g., in criteria for admission to universities, in the appointment of faculty, in promotions, in scholarships, etc.); alleged favoritism of other kinds toward women and ethnic minorities; the apparent abandonment of merit as the prime criterion for judging quality; speech codes (where offensive remarks about particular groups of people were banned); and "sensitivity" programs for incoming students and staff.

This chapter argues that Paulo Freire would oppose educational policies and practices based on politically correct assumptions.

Given his espousal of conscientization and critical literacy, political correctness is in tension with everything Freire stands for. To be a "politically correct Freirean," then, would be a contradiction in terms. The difficulty in asserting this, however, arises when one attempts to define *political correctness*. For, despite its widespread use and application in diverse contexts, the term has always been remarkably ambiguous (O'Keefe, 1992, pp. 123–126). This imprecision is significant for two reasons. First, it has allowed the label *political correctness* to become a multipurpose bludgeon for criticizing an enormous variety of new developments in education and other spheres of the social world (Dickstein, 1993, p. 542). Second, such ambiguity obscures the potential value of the term as a distinct concept in educational discourse. My analysis suggests that if the concept of political correctness is to have educational force, its pejorative connotation must be retained. Once conditions for its use have been clarified, useful comparisons can be drawn among political correctness, dogmatism, and pedagogical authoritarianism. The contrasts between politically correct approaches and the Freirean ideals of critical consciousness and critical literacy likewise become readily apparent.

The Many Faces of "Political Correctness"

During the 1990s, the lack of conceptual clarification in discourses on political correctness allowed the term to serve as a powerful device for attacking new ideas and practices. This section of the chapter comments on the politics of this process, paying particular attention to the views expressed by conservative commentators. Why the focus on conservative critics? There was certainly a critique of political correctness on the Left. Indeed, the term originated within Left circles, and was used, with a gentle mocking or ironic tone, to refer to the excessively serious adherence to a political position. It was on the political and cultural Right, however, that the most vigorous assault on political correctness was mounted. The aggressiveness of the attack reflected, in part, a change in the perceptions of those employing the label over time.

Roger Kimball, a prominent conservative commentator in the "culture wars," argued that political correctness had shifted from being something that was merely farcical to a phenomenon that was genuinely tragic. In 1993, he asserted that although in the past the label *politically correct* described "the self-righteous, nonsmoking, ecologically sensitive, vegetarian, feminist, nonracist, sandal-wearing beneficiaries of capitalism—faculty as well as students—who paraded their outworn sixties radicalism in the classroom and in their social life," in more recent times the situation had become far more serious: "Anyone who has taken the trouble to observe what has happened in the academy knows that over the last couple of years political correctness has evolved from a sporadic expression of left-leaning self-righteousness into a dogma of orthodoxy that is widely accepted, and widely enforced, by America's cultural elite" (Kimball, 1993, p. 565).

For some critics, "political correctness" appeared to encompass almost every political position, academic development (i.e., new course, program, etc.), or theoretical perspective that did not comfortably mesh with a conservative view of the world. Take, for instance, the following statement by William Phillips (1993, p. 671):

> What is political correctness? It is a loose but useful term, denoting a wide movement with many facets and differences, but essentially a new left configuration. It includes extreme and radical feminist theories, gay and lesbian liberation studies and activities, ideas stemming from the deconstructionists, neo-Marxists, and remnants of old, revolutionary postures. It is not basically Marxist or revolutionary, but it is to a large extent anti-American, in some quarters anticapitalist, pro–third world, pro-minority, and anti-Western cultural and political interests.

The same approach was evident in Jerry Martin's (1993) critique of what he calls the "transformationist view" of education. Martin collapsed deconstruction, Marxism, feminism, the work of critical pedagogues such as Giroux and McLaren, and a range of other critical perspectives into a single homogeneous category: "the postmodern argument for the transformationist view." According to Martin (1993, p. 653), "The postmodern argument for making the university an agent of social transformation protects itself from criticism, not only theoretically, but institutionally as well. The early steps of the postmodern argument may be questionable, but only grant them, and the remaining steps—including political correctness, critical pedagogy, speech codes, and denial—follow."

We might object to characterizations of this kind in several different ways. On one level we might protest that this form of reductionism demonstrates an ignorance of the complexities of the traditions in question and renders invisible the conflicts and contradictions within and between different pedagogical approaches. Or, doubt might be cast on the appropriateness of the label *postmodern* in Martin's article: Some of the principles alluded to as typical of the "postmodern view"—elements of Marxism, for instance—are among the key ideas postmodernists seek to position themselves *against*. Alternatively, specific mention could made of gross inaccuracies in Martin's portrayal of critical pedagogy. He asserts, for example, that "one of the main tasks of critical pedagogy is to overcome 'patterns of resistance' from students who resist ideas that challenge prevailing norms" (1993, p. 643). Similarly, confusing the exercising of academic authority with political authoritarianism, Martin claims: "The transformationist proposes to mould students into, among other things, radical egalitarians; but to do so would give teachers authority over students that is incompatible with radical egalitarianism. The dictatorship of the proletariat may have been replaced by the dictatorship of the professoriate, but the dilemma remains the same—how to achieve antiauthoritarian ends by authoritarian means" (p. 652).

Distortions of this magnitude were not uncommon in 1990s debates over political correctness. Complex political positions, intellectual traditions, and pedagogical theories were all lumped together as part of a common "disease": the scourge of political correctness in the academy. Wielding the label *political correctness* as a multipurpose weapon could, as many on the receiving end of the attacks attested, be highly effective in silencing debate and squashing resistance (cf. Carey 1992, pp. 58–59). If the debates over political correctness in the period are conceived as a kind of war that occurred between two broad factions—the conservative Right and a "rainbow coalition" of groups on the Left—then the former can be seen as having achieved a major victory in at least one sense: With such a multifaceted concept, almost any development incompatible with conservative ideas was open for criticism.

Using a term to roundly dismiss a diverse array of opposing perspectives is arguably more consistent with *promoting* political correctness (as I shall define it below) than resisting it. Of course, where the goal is ideological and material domination, conceptual contradictions and confusions do not necessarily matter. If the meaning of political correctness is sufficiently vague, but the connotations of being labeled politically correct are clearly and invariably negative, care in using the term is no longer necessary: The *accusation* of political correctness becomes, on its own, sufficient to cause the desired effect. This is precisely the situation that evolved in the 1990s.

Ellen Messer-Davidow (1993) discussed the politics of this process in some detail. She argued that the Right played a significant role in both initiating the attacks and creating an aura of suspicion around moves to reform the curriculum in universities. This does not mean that the *ambiguities* that attended many references to political correctness were the result of a carefully crafted plan by conservatives; indeed, these confusions were seldom noticed and only infrequently analyzed by those on the Right (see Dickstein, 1993). There was little doubt, however, that the ferocity and breadth of the assault gave "political correctness" an unquestionably pejorative connotation, and this was used to good effect by defenders of a certain form of tradition in universities and other institutions. Reformists, whether avowedly left-wing or not, often ended up on the back foot—defensive, and, at times, apparently stunned by the force of the onslaught.

Given this situation, it becomes especially important to clarify conditions for the term's use, if political correctness is to have any ongoing educational significance. In this chapter, I want to concentrate on one of the few points on which agreement could be found among many critics from both the Right and the Left: namely, that political correctness has something to do with *intolerance*. I begin from the assumption that a worthwhile connection can be made between political correctness and what David Lehman (1993, p. 598) describes as "the inability or unwillingness to tolerate a rival point of view." (On the theme of intolerance, and related notions such as conformism, compare, Delbanco, 1993; Loury, 1993; Marcus, 1993; Merkin, 1993; M. Phillips, 1994; Hall, 1994.) The concept of political correctness advanced in the pages that follow focuses on orthodoxy, conformism, intolerance of differences, and the suppression of questioning. Political correctness, when seen in this light, might relate to the enforcement of a "party line," the refusal to allow or acknowledge alternative or opposing views on political and ethical matters, the censuring of criticism, the banning of questions, or the stifling of debate. Political correctness, in short, is the enforcement of one position as the only possible or acceptable or legitimate position.

In emphasizing intolerance, conformity, and the suppression of criticism and questioning as key criteria, I am attempting (1) to capture a key element in the 1990s (and twenty-first century) discourses on political correctness, and (2) to develop a construct that might be meaningfully related to the work of Paulo Freire. My suggestion is that if political correctness is to have any value in a theory of education based on Freirean principles, it must remain a pejorative concept. It is important to acknowledge, however, that not all commentators, past or present, see it this way. Some, in defending changes to curricula and policy, have said that if the term *political correctness* is to be used at all, it should correspond to positive developments. Lisa Jardine (1994, p. 106), for example, submits that "insofar as it is a term which means anything, [political correctness] ... describes the teacher's commitment to making all teaching inclusive, faced with an increasingly diverse undergraduate population." Others have denied that political correctness exists at all: It is, they argue, simply a malicious fabrication by the Right.

As far as the first option is concerned, I believe that if political correctness is to name a positive set of attitudes or practices, the ambiguities long associated with the term can only increase. In asserting this, I am presupposing that the aim is to find something meaningful to say about political correctness *in relation to Freire's work*. If this is the case, a pejorative reading is more effective than a positive interpretation of the term. Although it is true that the label *political correctness* has been used as a referent for developments Freire would support—for example, certain multicultural policies, the growth of women's studies programs, the discussion of literary works from Marxist and feminist points of view, and so on—it is not the case that Freire would endorse *all* practices associated with these developments.

It could be argued that the criteria for distinguishing practices Freire would support from those he would not should spring from the ethical and educational imperatives in Freire's work. Hence, being politically correct might mean being critical, dialogical, rigorous, and so on. But what would give the term *political correctness* special significance, if this were the case? Distinct concepts for describing these characteristics are already in place in Freire's work: The Freirean ethical ideal is encapsulated in the notion of humanization; *liberating education* is the generic term for a family of pedagogical principles, practices, and attitudes consistent with this ideal; and *critical literacy* captures the essence of Freire's approach to literacy. It is not clear what political correctness would name that is not already covered by these concepts.

If the term is given a pejorative reading, however, *political correctness* might usefully be employed to describe a series of related practices for which there is no generic concept in Freire's work (including his posthumously published texts). Freire talks about dogmatism, sectarianism, intolerance of differences, the confining of investigation within overly restrictive boundaries, the silencing of questions, enforced conformity, and the denial of dialogue, but he does not have an overarching concept for collectively naming these practices. A staunch member of a political party (whether on the Right or the Left) might hold to a position slavishly in the face of criticism: This is dogmatism. Or, teachers might actively impede discussion and debate in a monologue on political ideas: Such a stance is antidialogical. Or, political leaders might refuse to allow consideration of opposing views: This is intolerance. The notion of *political correctness* allows all of these (undesirable) practices to be described under a single heading.

Education, Conscientization, and Critical Literacy

As discussed in more detail elsewhere in this book and in earlier writings (e.g., Roberts, 2000), Freire argues that all human beings have an ontological and historical vocation of humanization. People pursue this vocation when they engage in critical, dialogical praxis. Praxis, for Freire, represents the synthesis of reflection and action. Where opportunities for pursuing authentic praxis are impeded, a situation of oppression emerges. Impediments to praxis might take the form of overt constraints to human action (e.g., exploitative working conditions), structural barriers to democratic participation in social life (e.g., being denied the vote because of one's illiteracy), or hegemonic control of patterns of thought (e.g., fostering the view that poverty is "God's will"). Relations of oppression are dehumanizing for both oppressors and the oppressed. The oppressed pursue their liberation (and hence humanization) when they struggle against the conditions that oppress them, seeking, collectively, to reclaim their role as subjects in the historical process.

Education is vital in this process. Freire calls upon educators to side with the oppressed in building a better social world (Weiler, 1991). Education, on the Freirean view, should be based on a structured, purposeful, and rigorous form of dialogue between the teacher and students, and among the students themselves, rather than a monological, one-way, vertical relationship, where the teacher issues communiqués to passive, docile, patiently listening pupils (Freire, 1972a, ch.2, 1976, pp. 45–46). Through education, participants undergo "conscientization," attaining a (more) critical awareness of social reality generally and the nature of oppression in particular. Conscientization implies the movement from "magical" or "naïve" levels to understanding toward critical consciousness (Freire, 1972b; 1976, pp. 17–20). In *Education: The Practice of Freedom*, Freire suggests that critical consciousness is characterized by:

> depth in the interpretation of problems; by the substitution of causal principles for magical explanations; by the testing of one's "findings" and by openness to revision; by the attempt to avoid distortion when perceiving problems and to avoid preconceived notions when analysing them; by refusing to transfer responsibility; by rejecting passive positions; by soundness of argumentation; by the practice of dialogue rather than polemics; by receptivity to the new for reasons beyond mere novelty and by the good sense not to reject the old just because it is old—by accepting what is valid in both old and new. (1976, p. 18)

These ideas are extended in later writings, where Freire speaks of the importance of adopting an investigative, probing stance in the act of studying, reading, and thinking (Freire, 1985, pp. 1–4; Freire and Shor, 1987, pp. 10–11, 82–87; Horton and Freire, 1990, pp. 23–27). Readers, he stresses, should never simply accept the ideas presented in books; rather, they should always be prepared to question what they read, and, in turn, to be challenged by authors and by other readers (see Roberts, 1993, pp. 172–173). Freirean critical literacy is distinguished by the linking of "word" with "world," the relating of theory to practice, the overcoming of pedagogical and political passivity, the rejection of fragmented and decontextualized readings of an author's work, and the reinterpretation of personal experience, among other features (Peters and Lankshear, 1996; Aronowitz, 1993; Freire and Macedo, 1995; Roberts, 2000). Freire sees the process of critically reading both "texts" and "contexts" as necessarily incomplete. Insofar as the world is constantly changing, we can never *know* absolutely or completely (Horton and Freire, 1990, p. 101), but instead must be ever restless—perpetually curious—in our quest to uncover deeper and deeper layers of meaning in social phenomena and problems.

Becoming critically conscious demands a deliberate effort to probe beneath the surface: to seek out "the *raison d'etre* which explains the object [of study]" (Freire and Shor, 1987, p. 82). Through this process of engaging word and world, human beings "create" history, and, in so doing, "recreate" themselves.

To judge by both his theory and his practice, it seems certain that Freire would have been fundamentally opposed to any policy or practice that compelled or coerced people to accept a position without question. (A "position" might be an interpretation of a text, a stance on a contentious issue, or a reading of social reality.) To abandon the right to question is to forsake the very essence of the Freirean educational ideal: the development of a critical approach toward understanding the world. "Political correctness," I maintain, can be seen as the exact opposite of critical consciousness, and, hence, as incompatible with any program of education based on the principle of conscientization. I want now to elaborate on this argument, drawing in particular on Freire's later writings.

Freire on Tolerance, Dogmatism, and Diversity

Although Freire was always clearly (and openly) to the left end of the political spectrum (see, for example, Freire's comments in Freire and Faundez, 1989, p. 49; Horton and Freire, 1990, p. 219), he frequently criticized intolerance on the part of both the Left and the Right. In reflecting on the politics of life in Chile several decades ago, for example, Freire states:

> Only a radical politics—not a sectarian one, however, but one that seeks a unity in diversity among progressive forces—could ever have won the battle for a democracy that could stand up to the power and virulence of the Right. Instead, there was only sectarianism and intolerance—the rejection of differences. Tolerance was not what it ought to be: the revolutionary virtue that consists in a peaceful coexistence with those who are different, in order to wage a better fight against the adversaries. (Freire, 1994, p. 39)

Dogmatic stances, like reactionary responses, deny the reflective, critical component of humanizing praxis; neither position can be conscientizing. Indeed, dogmatic and reactionary positions both positively *impede* the development of critical thought and action;

both constrain, rather than enhance, opportunities for expanding the discursive universe within which people might participate. For Freire, there are important similarities, as well as certain differences, between the dogmatist and the reactionary. The dogmatist holds steadfastly and unreflexively to a particular view of the world (cf. Roberts, 1999a). He or she either refuses to acknowledge the existence of alternative perspectives, staying with a particular "line" on a given issue no matter what, or denounces counter positions without engaging them. The dogmatist might, like the reactionary, be defensive in the face of criticism, attacking opposing ideas with vigor or even violence; or, he or she might simply ignore criticism and hold resolutely to existing views. For the reactionary, opposing positions represent a threat; for the dogmatist, they might simply be considered irrelevant. For dogmatists, there is only one way to view the world, *period*; for reactionaries, there is only one *acceptable* or *legitimate* way to view the world.

For Freire, dogmatic and reactionary stances are both closely related to authoritarianism. Dogmatic and reactionary educators wish to impose their view of the world on students, stifling criticism and discouraging (or explicitly prohibiting) questioning. If there is only one correct, acceptable, or legitimate way of understanding an issue or subject or object of study, and if one's task is to teach others about this object of study, then it follows that this must be the view conveyed to students. The dogmatic teacher *knows* (or thinks he or she knows) what others need to know; thus, the ideas students bring to the educative situation are neither relevant nor valued. This, Freire says, "is the certitude, always, of the authoritarian, the dogmatist, who knows what the popular classes know, and knows what they need even without talking to them." Freire continues: "What makes sense to them is what comes from their readings, and what they write in their books and articles. It is what they already know about the knowledge that seems basic and indispensable to them, and which, in the form of content, must be "deposited" in the "empty consciousness" of the popular classes" (Freire, 1994, p. 116).

These points lead usefully to a consideration of intolerance, conformity, and the suppression of criticism—and their opposites (tolerance, difference, and criticalness)—as pivotal themes in a theory of political correctness based on Freirean principles. In later publications, Freire emphasizes the value of tolerance as a key virtue in the university (see especially Escobar et al., 1994). He speaks of the need to accept—though not uncritically—ways of thinking other than one's own. In *Learning to Question*, Freire notes: "Tolerance doesn't in any way imply giving up what seems to you to be right and just and good. No, tolerant people do not give up their dreams: they are determined to fight for them. But they do respect those who have a different dream from themselves" (Freire and Faundez, 1989, 17). Tolerance, for Freire, does *not* mean accepting all views without question; on the contrary, respect for others positively demands that their ideas be open for discussion and debate. Tolerance makes ethical and educational sense to Freire precisely to the extent that it enables one to *engage* views other than one's own. Teachers have a right—indeed, a responsibility—to challenge the students' perceptions of the world. But, Freire (1994, p. 83) says, "what is not permissible to be doing is to conceal truths, deny information, impose principles, eviscerate the educands of their freedom, or punish them, no matter by what method, if, for various reasons, they fail to accept my discourse—reject my utopia."

Freire argues that the university ought not to become a homogeneous institution where all students have, or are encouraged to adopt, the same views and commitments. Freire sees difference within a university as potentially enriching, provided it is "lived with faith, loyalty, honesty, and integrity." He suggests: "Instead of engaging in controversy about the difference, we must hold a dialogue about the difference. For it is very important that the young student perceives a different vision of reality and that this reality is not the same for all university students. In this manner, the young student will know that there is a diverse educational context within the university. Thus, his or her political and ideological education will be ensured" (Escobar et al., 1994, p. 91). The university, Freire argues, ought not to become a kind of "sacred temple where to be chaste is a virtue." An institution of higher education "that is beyond and above the social and political system of the society where it exists is unfeasible" (Escobar et al., 1994, pp. 79, 136). The university should be, and cannot avoid being, a thoroughly political institution, but this does not mean that it should prescribe or proscribe political positions for students. Freire supports an environment of intellectual pluralism within institutions of higher education, where students might, for example, be taught by both reactionary and revolutionary professors. The key is for all teachers to be open with students about their politics: "I belong to a political party in Brazil and the students know this; there is no reason to hide it. What I cannot do is change the academic policy of the university where I work for the policy of the Worker's Party and I must respect the students who do not have anything to do with that party" (Escobar et al., 1994, p. 138).

These points find further elaboration in *Pedagogy of Hope*, where Freire speaks of the impossibility of educating without "running risks." It is, Freire argues, "precisely the political nature of educational practice, its helplessness to be 'neutral,' that requires of the educator his or her ethicalness" (Freire, 1994, p. 77). Freire continues:

> What especially moves me to be ethical is to know that, inasmuch as education of its very nature is directive and political, I must, without ever denying my dream or my utopia before the educands, respect them. To defend a thesis, a position, a preference, with earnestness, defend it rigorously, but passionately, as well, and at the same time to stimulate the contrary discourse, and respect the right to utter that discourse, is the best way to teach, first, the right to have our own ideas, even our duty to "quarrel" for them, for our dreams—and not only to learn the syntax of the verb, *haver*; and second, mutual respect. (Freire, 1994, p. 78)

On the one hand, then, university teachers ought not to disavow their personal politics: To do so would be to deny the situatedness of their pedagogy within a particular conception of human beings and the social world. On the other hand, academics also ought not to take advantage of the spaces the university provides to engage in party politics, to coerce students into accepting certain policies, to punish those who do not conform to one's own view of the world, and so on. University teachers should be secure enough in their own convictions to leave their ideas open to refutation—by others, or by subsequent events. Taking a stance on ethical and political issues always involves risks and uncertainties. Paradoxically, greater certainty about the worth of a particular stance can, from Freire's point of view, only emerge through not being too certain of one's own position, and through continually exposing it to counterpositions. Working in a pluralistic way with others is not easy, because "pluralism within the university entails positions that are not only different but antagonistic" (Escobar et al., 1994, pp. 151–152), but it is the only way forward if the university is to become a site for genuine tolerance, critical analysis, dialogue, and debate.

Some Implications of a Freirean View on Political Correctness

Given the ideas just presented, what might be said about the various domains to which the term *political correctness* has been applied? Some of the implications of a Freirean view on political correctness are clear. With regard to debates over core curricula and required reading, for instance, on the criteria outlined earlier, any situations where students are prevented, or discouraged, from criticizing or questioning an author's ideas or the teacher's interpretation of texts can obviously be classed as examples of political correctness. Such cases overtly contradict the Freirean ideal of critical consciousness. Similarly, if certain books are categorically banned in a university context on the grounds that they do not "fit" the lecturer's personal political perspective, a charge of political correctness would be valid. The same would be true of cases where sections of texts are ignored, removed, or censored because the lecturer finds them "offensive" (sexist, racist, homophobic, colonialist, etc.). An indictment of "political correctness" would be ill-founded if university teachers merely attempted to incorporate feminist or Marxist perspectives (or various conservative and liberal views) into the curriculum; indeed, if these approaches represent major alternatives in addressing enduring questions, themes, and concerns, those who intentionally keep such perspectives *out* of core courses are acting in a politically correct way (cf. Roberts, 1997).

A crucial element in conservative assaults on reforms to university curricula was the charge that education had become "political" and "ideologically driven" (see, for example, Alter, 1993; Sidorsky, 1993). This accusation, Freire would have argued, betrays either a naïve understanding of the political dimensions to education or a mischievous attempt to disguise the politics of traditional pedagogical practices. Freire, along with dozens of scholars in critical pedagogy and the sociology of education, has convincingly demonstrated that teaching is *always* a political process. This point was established decades ago by theorists such as Michael Apple (1979, 1985), Henry Giroux (1983, 1988), Peter McLaren (1989), and many others. Educational programs always favor some values, beliefs, attitudes, practices, ideologies, and interests over others. This is not the same thing as saying that teachers cannot avoid being politically *correct*. From a Freirean point of view, it is not a matter of asking whether one ought or ought not to be political as a teacher, but rather of deciding what *kind* of politics to foster in the classroom (compare Freire, 1987).

An openly "political" teacher admits his or her political preferences, but allows these to be questioned, challenged, and debated; a "politically correct" teacher advances one way of thinking as the *only* (acceptable or legitimate) way. The former encourages tolerance and diversity; the latter impedes the development of these qualities. Recognizing and acknowledging the political character of education expands the students' discursive universe by allowing them to interpret policies and practices in a new way; political correctness more tightly wraps student views within existing enclosures. All teachers take certain assumptions about human beings and the world as (at least provisionally) given for particular purposes in the classroom; politically correct teachers take it for granted that their assumptions ought to prevail for all, no matter what the circumstances. If "political correctness" is equivalent to "bringing politics into the classroom," then *all* education is politically correct from a Freirean perspective. A Freirean would be neither in favor of nor against *political correctness,* because the term, if defined in this manner, would fail to give effective purchase—whether pejorative or positive—on anything: A "politically correct" educator would simply be an educator.

The equating or linking of political correctness with multiculturalism, as occurred in the 1990s and as is still evident today, is a peculiar, and at times revealing, phenomenon. The conjoining of the two during the most heated period of debate was almost exclusively a trait of conservative critiques of political correctness (see, for instance, Berger, 1993; Brustein, 1993; Phillips, 1993; Radosh, 1993). Where liberals or radicals mentioned the two in the same breath, it was invariably to defend allegedly politically correct practices or attitudes as a means toward a noble end: multiculturalism. Of the conservative accounts, perhaps the most blatant declaration of opposition to multiculturalism came from Hilton Kramer (1993, p. 571), who called it the "bastard offspring" of the political correctness movement. Others, however, were also surprisingly forthright. Brigitte Berger (1993, p. 517) claimed that "the multicultural agenda is overwhelmingly a political agenda and has very little to do with the essential tasks and mission of a modern university." Signaling the imminent arrival of an academic Armageddon, she writes: "A university wavering between the mindless visions of multiculturalist propagandists and the complacency of an intellectually slothful professoriate is about to abandon its *raison d'être* and civilatory mission. Rather than witnessing 'the end of history' as Francis Fukuyama argued a few years ago, today we must face up to the prospect of the end of a civilization" (Berger, 1993, p. 526).

William Phillips offered an equally alarmist account. Beginning with the premise that "multiculturalism is the battle cry of the politically correct and those under its influence," he claims that reformists are "promoting a largely inflated African heritage for blacks as a source for the knowledge and science of the West." Were such groups to succeed in realizing their goals, Phillips maintains, "Western culture would be wiped out, or at least demoted to the status of an evil past" (Phillips, 1993, p. 672).

Freire, needless to say, saw the issue of multiculturalism quite differently. He always viewed racism as deeply dehumanizing and campaigned for better recognition of nondominant cultural groups in educational institutions. In *Pedagogy of Hope*, Freire argues for a position of "unity in diversity" as a means of addressing the problems confronting various minority groups. Without this, he says, "the so-called minorities could not even struggle, in the United States, for the most basic ... rights, let alone overcome barriers that keep them from 'being themselves,' from being 'minorities for themselves,' *with* one another and not *against* one another" (Freire, 1994, p. 151). Pointing out that minorities often collectively make up the majority, Freire maintains that only through concentrating on their similarities as well as their differences can the different groups build a "substantial, radical democracy." Freire believes that the oppression of ethnic minorities (and women) cannot be understood in the absence of a class analysis: Any solution to problems of racism and sexism must therefore also address the question of class struggle.

Freire contends that in a multicultural society there is a need for a certain kind of tension between different cultures. This is a tension "to which the various cultures expose themselves by being different, in a democratic relationship in which they strive for advancement.... [It] is the tension of not being able to escape their self-construction, their self-creation, their self-production" (Freire, 1994, p. 156). *Cultural pluralism*, or *multiculturality* (these terms are synonymous for Freire), is an ongoing project: a continuous, unfinished process of social, dialogical struggle. Freire summarizes his position thus:

> The very quest for this oneness in difference [through unity in diversity], the struggle for it as a process, in and of itself is the beginning of a creation of multiculturality. Let me emphasize once more: multiculturality as a phenomenon involving the coexistence of different cultures in one and the same space is not something natural and spontaneous. It is a historical creation, involving decision, political determination, mobilization, and organization, on the part of each cultural group, in view of common purposes. Thus, it calls for a certain educational practice, one that will be consistent with these objectives. It calls for a new ethics, founded on respect for differences. (1994, p. 157)

Freire's acknowledgment of difference did not lead him to the view that one should never criticize cultures other than one's own. In *We Make the Road by Walking,* he notes: "My respect for the soul of the culture does not prevent me from trying, with the people, to change some conditions that appear to me as obviously against the beauty of being human." Using as an example the tradition in Latin American cultures that prevents men from cooking, Freire observes: "In the last analysis, men created the tradition and the assumption in the heads of the women that if men cook, they give the impression that they are no longer male" (Horton and Freire, 1990, p. 131). This confers an advantage on men and places an additional burden on women who have to work in both the field and the home. Freire argues that his respect for this tradition should not prevent him, as an educator, from challenging this practice and the assumptions on which it is based. Pointing out that such traditions are historical and cultural formations (rather than given destinies), Freire maintains that "if it can be changed, it's not unethical to put the possibility of change on the table" (Horton and Freire, 1990, p. 132).

Freire would not, of course, have supported every educational development initiated in the name of multiculturalism. His approach would have been to examine each educative situation in its context, and in the light of a clear set of ethical principles. Freire's discussion in *Pedagogy of Hope* makes it plain that, for him, issues of ethnicity (and gender, and homosexuality, and poverty) should be *debated* in a climate of open discussion, uninhibited by the paternalism of guilt (Freire, 1994, p. 152). He recalls the wrath he endured from a young black leader for advocating "unity in diversity" at a seminar in Chicago, and also notes resistance from friends and colleagues to the notion that problems of ethnicity and class are related (Freire, 1994, pp. 153–159). From a Freirean standpoint, multiculturalism would certainly *not* be "equivalent to," or "a symptom of," or "a dimension of," or (to use Kramer's shocking phrase) the "bastard offspring" of, political correctness. However, given Freire's commitment to "multiculturality" as one aspect of his wider ethical ideal, it becomes all the more important that struggles toward this end be subjected to the same standards of critical examination as all other educational endeavors.

If educationists are concerned with practicing, promoting, or enhancing Freirean critical literacy, it seems to me that they must—on ethical and educational grounds—be opposed to political correctness. In fact, the identification and analysis of, and resistance to, politically correct policies and practices might itself be an example of critically literate activity. The critical interrogation of popular media stories from a Freirean point of view would allow genuine examples of intolerance and the suppression of criticism to be distinguished from those where the allegation of "political correctness" is itself used as a silencing device. If it is true that many accounts of political correctness rest on vague conceptual criteria, poorly developed arguments, and contradictory assumptions, then the Freirean notion of critical literacy has much to offer in exposing such flaws. These tasks remain important at the present time, for inasmuch as politically correct practices continue to be perceived as overwhelmingly undesirable, there is a strong possibility that those accused of such activities will suffer considerable personal stress, if not outright humiliation. Equally, those who dare to challenge prevailing orthodoxy in environments where political correctness *is* fostered and enforced deserve the support of colleagues who are also willing to rub against the grain of conformity. The price to be paid for speaking out in such cases is sometimes high indeed, but, as Freire has often said, risks are an inevitable part of the educational process.

Concluding Remarks

The parameters for a Freirean perspective on political correctness should now be clear. Freire regards tolerance, difference, debate, and questioning as fundamental principles on which any university should be founded. Politically correct policies, practices, and attitudes are those that either negate or impede these principles. "Political correctness," as it has been defined in this chapter, relates to the promotion, whether this is direct or indirect, of one position as the only acceptable, legitimate, or possible one. From a Freirean perspective, teachers have a responsibility to not only tolerate views that oppose their own, but to actively stimulate engagement with alternative discourses. To confine discussion within overly narrow boundaries, in the full knowledge that alternative perspectives exist, and where opportunities for considering a wider range of positions are readily available, is thus as politically correct as banning questions or actively ruling out dissenting views. Hence, intolerance, which lies at the heart of political correctness, does not consist just in the refusal to *allow* opposition, questioning, and debate, but also in the failure to provide the conditions that make these critical processes possible. Political correctness, as discussed in this chapter, inhibits dialogue, works against the development of a critical orientation toward the world, restricts rather than expands the discursive universe within which people might reflectively and actively participate, and is thus thoroughly dehumanizing.

Chapter 5

Critical Literacy, Breadth of Perspective, and the University Curriculum

A Freirean Perspective

The question of what, how, and why students ought to read has long been an important topic for scholarly and popular discussion. This question was, for example, at the heart of debates in the United States during the late 1980s and early 1990s over "the canon" and core "Western Civilization" courses. At that time, two broad oppositional groups could be identified. First, there were those who sought to defend a "traditional" program of "Great Books," concentrating on philosophical works by Plato, Aristotle, Machiavelli, Hobbes, Locke, Rousseau, Marx, and Nietzsche, among others, together with literary classics by writers such as Shakespeare, Proust, Dickens, Milton, Joyce, and Tolstoy. Opposing the traditionalists was a coalition of diverse reformists calling for representation of a wider variety of authors (more women, more authors from ethnic minority groups, and so on) in core reading lists. Although several features of these debates are of ongoing interest to educationists, this chapter concentrates on one theme of particular significance for teachers and students in university settings, namely, the problem of finding the correct balance between breadth and depth in reading. This issue will be addressed from a Freirean point of view.

CHAPTER 5

There are arguably many features of Freire's work of potential value to educationists and others with an interest in universities. This chapter limits its focus to the Freirean concept of critical literacy. The chapter comprises two broad parts. Beginning with the notion of "reading the word and the world," the first part of the chapter explores Freire's approach to reading and the act of study. Freire encourages readers to adopt an investigative, inquiring, questioning posture. Critical reading, for Freire, is a demanding but potentially joyous process, in which "texts" are related to "contexts," and through which the reader's understanding of social reality is progressively deepened and extended. The second part of the chapter addresses the question of how depth might be balanced with breadth in core courses based upon the Freirean ideal of critical literacy. It is argued that if the constraints imposed by time are to be properly recognized in the curriculum, university teachers need to reduce the number of texts on core reading lists to a minimum while nevertheless attempting to enhance breadth in theoretical perspective. A three-tiered proposal for addressing this objective is advanced.

Freirean Critical Literacy

Over the past three decades, the notion of critical literacy has gained increasing prominence in discussions of reading, writing, and education. Although the term has been employed in a number of different ways, two broad orientations have been particularly well represented. The first draws on Freirean, neo-Marxist, and other radical strands of modernist social criticism; the second develops ideas from discourse analysis, the work of theorists such as M. A. K. Halliday and J. P. Gee, poststructuralist currents in literary theory, and postmodernist scholarship in a variety of fields (cf. McLaren and Lankshear, 1993, p. 380). This chapter concentrates exclusively on the Freirean view of critical literacy. Freire's position is elaborated through three related themes: the notion of reading the word and the world; reading and the act of knowing; and the theory-practice link in Freirean critical literacy.

Reading the Word and the World

Freire's central theoretical construct as far as literacy is concerned is the notion of "reading the word and the world." In his essay,

"The Importance of the Act of Reading" (Freire, 1983), Freire discusses the way in which his early experience of learning to read words and books was preceded by a certain awareness or growing understanding—that is, a form of "reading"—of the world around him. Freire describes the house in Recife where he grew up, with its bedrooms, hall, attic, and terrace. He talks about his backyard, his mother's ferns, and the trees surrounding the house. It was in this world that he first learned to walk, to talk—and to read. "Truly, that special world presented itself to me as the arena of my perceptual activity, and therefore as the world of my first reading. The *texts*, the *words*, the *letters* of that context were incarnated in a series of things, objects, signs. In perceiving these, I experienced myself, and the more I experienced myself, the more my perceptual capacity increased" (p. 6).

Freire paints a picture of a rich world of early observations and activities. He speaks of the songs of the different birds in his area, of the movements in the sky, of the changing of the mango as it ripens, of the habits of the family animals, of the "ghosts" that were said to haunt the neighborhood. All of these experiences formed a deep impression on Freire. His reading of this world—his emerging interpretation and understanding of his surroundings—was accompanied by a form of "writing" reality (cf. Freire and Macedo, 1987). For it was not only the trees, the animals, the clouds, and the ghosts that imprinted themselves on Freire's inner world of experience (and that remained with him as he grew older); Freire himself, as a young boy growing up in his house, his backyard, his neighborhood in Recife, played a part in shaping, or "writing," that world. Freire expresses this process as follows: "Reading the word is not preceded merely by reading the world, but a certain form of *writing* it or *rewriting* it, that is, of transforming it by means of conscious practical work" (Freire, 1983, p. 10). When it came time for Freire's parents to introduce him to the world of print, his learning of the *word* was a simultaneous extension of his reading of the world. He recalls, "I learned to read and write on the ground of the back yard of my house, in the shade of mango trees, with words from my world rather than from the wider world of my parents. The earth was my blackboard; sticks, my chalk" (p. 6).

Of course, Freire does not claim that his reading of either the word or the world at this stage was an especially critical one; indeed, he makes it plain that his encounter with these early forms of experience "did not make ... [him] grow up prematurely, a rationalist in boy's clothing" (p. 7). But the seeds were sown for the development of his later work with illiterate adults. Reading and writing, Freire discovered at an early age, only make sense when they relate to something within the realm of a person's lived experience (Freire and Macedo, 1987, p. 42). It was the expression of a *curious* attitude toward the world that characterized Freire's reading of his childhood environment. This curiosity forms the basis of a deepening restlessness—a searching—which is essential for the formation of a critical approach in reading the word and the world (cf. Freire, 1983, p. 8). When working with children in pedagogical environments, then, attention should always be paid to their experience, and teachers need to take into account the differing levels of knowledge children bring with them to the classroom (Campos, 1990).

Reading the world, Freire argues, is always *prior* to reading the word (Freire, 1983, p. 10). Freire's conceptualization of the sequence of experiences—reading the world first and the word second—has an anthropological and historical basis. Human beings first learned to act on their environment, using and modifying the products of nature, altering the material world. Freire conceives of this transformation of the objective world as a form of "writing reality" (Freire and Macedo, 1987, p. 50). As humans began to change the natural world, the reality they had created through conscious practical activity "acted back" on them, modifying their ideas, conceptions, and attitudes (Freire, 1972b, pp. 29–30, 56–57, 1976, p. 145). From this process of continual, reciprocal transformation, human beings emerged as "writers" and "readers" of the world—long before they became writers and readers of the word (Bruss and Macedo, 1984, p. 224). The same ordering of moments in human experience occurs within the individual human being. The child first learns to relate to his or her environment, then to speak and communicate with others. It is only at this point—once a complex but as yet incomplete relationship with the world and others has been established—that the child becomes ready to learn to read and write. Freire's preference for basing literacy on the lived histories and experiences of learners, then, is grounded in an understanding of human evolution and development.

Critical Reading as an Act of Knowing

Freire makes it clear that he is opposed to a mechanistic approach to reading and writing. Simply learning how to copy words, combine syllables, form sentences, or structure paragraphs becomes—at best—a lifeless exercise in drill and memorization. At worst, such a strategy represents a manipulative exercise in domestication: It signifies an attempt to impede the possibility of dealing critically with words, and it effectively precludes the possibility of moving beyond the words to a critique of social and political reality. For Freire, a mechanistic approach to the written word—where learners are encouraged to repeat phrases, to memorize words, to learn the techniques for making sentences, without at the same time going beyond mere technique and memorization to a critical engagement with the text and the world—does not constitute an act of knowing (Freire, 1983, p. 9). Knowing demands a conscious effort to get beneath the surface of the object of study—whether in the process of reading the word or in the act of reading the world—to uncover deeper and deeper layers of meaning. Reading, in Freire's view, is "not walking on the words; it's grasping the soul of them" (Dillon, 1985).

Taking a critical approach to reading involves "seizing" the text and "wrestling" with its ideas and themes: "The thing is to fight with the text, even though loving it.... To engage in a conflict with the text" (Freire and Shor, 1987, p. 11). Adopting such a stance requires a (considerable) degree of intellectual discipline, which Freire believes can only be acquired through practice (Freire, 1985, p. 2). "Banking" education is by nature antithetical to critical reading: It depends for its very existence on passivity in the act of study (Freire, 1972a, ch. 2). Whereas under the banking system the student waits to be "given" the meaning, the answers, or the message behind a text, under problem-posing education, active *engagement* with an author's ideas is encouraged from the very setting up of a "problem" to be (dialogically) investigated in the first place.

From Freire's point of view, a reader ought to assume the role of a *subject* in approaching a text (cf. Lankshear, 1993). He or she should never simply *accept* what has been presented in a book, as though "mesmerized by a magical force" (Freire, 1985, p. 2). The act of reading demands a "permanent intellectual disquiet" (p. 3): a curious, restless, probing, searching, questioning approach to study. For Freire, a critical posture also requires a sense of modesty. Notwithstanding the imperative to challenge the text, a reader ought to be humble enough—and sufficiently *critical*—to recognize (and respond) to difficulties in interpretation and understanding (p. 4).

CHAPTER 5

Theory and Practice in Freirean Critical Literacy

In a number of his writings on literacy, Freire is critical of the artificial separation of "word" and "world" in North American educational institutions. Economic crises, discrimination, struggle: All of these things, Freire points out, are a feature of the social world, but rarely do they become the object of critical reading, study, and debate within schools (Freire and Shor, 1987, p. 135). Students seldom transcend a surface-level understanding of either the word (school texts) or the world (social and political reality outside, as well as inside, the classroom). The emphasis in schooling is on description rather than interpretation or critical understanding. This tendency reinforces the split between the word and the world for those responsible for teaching the students, with teachers and academics becoming ever more preoccupied with concepts and increasingly less interested in social transformation. Freire gives the example of theorists who call themselves Marxists, but who "have never drunk coffee in the house of a worker" (p. 136). The gulf between theory and practice in such cases is, for Freire, highly problematic. Dealing with the word–world relationship in this way, Freire claims, amounts to nothing more than theoretical "play": Theorists become "Marx experts" but not "Marxists" (p. 136).

Freire is similarly direct in his attack on the myth of neutrality in the teaching of reading and writing. Working with texts is, in Freire's view, never a neutral process. Students are often encouraged to simply *describe* what they see in a text, in the belief that if they are to be "scientific" (or "objective") they must avoid *interpreting* the material (p. 12). The better one is able to avoid clouding investigation with "political" questions, so the argument goes, the better scientist one is taken to be. The influence of positivism generally, and those strands derived from the natural sciences in particular, is obvious here. Scientists, it is thought, should deal *just* with the text, not with the text in its social, political, cultural, and historical *context*. Freire objects to this and argues that nothing can be written, taught, read, or studied in a neutral manner. *All* forms of textual engagement—literary, scientific, philosophical, sociological, and so on—are structured and informed by presuppositions about the way the world is and ought to be. This is also true of any mode of teaching and learning involving the written word: Deciding what, how, and why texts should be read is a necessarily nonneutral, political, interest-serving process.

In later works, Freire touches on the possibility of reading becoming an "aesthetic" experience. Whether reading a novel, a poem, Marx, or Gramsci, he says, encountering a text ought to be a loving event. Reading should be a joyous, if demanding, activity (Horton and Freire, 1990, pp. 23–27). The beauty of the text—or, more precisely, of *reading* the text—lies in the possibility of reading becoming an act of knowing: "I have to grasp in between the words some knowledge that helps me not exclusively to go on in the reading and in *understanding* what I'm reading, but also to understand something beyond the book I am reading, beyond the text. It is a pleasure" (p. 23). Finding the aesthetic moment in reading the text does not come easily. Getting started on the task of reading—reading seriously—is especially difficult (p. 23). Part of the reason for this is that reading implies *risking* (Bruss and Macedo, 1984, p. 218). To engage a text is, among other things, to risk "being convinced by the author" and "being angry" (p. 218). Reading critically is demanding because it necessitates facing up to these risks and confronting them by rewriting not only the word (through interpretation) but also the world (through transformative action inspired by the text). This responsibility is fraught with dangers and fears, and is charged with emotion. For Freire, "knowing ... is not a neutral act, not only from the political point of view, but from the point of view of my body, my sensual body. It is full of feelings, of emotions, of tastes (Horton and Freire, 1990, p. 23).

Freire recounts his experiences with books as a young man, reading and studying into the early hours of the morning, and remarks that he had "an almost physical connection with the text" (p. 27). This, exactly, is the moment of joy, of happiness, of knowing—of being *critical*—that signifies reading as an aesthetic, loving event: It is the moment of *entering into* the text, curious, searching, and exploring, all the time linking the word in the text to the wider text that is the world itself.

Freire also speaks of the need for writing to be beautiful. He challenges the notion that the only place for elegance and beauty with the written word is in literature. Scientists, too, must take hold of the "aesthetical moment" in language and write beautifully (p. 32). A written text, whether by a novelist, a scientist, or a philosopher, should embrace a clarity and simplicity (without being *simplistic*) that aids understanding. Writing should become a "noble form, as serious as science" (though, interestingly, Freire says of his own work, "I do not write beautifully") (Bruss and Macedo, 1985, p. 21).

The value of books abides in their potential—realized only through critical reading—to serve as vehicles for re-creating practice. Freire insists that a dialectical unity be maintained between theory and practice, between reflection and action (Horton and Freire, 1990, p. 21). Reading books allows one the opportunity of "remaking" one's practice theoretically (p. 36). That is, the act of reading—when it moves from a mere "walking over the words" (cf. Freire and Shor, 1987, p. 10) to the active, critical engagement with the text necessary for theorizing—encourages one to reexamine or "reread" one's practice and, if necessary, to change ("rewrite") it.

Balancing Breadth and Depth in Reading at the University Level

The battle between traditionalists and reformists in debates over the canon can be conceived as a struggle for "voice" and political influence through the curriculum. There is, of course, only so much "educational space" available. Given the tight constraints imposed by university timetables, time for reading is in short supply. To read texts *well*—by which we can mean, among other things, reading them critically (in the Freirean sense)—takes far more time than many educationists and others seem to presuppose. This was especially evident in debates over "Western Civilization" courses (and their successors) in the United States during the late 1980s and early 1990s (cf. Pratt, 1992, pp. 17–18). In an insightful examination of workload and student learning, Ellie Chambers observes that "when teachers overburden students, demanding more work of them than they might have time to do, they create conditions in which what is to be learned is likely to be unintelligible, and in which students cannot possibly learn well" (Chambers, 1992, p. 144). Teachers have a responsibility not just to convey essential subject matter in their domain of expertise, but to consider how much time is likely to be necessary, given the difficulty of the material, for effective learning to take place. Calculating the time required for reading, writing, thinking, and completing assignments is thus an essential part of course planning. In Chambers's words, "'having sufficient time' to do the work required should be seen as a *precondition* of good learning, rather than just one among many conditions in which it may flourish" (p. 145). As a preliminary exercise, then, it is instructive to contemplate how many books academics might reasonably expect students to read, given the constraints dictated by a university teaching year.

Time: A Fixed Constraint

Suppose, for the sake of argument, that students are required to complete one compulsory course in which a number of key philosophical texts are to be read. Let us assume that for the bulk of the students, this is one course among seven (of equal weighting) to be completed in an academic year. Now, if approximately equal time is to be devoted to each of the seven courses, and if it is taken as given that students will have an average of fifty hours per week to devote to their studies, then—even allowing for the possibility of students stretching their reading time across a full calendar year instead of a university teaching year—this leaves only 371 hours per course available for study. Not all of this time, though, can be devoted "purely" to reading: Several written assignments based on the set texts are likely to be necessary, given the standard university assessment requirements. This could conceivably cut the time available for actually reading the words on the pages of texts back enormously, but let us suppose (optimistically) that there are still 250 hours left. If an average university student is able to read with reasonable comprehension at a rate of 250 words per minute, this translates to 15,000 words per hour. Taking some time off for fatigue and distractions here, it might be safe to assume that perhaps 12,000 words per hour would be an acceptable maximum. Given the remaining 250 hours, then, students could read no more than 3 million words per course per year. If the set texts average 100,000 words in length, this allows a maximum of 30 books to be set.

These calculations are premised on artificially "pure" reading conditions. In practice, students must weather a wide variety of pressures on their concentration and time. These might include struggling to find and stay in part-time employment, juggling very limited finances, attending to the myriad chores of everyday life in an apartment or house (washing, cooking, ironing, cleaning, etc.), maintaining personal relationships, and attempting to stay moderately fit and healthy. Students who are parents or caregivers have added responsibilities. Becoming involved in social causes, pursuing sporting interests and hobbies, or continuing a social life can seem like luxuries. It is difficult to maintain a steady focus on one's studies under any circumstances, but given the pressures many contemporary students endure, it is perhaps surprising that more do not fall by the wayside.

The estimates formulated above assume a "best case" scenario in almost every respect. Written assignments and other assessment tasks might more realistically be expected to cut reading time back to one hundred to one hundred fifty hours per course, and for those fortunate enough to find employment over the summer period, there is likely to be little spare time for reading. The calculations also assume far more continuity in reading intensity than is realistic, given other distractions, over a sustained period of time. Although it might not be difficult for a student at university level to read twelve thousand words in any given hour, it seems unlikely that this rate could be continued hour after hour, week after week. The whole process would almost certainly be far more disjointed and discontinuous than the previous characterization suggests. In light of these factors, twenty to twenty-five books per course per year seems more plausible.

This estimate is still generous, however, given the nature of the reading material in question. It is one thing to ask students to read twenty romance novels (as a form of light relief) in a year, but it is quite another to demand of them that they do the same with philosophical texts. It might be possible for a student to read Plato's *Republic* in two days in the sense of decoding each word in the text, but to suggest that the book could be properly comprehended in this time is preposterous. For undergraduates with little or no background in philosophy, the task of getting to grips with complex arguments and ideas is doubly difficult. For most students at this level, attempting to understand Plato is likely to involve reading many sentences several times, revisiting whole sections, and rereading the book in its entirety at least once. Some would argue that Plato is one of the "easier" thinkers to read: Grappling with Hegel or Heidegger, for example, could prove even more burdensome. Allowing for at least some rereading, then, the number of books on our one-year list might be whittled down to perhaps, at most, fifteen.

The magnitude of the task has still not been adequately conveyed, though, for thus far we have only considered what might be involved in "reading for comprehension" in the narrowest sense. By this I mean that if a student had read a book in the terms articulated to this point, he or she should have comprehended enough of the detail in the text to be able to recount some of the main points if asked to do so in an examination. To be able to do this with fifteen books—remembering that this is only one course among several, and mindful also of the other activities competing for a student's time—is a respectable achievement by any scholar's standards. Yet it is surely desirable that students go beyond mere comprehension in this narrow sense to some form of reflective or critical engagement with an author's ideas. Modes of critical engagement vary widely, but all imply a more time-consuming process than the form of reading alluded to thus far. For theorists as different as Paulo Freire and Allan Bloom, the idea of students reading fifteen philosophical or literary texts for a course that constitutes only one-seventh of a student's program would seem nightmarish (see Bloom, 1988, 1991; Roberts, 1993). What, then, might be considered a reasonable workload, if the Freirean ideal of critical literacy is to be upheld?

Quality and Quantity in Freirean Critical Reading

In *A Pedagogy for Liberation,* Freire outlines the case of a student who once approached him in desperation after enrolling in a course that had, for one semester, a bibliography of three hundred books (Freire and Shor, 1987, pp. 83–85). The student found he had no time for anything but reading, and the situation was creating problems for him at home. Freire questions whether the professor who set the reading list would have read all the books and goes on to imply that even if the books had been read they might not have been understood (p. 83). In stark contrast to this excessive emphasis on quantity, the case is given of a six-page transcript of an interview with a Brazilian peasant, used by Freire in one of his graduate classes. The interview, which was a critique of Brazilian education in the 1980s, served as the focus for class reading and discussion. Freire describes how (in his efforts to encourage a critical stance in the act of reading) he would read a sentence of the text of the interview, pause, then reread the sentence to show how he might attempt to understand and interpret what the peasant was saying. After several demonstrations of this slow, reflective mode of reading, he handed the task over to the students to continue. The class ended up spending twelve hours studying this single, six-page text. In Freire's estimation, after this exercise, members of his class would have understood "what it means to read" (p. 85).

It is difficult to imagine students being able to read more than half a dozen texts in a single course in this manner; indeed, depending on the texts, even this estimate is likely to be excessive. Freire clearly wants students to read slowly and carefully. The critical reader penetrates beneath the surface appearance of words, stops to ponder the meaning of passages, questions assumptions and arguments, and relates ideas in the text to the wider (con)text of their social world. If students are to engage texts with such rigor, the number of books on reading lists must, it seems clear, be far fewer than many commentators in debates over canons and core curricula have suggested. The emphasis in Freire's work is on quality rather than quantity, on in-depth analysis in place of superficial skimming or "reading for entertainment," on a complex and intimate relationship between text, reader, and world.

Yet, if critical reading of the kind promoted by Freire is to proceed, a certain breadth in prior reading seems imperative. Breadth is necessary in order to "make the connections" between different ideas and theorists, to enable one to see why particular views might be labeled in a certain way (e.g., as postmodern, Marxist, feminist, liberal, conservative, humanist, etc.), and to place what one is studying in its broader relevant contexts (disciplinary, social, historical, cultural, policy, and so on). An in-depth understanding of a text requires some sort of knowledge of what it *is not*. We cannot fully understand what is distinctive, special, or valuable in Marx unless we have some knowledge of thinkers *other* than Marx. In particular, we need to know something about those theorists who offer opposing points of view on questions similar to those addressed by Marx. To better appreciate Marx's critique of capitalism, then, some knowledge of Adam Smith's work is necessary. Similarly, to grasp the significance of Marx's stance on the dialectical relationship between ideas and material reality, it is essential to know something of Hegel (for whom Marx believed the dialectic was standing on its head). In broader terms, a Marxist position on ethics and politics cannot be deeply comprehended without consideration of other conflicting ethical traditions (e.g., certain strands of liberalism). At a wider level still, students cannot be expected to make much sense of, say, postmodern cultural criticism unless they have some idea of the elements of modernist thought postmodernists oppose.

Freire's appreciation of the need for students to have some understanding of a range of theoretical positions and perspectives is evident in his statements on the reading of key works in given subject areas. He argues that students ought to read "the classics" in their field of study, but stresses the importance of grasping a sense of conflicting intellectual traditions. Hence, in a sociology class, the work of positivists, structuralists, functionalists, Marx, and various Marxists would be indispensable, irrespective of one's acceptance or rejection of any of these perspectives (cf. Freire and Shor, 1987, p. 83). Attempting to read the classic texts within each of these traditions by focusing, for example, on a selection of books by Comte, Marx, Durkheim, Weber, and so on, is likely to prove a demanding if not impossible process if the depth of critical engagement advocated by Freire is applied in every case. This, of course, relates to just *one* field of study; those embroiled in battles over the canon in United States in the late 1980s and early 1990s were generally dealing with the problem of what to include and exclude in a single course (traditionally organized around themes such as "Western Civilization" or "Western Culture") to be taken by students from a multiplicity of disciplines and programs. If the Freirean approach to critical reading is taken seriously in these courses, the number of books that might be "truly" read (in the Freirean sense) would be so few—no more than half a dozen, perhaps—that, paradoxically, the breadth of perspective necessary for critical reading could be readily compromised.

The problem of finding the right balance between breadth and depth has its genesis in debates that stretch back to the earliest medieval universities and goes to the heart of degree planning in (post) modern institutions of higher education. Even in universities without compulsory courses of the kind discussed in the U.S. debates over the canon, issues of breadth and depth are central in structuring degrees. In contemporary bachelor of arts degrees in many countries, for example, students are required to complete a certain number of papers in given subjects at each of three stages. In their first year, students are typically advised to take one or two papers at Stage One level in three or four subjects, nominating one or two of these as their "major" or "double major." In the second and third years, the spread of subjects is usually reduced and an increasing number of papers in the major subject(s) are taken. By the end of their degrees, bachelor of arts students might have completed at least one paper in perhaps half a dozen subjects and six to eight papers in one or two of those subjects. Breadth at the beginning of the degree thus gives way to greater depth in later stages. For students who progress on to master's and doctoral degrees, this trend continues, with increasing specialization the farther a student goes. The path from year one of a bachelor's degree to the completion of a doctorate is neatly captured in the colloquial expression that at the beginning of a first degree a student knows "nothing about everything," whereas at the end of a doctoral thesis he or she knows "everything about nothing"!

Of course, students have lives beyond one course or program in a given year of their academic studies. Other opportunities for reading the "classic" works in given fields of study exist—at least potentially—later in degrees: Compulsory courses do not have to be confined to the early stages of a student's career. Additionally, students have their whole lives to lead after they leave university: If they so wish, their reading might (circumstances permitting) continue for fifty years or more. Given the time constraints imposed by a three- or four-year degree (or even a six- to eight-year period of several degrees), educators must face the possibility that they cannot promote *both* breadth and depth in reading at all stages in the student's total period of study. Courses of the kind under discussion in debates over canons and core curricula generally occur in the early stages of a degree or program. If it is this period with which we are dealing, and if the aim is to consider the issue from a Freirean point of view, then there are at least two possible responses to the problem of balancing breadth with depth in reading. From one vantage point, it might be argued that depth must initially, and of necessity, be sacrificed in favor of breadth, for without a certain breadth of perspective critical reading (of the Freirean variety) is impossible. From a different angle, however, the claim might be made that a student must learn to read *something* critically before proceeding to other reading: This demands that breadth give way, in the first instance, to depth. The discussion that follows attempts to address the tension between these two positions.

few Books, Multiple Perspectives?

"Breadth" and "depth" can both be maintained, in one sense, if we think of the former in terms of "perspectives" and the latter in terms of the number of books one reads. Elsewhere, I have argued that instead of trying to read books from every major political and ethical position, core courses might serve a more useful purpose (and keep the Freirean ideal of critical literacy intact) if they concentrate on a few texts but examine them from a variety of perspectives (Roberts, 1997). Plato's *Republic* was used as an example of a text that might be suitable for this kind of approach (though many other books might serve equally well). Accepting the view that certain metaphysical, ontological, ethical, and political questions are of enduring human importance, I suggested that a multiplicity of perspectives—feminist, Marxist, liberal, conservative, and so on—could be brought to bear on a small number of key texts in which questions of this kind are addressed. These books would be debated and discussed in detail, from a variety of different angles. Students would be encouraged to relate the themes addressed in these books to contemporary social problems, practices, structures, and struggles, and to place the texts in their appropriate historical and social contexts.

Although I believe the general principles underlying this proposal are sound, there are some serious risks in adopting such an approach. Of greatest significance for present purposes, there is a danger that the maximization of breadth will lead to superficiality, with an apparently seamless smorgasbord of perspectives and questions. This danger might be avoided to some extent were a university classroom to exhibit some of the characteristics Freire regards as ideal. Freirean education demands, among other things, dedicated teaching, enthusiastic participation by all, a passion for ideas, discipline and rigor in critical reading, a willingness to question, and a commitment to understanding and changing the world for the better. An educative situation with these characteristics is, of course, seldom easy to create! However, even if such circumstances did eventuate, the range of questions around which discussion would be based might easily become excessive if the requirements of critical reading in the Freirean sense were to be met. Conceivably, students and teachers might be unable to "finish" reading *one* book if the full range of questions outlined in my earlier essay (Roberts, 1997) were to be thoroughly addressed from a multiplicity of perspectives. This difficulty could, ironically, be *exacerbated* rather than overcome if a university class displayed the ideal qualities previously noted. For the more closely a class follows the Freirean ideal in its educational approach, the more thorough (and hence time consuming) reading, questioning, and dialogue are likely to be.

Narrowing the Focus

One way of dealing with this problem, should time be particularly limited in a given program, would be to narrow the full range of key questions down to a single, overriding question, namely: "What human ideal(s) ought we to work toward?" This question lies at the heart of Freire's philosophy, and his response to it informed every pedagogical decision he made. Although overtly ethical, the question also allows metaphysical, ontological, epistemological, political, and aesthetic concerns to be addressed. Asking what *ought* to be the case requires some reflection on that which might prevent or impede an ideal being realized or pursued; political questions become significant here. Similarly, before we can ask what *ideals* we wish to work toward as human beings, we need to first pay some attention to the question of what it means to *be* human; ontological and metaphysical themes would thus also almost certainly be traversed. There would, however, be a single question at the *center* of classroom dialogue and student reading. This would act as the pivot around which all aspects of the educative situation would revolve.

The question "What human ideal(s) ought we to work toward?" is sufficiently broad in scope to allow a diverse array of theoretical perspectives to be brought to bear on key texts. Indeed, it might be claimed that this question lies behind many theoretical perspectives in the social sciences and humanities; certainly the question provides at least an *implicit* focus or "reason for being" in many cases. Any rigorously developed theoretical perspective that has something to offer in addressing this question might be included. The question is obviously vital in many strands of feminism, Marxism, and liberalism. A key concern of feminists in the past has been to work toward a world free of patriarchy; Marxists have spoken about paths to socialism of one kind or another; and liberals have often valued ideals such as individual rational autonomy. However, there would also be merit in problematizing the question itself via, for example, various postmodern or indigenous or ecological positions.

To speak of "human ideals" is to permit discussion of both "individual" and "social" ideals. From a Freirean point of view, liberation is always a social process (Roberts, 2000). However, not all thinkers see it this way, and Freire was, as I noted in the previous chapter, always quick to argue that perspectives other than his own ought to be given careful consideration. Indeed, it cannot be presupposed that "liberation" of any kind should necessarily be the goal. Using the term *human ideals* does not prejudice the inquiry in favor of a particular construct, but leaves the door open for any number to be examined. Whatever concepts are explored, it seems probable that many of the themes that might be addressed would overlap with fundamental concerns in Freire's work.

Without denying that many theorists use categories other than those Freire employs in addressing questions about human ideals, the twin themes of "oppression" and "liberation" might feature strongly in a contemporary course of the kind envisaged here. We have seen earlier that for Freire, liberation was a fundamental human task. If, for the sake of argument, we accept Freire's position on the nature of this task, the possibilities for relating texts to contexts in addressing liberation and oppression as key themes become obvious. If the task is as pressing as Freire believes it to be, this process of linking "word" with "world" in the university curriculum assumes new significance. Classroom dialogue might address any number of contemporary issues of local, national, or international interest. Students might, for example, examine problems of homelessness, poverty, starvation, unemployment, environmental destruction, domestic violence, exploitation in the workplace, colonialism, and so on. All of these problems can be confronted from a range of perspectives on "liberation" and "oppression." At the same time, the very idea of understanding the social world in this way should be open to debate and critique.

Allowing the pressing social problems of the day to become the object of critical investigation is one way of linking "word" with "world" through core courses. This is not to say that course content should be determined purely on the basis of its perceived "relevance" for contemporary issues or for specific professional contexts. The "tailoring" of programs of study toward directly vocational ends contradicts the purpose of having core courses, and should, if such courses are to have a distinctive place a university curriculum, be resisted. The linking of texts with contexts, however, is an important aspect of Freirean critical literacy. Upholding this dimension of Freire's ideal while avoiding vocationalism and a "trendy issues" approach is a matter of turning the question of "relevance" on its head. It is not a case of making core courses relevant to something else, but of making elements of the students' world relevant to the purposes of core courses.

From a Freirean point of view, books become worthwhile when they are *engaged* in particular ways. The extent to which critical engagement might take place, and the exact character of that engagement, will vary from one context to another. The one factor that remains fixed in all cases, however, is time (the lack of it). The *potential* value of certain texts, given that very few can be selected if the Freirean ideal of critical literacy is to met, must therefore be carefully considered. This is where Freire's insistence that teachers become conversant with the key ideas in their field of study becomes important (see Freire, 1987). This is part of the directiveness of teaching in any educational program, but in core courses such preparation is especially crucial. Teachers have a responsibility to select texts that appear to offer the greatest potential for allowing diverse perspectives to be brought to bear on the themes addressed in them, while *also* setting up a pedagogical environment that maximizes the chances of this potential being realized.

A Third Level: The Bottom Line

In some circumstances, even the more specific focus just suggested (concentrating on the theme of "human ideals" instead of the full range of ontological, metaphysical, ethical, and political questions) might be far too ambitious. Several variables become significant in setting limits here, including: the students' prior learning, the teacher's knowledge, the form of pedagogy fostered in the classroom, distractions and responsibilities outside the university, the relationship between the "core" course and other courses, and so on. Although there will obviously be wide variations in the impact these factors have on the learning process, a program of the kind envisaged in the foregoing text could still prove too demanding for some students. I want, then, to suggest a third level at which a core course might proceed: This represents the "bottom line" in addressing the need for both depth and breadth in Freirean critical literacy.

Instead of seeking to address one theme or question, via a handful of texts, from a multiplicity of perspectives, an ongoing debate might be set up between just *two* competing discourses. The program would be built around two key texts, both addressing the ethical concerns articulated in the previous section, but from different points of view. Reducing the number of texts and ethical positions down to this bare minimum acknowledges the immensely demanding, and time-consuming, nature of Freirean critical reading, while nonetheless allowing students to see that different theorists can address the same question, theme, or problem in quite distinct ways. Minimizing texts and perspectives in this manner does not prohibit the teacher from alerting students to the existence of other theoretical positions; indeed, the creation of this form of awareness would be a necessity if the imperative for breadth as well as depth were to be upheld. Teachers would, however, have to recognize the difficulties involved in telling students "about" other perspectives without making these perspectives the subject of extensive class debate. The whole point of this approach, though, is to make *sure* (as far as any teacher can) that students read in some depth, without the curriculum becoming "cluttered" with a whole range of different texts, questions, and positions. The aim is to promote the *habit* of critical reading—and, more profoundly, a critical mode of being—without trying to cover "all the ground" from the start.

The emphasis, then, would be on fostering depth in early reading such that later reading, which would be progressively broader in scope, might have a better chance of being genuinely critical. The criterion of breadth would still be present in the program; it would simply take on a slightly different form. Students would gain a sense of what "breadth in perspective" might mean *and* deepen their understanding of the texts under investigation, through the principle of "contrast." This is the idea, readily supported by Freire's educational theory, that one can gain a more critical comprehension of one book (or position) by comparing it to that which it is *not*. With only two competing positions under (thorough) consideration, contrasts can, if anything, be sharpened. Provided students do not assume that *all* ethical and political perspectives fall into neatly contrasting categories, this sharpening of contrasts can serve a useful educational purpose.

Concluding Comments

To a large extent, the number and range of themes, texts, questions, and perspectives that might be engaged depends on the time available, the students' other commitments, and the nature of the institution within which the course is operating. Obviously, if there is more than one course set aside for this sort of program, greater breadth *and* depth in reading becomes possible. Whether the focus is on one question or several, on a single text or half a dozen, the key is to extend rather than restrict the range of possibilities open to students. Core courses, I want to suggest, have a potentially significant educational role to play in expanding the range of discourses within which students might critically participate. They are, it must be stressed, but a part—one "moment" or "layer"—of the broader process of lifelong education. Their distinctive contribution to this process is to give students some sense of the different ways in which a range of groups have addressed questions of longstanding human interest.

Although there are real limits to what can be achieved given the time available, students might, if these courses are successful, be expected to at least develop a deeper appreciation of why it might be important to address certain questions. Of course, this notion would itself be contestable: It cannot be taken for granted that questions of the kind articulated earlier *are* of (considerable) human significance. But teachers, from a Freirean point of view, must put something forward; they can play a key role in providing direction and structure in a student's program of study. Questions about human ideals, especially when coupled with wider metaphysical, ontological, and epistemological questions, provide a starting point from which deeper reflection—a crucial element of which is the development of *other* questions—can begin.

For Freire, learning how, why, when, and where to ask questions is an indispensable part of a university education. Freire does not issue a formula, or a set of fixed procedures, for addressing this objective, but he does develop a detailed view of critical reading that takes as its starting point the adoption of a curious, probing, searching, investigative stance toward the world. The Freirean ideal of critical literacy provides both the basis upon which a program of the sort I have proposed is founded and the means through which students might go *beyond* this program to other worthwhile forms of learning. Knowing, through experience in core courses, what it means to pose and address well-defined key questions lays the foundation for continuing critical inquiry.

No matter what approach is taken, there will always be serious limits to what can be achieved in a single course. From a Freirean point of view, the development of a critical orientation toward the world—an ideal to which core courses might contribute—is a crucial part of the ideal of liberating education. Arguably, however, the habit of critical reading—once acquired—need not be applied to *every* text, in all situations. (This point was also discussed in Chapter 2.) Fostering breadth in reading, or literary enjoyment, sometimes demands the temporary suspension of critical judgment. Nevertheless, if the intention is to consider the distinctiveness of a Freirean perspective on canons, core courses, and university curricula, the formation of a critical stance in reading, writing, and studying must be regarded as pivotal. Freire's educational ideal demands an awareness of, and a willingness to pay respectful (but not reverent) attention to, alternative conceptions of human beings and the social world. If core courses were to encourage rigorous study habits, enhance opportunities for dialogue and debate, and allow students to forge a dynamic link between "word" and "world," they would represent one way of bringing Freirean principles to life in a university context.

Chapter 6

Freire and Dostoevsky

Uncertainty, Dialogue, and Transformation

Paulo Freire and Fyodor Dostoevsky: What an odd combination this appears to be! What possible connection, for those interested in education and transformation, could there be between these two individuals? Paulo Freire's name is a familiar one for most educational theorists in the Western world. Known internationally for his work with illiterate adults in Brazil and for his influential book, *Pedagogy of the Oppressed* (Freire, 1972a), Freire devoted his life to the theory and practice of teaching and learning. Dostoevsky, by contrast, had relatively little to say about education. A Russian writer of the nineteenth century, he is best known for his fiction, and particularly for his major later works: *Crime and Punishment, The Idiot, Demons, The Adolescent,* and *The Brothers Karamazov.* Dostoevsky was not a teacher by profession; nor, on the face of it, was education a key theme in his novels (or his shorter stories, or his journalistic writing). Why, then, should educationists bother with his work? And how might we understand the relationship between Dostoevsky and Freire?

To the best of my knowledge, Freire has never quoted Dostoevsky in any of his publications. I am also not aware of any detailed comparative analysis of the two thinkers in commentaries on Freire's or Dostoevsky's work. Yet, I want to suggest in this chapter that productive links can be made between these two writers. I try to show that Dostoevsky allows us to deepen our understanding of key Freirean ideas. Equally, by paying attention to Freire's pedagogical theory and practice, we can come to appreciate Dostoevsky's novels in a fresh light and enhance our ability to learn from them.

The chapter begins with brief comments on the biographies, political views, and writing styles of the two thinkers. Attention then turns to the importance, for both Dostoevsky and Freire, of uncertainty, dialogue, and the interplay of different voices. This leads to a broader consideration of the relationship between reason and emotion, and the significance of the concept of love, in the work of the two writers. It is argued that for both Freire and Dostoevsky, education is a difficult, complex process of transformation through *struggle*. The penultimate section of the chapter explores aspects of the transformative process in the lives of some of Dostoevsky's characters and in Freirean pedagogy. The chapter concludes with brief remarks on weaknesses, points of difference and compatibility, and possibilities for further study in the work of Freire and Dostoevsky.

Life, Work, and Influence

Both Freire and Dostoevsky have been influential well beyond their specialist areas. Freire's work has been studied not only by educationists at all levels (both within and outside the formal education system), but also by scholars in theology, indigenous studies, political science, women's studies, linguistics, literature and language studies, sociology, cultural studies, geography, peace studies, counseling, and the health sciences. Dostoevsky's writings, similarly, have been discussed and debated not just by literary critics and specialists in Russian studies but also by scholars in philosophy, theology, political science, sociology, psychology, film studies, jurisprudence, and medicine, among other fields. Both Freire's and Dostoevsky's writings are deeply entwined with their biographies. Both paid a heavy price for their political activities. Dostoevsky was imprisoned in Siberia for his involvement with the Petrashevsky Circle, a utopian socialist group, while Freire was arrested and exiled for his allegedly "subversive" approach to adult literacy education in Brazil. Dostoevsky was later to reject, emphatically, the views of his former colleagues in the Petrashevsky Circle. He became an opponent of socialism, or at least a certain kind of socialism. Freire, on the other hand, remained a democratic socialist until his death in 1997. Freire and Dostoevsky appear to differ quite substantially in their political views, yet there are some significant points of compatibility in the principles to which they adhered. Both advanced sharp criticisms of materialist greed. Both were heavily influenced by the Gospels. Dostoevsky's faith was ultimately strengthened as he grew older, and by the time he published *The Brothers Karamazov* (1991), Christian ethics would provide the primary ground for his moral philosophy. He did not, however, reach this position uncritically; rather, he arrived at it precisely through "fighting" with himself over this issue, for decades, wrestling with doubts, posing difficult questions, and considering alternative points of view. Freire read the Gospels as a call to social action. Together with his first wife, Elza, he became involved with radical Catholic groups in Brazil and was sympathetic to the ethical and political stance adopted by liberation theologians in their contestation of oppression in Latin America (Mackie, 1980). Freire would have found Dostoevsky's anti-Catholic, anti-Polish, anti-Semitic tendencies distasteful, just as Dostoevsky would have had little time for the language of revolution and the support for socialist political change in Freire's work.

Both Freire and Dostoevsky wrote about what they knew from personal experience. Freire claimed that his books were all, in one way or another, reports on or reflections of his educational practice. Several of Dostoevsky's books have close parallels with events in his own life. His *Memoirs from the House of the Dead* (1983) captures his experience of prison in Siberia; the descriptions of Prince Myshkin's epilepsy in *The Idiot* (2001) mirror, to a considerable extent, Dostoevsky's own experience; and Dostoevsky shared Alexei's compulsive need to keep returning to the roulette table, as depicted in the novella *The Gambler* (1981). More than this, many of the *ideas* conveyed and enacted by key characters in Dostoevsky's novels—Myshkin's views on Catholicism in *The Idiot*, the Underground Man's assault on rational egoism in *Notes from Underground* (2004), the ethics of Christian love lived and taught by Father Zosima in *The Brothers Karamazov* (1991)—were *Dostoevsky's* ideas. Dostoevsky also allowed his characters to demonstrate the weaknesses, contradictions, and absurdities of some ideas. In *Demons* (1994), for example, he provides a devastating critique of Russia's anti-czarist nihilists through parody. At a deeper level still, many of the *debates* played out in the great novels, sometimes among characters, sometimes *within* characters, bring to life the workings of Dostoevsky's own "divided conscience," as Aileen Kelly (1988) calls it. Freire, too, mixes recollections of events from his life with what we might call "ideas in formation." In a number of later works in particular, Freire appears to still be working through the ideas, debating them in his own mind, and playing them out through writing, in the text. Just as we see an interplay of ideas in the interactions among Dostoevsky's characters, so, too, in Freire's "talking" books of the 1980s and 1990s (Freire and Shor, 1987; Freire and Macedo, 1987; Freire and Faundez, 1989; Horton and Freire, 1990; Escobar et al., 1994) do we see ideas evolving as Freire engages in structured dialogues with his coauthors. Admittedly, possibilities for dramatic *clashes* among participants in the conversation, or between the ideas themselves, are somewhat reduced in these dialogical books, given that in each case Freire's coauthors are largely supportive of his philosophy and pedagogy. Nonetheless, from time to time, some noteworthy tensions arise, as in Freire's dialogue with Antonio Faundez (Freire and Faundez, 1989), where a significant difference of opinion over Freire's work in Guinea Bissau emerges.

The Importance of Uncertainty

One of Freire's favorite claims in the latter part of his career was that one should not become "too certain of one's certainties." Taken out of its appropriate contexts, this statement might seem rather meaningless or banal. Yet, I believe this was more than a catchy phrase for Freire. Uncertainty was fundamental to Freire's epistemology, ethic, and pedagogy. Uncertainty provides the basis for investigation: for *seeking to know more*. Freire's arguments against the reactionary and conservative tendencies of the political Right and the dogmatism of some of his colleagues on the Left were, at least in part, borne out of his sense that such stances *lack respect for uncertainty*. Reactionary and dogmatic positions convey a certain arrogance: a lack of humility, an unwillingness to pause for reflection, and a false sense of assurance that one need not investigate any further (cf. Freire, 1997a). For Freire, uncertainty does *not* imply an "anything goes" point of view. Freire argued strongly against laissez-faire approaches to education, stressing the need for structure and direction in the learning process (Freire and Shor, 1987; Horton and Freire, 1990; Freire, 1998a). As noted earlier in this book, he was no relativist, in either epistemological or ethical terms: He made it clear that he believed some ways of understanding the world and of living in it were better than others. But his views were not *fixed*. Although it is true that he retained some fundamental philosophical and pedagogical principles across his career, he also changed in certain ways—bringing greater depth and complexity to his ideas as he grew older (Mayo, 1999; Roberts, 2000; Morrow and Torres, 2002). This was, in part, a result of learning from his mistakes. On a number of occasions, he recalled how, in his earlier years, he had brought ideas from *his* world—the highly theoretical world of the university—to the world of impoverished workers and peasants, naïvely assuming that he could "lecture" to participants in an educational setting while largely ignoring the realities of *their* world. Chastised by both his wife, Elza, and some of the adult students with whom he worked, Freire learned the importance of integrating literacy learning with the experience, the lived reality, of participants (see Freire, 1972b, 1976). Toward the end of his life, Freire became both less certain of his views and more convinced than ever of the need to take a stand despite this (see, for example, Freire, 1998b). For Freire, uncertainty prompts us to action, not to a position of despair and immobility. We *need* uncertainty in order to know, but we cannot allow the feeling of uncertainty to become so overwhelming that it distorts or destroys our capacity to ask questions, make decisions, and move on.

But what does this mean in daily life? How does uncertainty *play itself out* in our conversations, in the decisions we make, in the actions we take, in the way we respond to the real problems and dilemmas that structure our lives? Freire, as an educational theorist, can only tell us so much about this. Although Freire's style of writing in later books is less formal, more relaxed, sometimes less highly structured than the style adopted in many other educational texts, he is nonetheless still working with a form of writing that sets its own limits on what it can tell us about uncertainty. We can gain something more by examining Freire's biography, or by talking to those who knew him, or by listening to him talk. But we do not *live with Freire* as he goes about his daily life, teaching, writing, thinking, feeling, interacting with others, and moving about in the world. We do not experience the way *others* respond to Freire in face-to-face situations; we cannot enter their inner world or see how they influence the development of Freire's ideas. One way to more deeply appreciate the importance of uncertainty is through the form of the novel. Dostoevsky's novels are particularly helpful in this regard, for they convey, with great power and effectiveness, the way uncertainty works on and through human lives. Nowhere is this more apparent than in *The Brothers Karamazov* (1991), where some of the most searching philosophical and theological questions are raised, pondered, and discussed. In parts of the novel, the debate is played out quite directly between characters; elsewhere, we are left to draw inferences about characters' views through their actions. At times, as in the famous "Poem of the Grand Inquisitor," one character (Ivan) conveys his views with great passion, and the other (Alyosha) demonstrates his values and commitment precisely through his ability to listen patiently and, in a certain way, *accept* a position contrary to his own. Throughout the book, Dostoevsky maintains a tension between Christian and humanist ethics. Dostoevsky, through the structure, form, and content of his novel, shows us the significance of uncertainty for human life in a way that Freire, working within the constraints of *his* form, cannot.

Dialogue in Freire and Dostoevsky

Russia in Dostoevsky's time was undergoing some important and unsettling changes. The czarist system was starting to be questioned, and the authority of religion in structuring everyday beliefs and practices could no longer be taken for granted. Dostoevsky was intimately involved in all of this, first through his membership of the Petrashevsky Circle and later through his vehement criticism of groups of this kind. His articles and commentaries in his *A Writer's Diary* (2009), along with several of his books—particularly *Notes from Underground* (2004) and *Demons* (1994)—served as vehicles for conveying his opposition to Russia's new liberal reformists, "rational egoists," nihilists, and socialists. (This was, of course, not Dostoevsky's only purpose in publishing these works.) Dostoevsky's reading of his historical moment in Russia, with all of its questioning of traditional structures and beliefs, does not lead him to a position of utter helplessness, meaningless, or despair. Dostoevsky wrestled with many of the same problems as those confronted by Ivan in *The Brothers Karamazov* (1991). All might be permitted if "God is dead," as Ivan ponders, but this does not—for Dostoevsky himself—mean that all choices about how we should live our lives once so permitted will be equally worthwhile. Dostoevsky questioned and doubted and agonized over metaphysical, ontological, and ethical questions. Yet, he was, like Freire, no relativist. Dostoevsky does not tell us how to live, but he does show, through all of his major works, why we must *ask* and *address* this question. Dostoevsky, in my view, does ultimately favor the ideal of Christian love set out in the Gospels, but this is a position he reached only through taking uncertainty seriously. He puts his ideas into radical interaction—highly critical dialogue—with their opposites.

If in doing such a good job of putting conflicting voices into conversation with each other Dostoevsky created a certain ambiguity over which of his characters best expressed his own views, this does not diminish the educational value of reading his work. It is the ideas themselves—and the thoughts, feelings, utterances, dialogues, relationships, and actions through which they are raised, debated, and conveyed—that matter. One of Dostoevsky's distinguishing characteristics as a novelist is precisely this: He radically "decenters" himself as author, leaving the characters to live out the drama that is their lives, and leaving it to *readers,* similarly, to reflect upon, work with, and be moved by the events, dialogues, and ideas. As the great Russian critic Mikhail Bakhtin observes, Dostoevsky's characters are "*free* people, capable of standing *alongside* their creator, capable of not agreeing with him and even of rebelling against him" (Bakhtin, 1984, p. 6, emphasis in original). What makes Dostoevsky's novels distinctive, Bakhtin contends, is their *polyphonic* character. In monological novels, the views of characters are ultimately subservient to the views of the author. In Dostoevsky's polyphonic novels, what we find is "not a multitude of characters and fates in a single objective world, illuminated by a single authorial consciousness"; rather, we encounter "a *plurality of consciousnesses, with equal rights and each with its own world*" (p. 6, emphasis in original) combining but not merging in the unity of the event. Characters in Dostoevsky's novels become *subjects* rather than objects, with their own signifying discourses. Characters do not serve merely as the mouthpieces for the author's ideas but enter into radical interaction with both the author's voice and the voices of other characters.

There are clear implications for education here, as Timothy Lensmire (1997) demonstrates. Lensmire ponders what it might mean to think of the writing teacher as a Dostoevskian novelist. Such a teacher, in conducting writing workshops, abandons the pedagogical straightjacket of monologism and works to "create a space, a context, within which student-characters are free to live and reflect upon and tell stories about an adventurous life" (p. 380). For Lensmire, Dostoevsky shows, through the structure and content of his novels, the importance of decentering the teacher and of considering multiple voices and points of view in interaction with each other in pedagogical settings. My view is that there is still an *implied* preferred ethical position in at least some of Dostoevsky's great novels (particularly *The Brothers Karamazov*), but not one that Dostoevsky pushes either his characters or readers into. To put this another way, although Dostoevsky does ultimately favor a Christian ethical worldview (cf. Scanlan, 2002), he gives us, through his characters, every opportunity to see why we might also reject this. Dostoevsky grants genuine freedom to his readers, not by suggesting or implying an "anything goes" position, where all ideas or practices or social arrangements are as good as any others, but by having his characters take different possibilities seriously. He thus exposes readers to the alternatives necessary for authentic deliberation and choice.

Freire's pedagogical theory is helpful in developing these points further. Like Dostoevsky, Freire places a premium on the interplay of different voices. Freire's focus is principally on the interaction between students and teachers in educational settings, which may be in or outside the classroom. As is the case in Dostoevsky's novels, the voices in a Freirean dialogue are given full, respectful consideration. But Freire also stresses the importance of structure, direction, and rigor in educational dialogue (Roberts, 1996d). Freirean dialogue is not idle conversation, without a clear point or purpose. Teachers have a right, Freire argues, to intervene where necessary to allow further productive, purposeful dialogue to occur. There are more implied "rules" (principles) in a Freirean dialogue than a Dostoevskian one. Where some people are dominating a conversation, impeding others who wish to contribute from doing so, teachers have a role to play in ensuring that all voices are heard (Freire and Shor, 1987). At the same time, although all participants are encouraged to speak, they are not pressured into doing so. Freire, like Dostoevsky, wants to encourage active *engagement* with the ideas that lie at the heart of a dialogue. This may be *silent* engagement, and those who speak might, in some instances, *not be engaging at all*. Alyosha in *The Brothers Karamazov* teaches others the importance of *listening*, and he is, as Richard Pevear (1991, p. xviii) points out, almost the only person in the novel who can truly *hear* what others have to say. Freire, too, sees the ability to listen—carefully, respectfully, critically—as a key pedagogical virtue. We need to know how and when to "pull back" from an educational conversation, suppressing the urge to have our own voice heard. Freire, like Dostoevsky, values *humility* highly, and learning how to listen is a significant demonstration of this quality (Freire, 1995, 1998a, 1998b). If in Dostoevsky's work there is an *implied* normative position, in Freire's case, ethical preferences are brought more to the fore. Freire stresses that teachers cannot be neutral (Freire, 1972a, 1985). He is happy for teachers, when asked and where appropriate, to disclose their political views when working with students. He stresses, however, that disclosing is not the same as *imposing*. Just as Dostoevsky goes out of his way to put opposing views into active conversation with each other and to allow his readers the freedom to deliberate and choose between them (or to reject both, or to question the merit of setting them in opposition to one another), so too does Freire argue that teachers have a duty not merely to allow but to *actively stimulate* contrary discourses (see Escobar et al., 1994). Freire argues that teachers have a responsibility, as far as this is possible within the constraints of a given educational context, to foster awareness of alternative ideals, perspectives, and ways of life and to give students every opportunity of pursuing these.

Freire and Dostoevsky on Reason and Emotion

In later publications, Freire spoke increasingly about the educational and ethical significance of emotion. Although Freire's work in this area remained underdeveloped, it is clear, as I argued in Chapter 2, that he rejected a narrow rationalist approach to education, emphasizing instead the interconnectedness of reason, emotion, and politics in pedagogical activity. Freire, I believe, would have shared Megan Boler's (1999) view that emotions "are inseparable from actions and relations, from lived experience" (p. 2). To judge by the comments of those who knew Freire well, he was, as noted in Chapter 2, a highly passionate person. He expressed his ideas with enthusiasm and conviction, but also with patience and humility. His style of writing in later books is strongly emotional in character. Freire reveals more of his feelings (e.g., his anger at the politics of neoliberal capitalism), confesses his discomforts (e.g., in talking about his faith) more readily, and discusses some of his weaknesses (as a writer, a teacher, and a family man) at greater length. Freire's language, both in writing and speaking, was, in the words of his second wife, Ana Maria, "loaded with feelings" (Borg and Mayo, 2000, p. 112). Freire also sees *knowing* as something more than a purely rational process. He speaks of knowing with his whole being: with his *body*, and with feeling and reason (Freire, 1997a, p. 30). Freire stresses the importance of virtues such as openness, tolerance, and commitment in teaching and learning situations (Freire, 1998a, 1998c; Escobar et al., 1994). "We are not born with virtues or faults," Freire points out; "[w]e create them" (Freire, 1995, p. 19). Freire wanted to hold on to the importance of *hope*, all the more so in the face of seemingly overwhelming problems of impoverishment, starvation, homelessness, and ecological destruction across the planet (Freire, 1994, 1998b). Most of all, he emphasized the importance of *love*: love of one's fellow human beings, love of the students with whom one works, love of reading and study (see Fraser, 1997; Darder, 2002; McLaren, 2000).

The relationship between reason and feeling was also a lifelong preoccupation for Dostoevsky, and was explored, in different ways, in all of Dostoevsky's major works. Aileen Kelly (1988) notes that in the early part of the twentieth century many radical Russian intellectuals believed Dostoevsky had anticipated the moral dilemmas they would face in the period of great upheaval from 1905 to 1917. Dostoevsky discovered something of profound significance in addressing questions of moral choice, namely, that "there existed no single system of beliefs, no coherent ethical code, that could resolve all problems of ends and means and that this was so because, on some of the most fundamental issues of moral choice, the promptings of reason and feeling could not be reconciled" (p. 239). A number of scholars, Joseph Frank foremost among them, have concluded that Dostoevsky, in attacking reason and insisting on the primacy of religious faith as the ultimate source of moral values, was an "irrationalist" (Frank, 2003, p. 345). Others, notably James Scanlan (1999, 2002), have questioned the appropriateness of the label *irrationalist*. Scanlan maintains that even in *Notes from Underground*, where the assault on reason appears most irrational, there is a logical structure, and thus an implied commitment to rational argument, in the work. I share Scanlan's unease with the term *irrationalist*. To my way of thinking, reason and feeling for Dostoevsky, in both his novels and his own life, are in *tension*, but they are not mutually exclusive. Dostoevsky demonstrated the *limits* of reason, but he neither rejected it entirely nor responded to it in purely irrational terms. Appealing to Christian ethics as the ultimate ground for human conduct, and accepting that in the end we must rely on faith in making such an appeal, even if one does so in an "emotional" or "intuitive-emotional" way, does not commit one to an "irrationalist" position. Dostoevsky's position is, as Richard Neuhaus (2003) shows, close to Pascal's: The heart has its reasons. Reason might not always be able to comprehend the way feelings move us, but this does not mean those feelings are irrational.

One of the ways Dostoevsky teaches us is through what Harvey Siegel (1997) calls *felt* reasons: "by portraying characters who are themselves moved by reasons, Dostoevsky moves us" (p. 53). Siegel asks what it is in Dostoevsky's presentation of the problem of evil in *The Brothers Karamazov* that makes it so powerful, and responds: "The answer, I think, has to do with the visceral quality reasons sometimes have; with the impact that reasons sometimes have on us as feeling persons. We *feel* the force of reasons in some circumstances in entirely different ways than we feel the force of (what are propositionally) the same reasons in other circumstances" (pp. 48–49). Felt reasons differ from other reasons not in kind but in the way they are presented. A philosophical novelist of Dostoevsky's ability can show, in ways that are not possible through, say, teaching a philosophy class, or reading a philosophical textbook, the motivations and reasons behind alternative views. As Siegel puts it, "No matter how good a Philosophy 101 teacher I am, I cannot, by discussing arguments for and against atheism (for example), convey what it feels like to suffer Ivan's torment, nor Zossima's simple faith, nor Alyosha's somewhat less simple faith" (p. 53). Felt reasons can be helpful in "generating in students a sensitivity to reasons, and a recognition of their normative, directing power; they can help, consequently, in developing in students the disposition to be moved by reasons" (p. 52). And this disposition, Siegel argues, is fundamental to education.

Dostoevsky, like Freire, placed great importance on the concept of love. Indeed, I believe love is the key to Dostoevsky's view of teaching. One of the principal teachers in *The Brothers Karamazov*, Father Zosima, tells us: "love is a teacher, but one must know how to acquire it, for it is difficult to acquire, it is dearly bought, by long work over a long time, for one ought to love not for a chance moment but for all time" (Dostoevsky, 1991, p. 319). Dostoevsky shows, through his characters—their thoughts, feelings, actions, conversations, interactions, and struggles—that we *learn through living,* and, in particular, through *active love*. Learning must thus be seen as a *lifelong* process. From a Dostoevskian perspective, questions of teaching and learning do not belong merely in the school or the formal education system. There are teachers all around us, but we must know how and why to learn from them. Some characters in Dostoevsky's novels learn a great deal (e.g., Dmitri in *The Brothers Karamazov*, Raskolnikov in *Crime and Punishment*, Alexander in *Memoirs from the House of the Dead*, Arkady in *The Adolescent*); others—the Underground Man, for example—*fail* to learn, or at least *appear* to fail to learn, even when they encounter good teachers. *We*, as readers, can learn from examples of both kinds and, in the process, enrich our understanding of lifelong education.

Education and Transformation

For Freire, education is a process of transformation. As we engage in critical, dialogical, praxical teaching and learning activities, we transform ourselves and the world (Freire, 1972a). Dostoevsky allows us to understand, in greater detail, *how* transformative educational processes work. In some of Dostoevsky's characters, the process of transformation is more obvious than in others. In *The Brothers Karamazov* (1991), Dmitri clearly changes and *grows* as the events of the book unfold. The same is true of Katerina, Grushenka, the young boys Alyosha befriends, and Alyosha himself, among others. In Ivan's case, the nature of the transformative process is less self-evident. Ivan is presented as the tortured intellectual, questioning both himself and the central tenets of Alyosha's—and Dostoevsky's—faith. Ivan, goaded by Smerdyakov and by a devil who appears to him in a dream, goes mad. He seems to fail to learn from Alyosha, Dmitri, Katerina, and others, and ends up a shattered man. Yet, as Joyce Carol Oates (1968, p. 204) points out, arguably every significant character in the book is transformed. Ivan's "brain fever" is the price he pays for his sin of intellectual pride, but this also, in Oates's view, points the way toward his future regeneration. Dostoevsky, in my view, shows us—perhaps more vividly in the character of Ivan than anyone else in the book—what is at stake in a lifelong process of learning. Both Freire and Dostoevsky demonstrate, in different ways, that we learn through living, but they also remind us that life is cruel, messy, and difficult—sometimes overwhelmingly so. Ivan might be seen to be undergoing what Stanislav Grof (2000) terms a *spiritual emergency*: a deep process of change, often borne out of a crisis or series of crises, where there is the potential for both great distress and significant spiritual advancement and learning. To this extent, Ivan is, in many ways, the most interesting character of all from an educational point of view. He seems to be crushed by the weight of reason, by the workings of his own intellect; and yet there is an unspoken sense that he can emerge from his breakdown as a different man.

Freire, it will be recalled from earlier chapters, speaks of liberation not as an endpoint to be reached but as a process of *struggle* against oppression. The theme of struggle is important for Freire in other ways as well. As noted previously, Freire's stance toward reading, at least in an academic context, is one in which he "fights" with the text while *loving* it (Freire and Shor, 1987). Education, for Freire, is a difficult, complex, always unfinished process of striving: of seeking to *know*, while being aware that one can never know absolutely or completely; of attempting to engage in genuine dialogue while properly acknowledging and working with difference; of struggling to fulfill an ontological and historical vocation of humanization while realizing that we can only ever become *more* fully human. Liberation, for Freire, is pursued *through* struggle, not in spite of it. There are important connections here with Dostoevsky's work. Dostoevsky once said, after listening impatiently to a young fellow Russian's early efforts at poetry: "Weak, bad, worthless ... In order to write well, one must suffer, suffer!" (cited in Pevear, 2002, p. 497). In his novels, Dostoevsky shows, again and again, the power of suffering in changing lives. This was his own experience in Siberia, where, in the harshness and brutality of his prison conditions, he was to find a new spiritual strength. This process is described, in a deeply moving way, in the largely autobiographical *Memoirs from the House of the Dead* (1983), a fictional work but one filled with similar events, experiences, and feelings to those Dostoevsky lived with while in confinement as a young man. Raskolnikov in *Crime and Punishment* (1993) must find redemption for his act of double murder through confession and suffering. And in *The Brothers Karamazov*, we find that Father Zosima has attained wisdom, humility, and respect not merely through a life of prayer and devotion but also by learning from mistakes, wrongs he and others have committed, hardship, and anguish. Freire does not *support* suffering as a condition for learning; indeed, his work is driven by the motivation to *address* the suffering and hardship of others. At the same time, he would not deny that those who *have* suffered can learn from their experiences: They can, through structured dialogue with others, reflect critically on those experiences, begin to understand the conditions that contributed to the experiences, and consider how such conditions might be transformed.

Concluding Remarks

There are weaknesses in the work of both Freire and Dostoevsky. Some of Freire's earlier writings suffer from an unnecessarily abstract mode of written expression. His theory of liberation appears to depend on the existence of oppression for its intelligibility. As noted in Chapter 2, his emphasis on critical reading leaves unanswered questions about what might be *lost* as well as gained when we adopt such a stance, and Freire does not draw in any detail on bodies of work (e.g., the philosophy of emotion, feminist theory, virtue ethics) that might have been helpful in developing his ideas on intellectual dispositions and the relationship between reason and feeling. Freire could have said more about postmodernism, the politics of difference, questions of ethnicity and gender, the ecological crisis, and the spiritual dimensions of education. Dostoevsky helps us to address only some of these shortcomings. His own weaknesses included, at times, anti-Polish and anti-Semitic tendencies, a relatively superficial understanding of some of the ideals he criticized (e.g., socialism), a perplexingly vicious dismissal of Catholicism, and a somewhat unbalanced and inward-looking Russian nationalism. Freire's emphasis on tolerance, openness, and informed political critique assist us in identifying and addressing some of these problems.

Despite these shortcomings, there is much that educationists might continue to gain from reading both Freire and Dostoevsky. Freire and Dostoevsky lived in different centuries, in different countries, and faced different challenges in their personal and working lives. They diverged on some significant political issues, wrote for different audiences, and have seldom been studied together. Yet, for all their differences, these two thinkers share much in common. Both emphasize the importance of dialogue, the interplay of voices, and engagement with ideas. Both place considerable moral and pedagogical value on qualities such as humility, commitment, and love. Both show us why we must learn to live with, indeed *work with*, uncertainty. Both see learning as a difficult, lifelong, necessarily incomplete process. The themes addressed in this chapter are by no means the only ones of importance in Dostoevsky's or Freire's work. Similarly, undertaking a comparison with Freire is, of course, only one of the ways in which we might begin to tease out some of the educational implications of Dostoevsky's work. The analysis undertaken here is intended to complement the efforts of others (e.g., Siegel, 1997; Lensmire, 1997) who have seen the potential in Dostoevsky for enhancing our understanding of teaching and learning. Further studies by educationists of this great Russian writer's extraordinary novels will, in my view, be long overdue and should be welcomed.

Chapter 7

Conscientization in Castalia

A Freirean Reading of Hermann Hesse's *The Glass Bead Game*

Paulo Freire wrote primarily as an educational philosopher, political activist, and teacher. He was a theorist and a practitioner, not a novelist or dramatist. It would not be unreasonable to claim that Freire's later publications exhibit certain literary qualities. Several of his books were constructed in the form of dialogues (e.g., Freire and Shor, 1987; Horton and Freire, 1990; Freire and Faundez, 1989) or letters (e.g., Freire, 1996, 1998a), and one more recently published volume (Freire, 2004) includes a poem Freire wrote in 1971. Even the texts Freire composed in a more traditional academic format during his post-1986 writing period have, at least in some cases (e.g., Freire, 1994, 1997a, 1998b), a more "conversational" tone than most books published by theorists in critical educational studies. Yet, despite these departures from scholarly orthodoxy, it is clear that Freire's primary intention as an author was to develop, convey, and discuss his educational ideas via the medium of nonfiction prose. The thinkers to whom Freire has referred in his work have, similarly, been predominantly (but not exclusively) nonfiction writers. Freire's commentators have tended to follow suit, and hundreds of theoretical books and articles on Freirean themes have been published over the past four decades. Among philosophers of education in particular, Freire has typically been engaged via the work of other scholars who have read, reflected on, and published nonfiction academic writing.

Arguably, however, there is much that might be gained from putting Freirean ideas into conversation with writing of other forms. Freire has sometimes been criticized for the somewhat abstract nature of his written expression. This line of critique has been directed principally at his classic work, *Pedagogy of the Oppressed* (Freire, 1972a). The criticism becomes less convincing when *Pedagogy of the Oppressed* is read alongside other books with a strong practical focus (e.g., Freire 1976, 1998a; Freire and Shor, 1987; Horton and Freire, 1990). Nonetheless, even where Freire shows how his ideas might be, or have been, applied in (and developed from) practice, there is often still something missing. We cannot "get inside the heads" of those who think, feel, and act out the drama that is their educational lives. The limits of the scholarly form, even as stretched by Freire in his more conversational style, do not allow us to explore the particulars—the circumstances, the interactions, the relationships, the inner workings—of an educational situation or individual life in the manner permitted by some other forms of writing. Novels, by taking us into the hearts and minds of characters, provide an especially helpful means through which to explore the nature and significance of ethical, epistemological, and educational ideas for human lives (cf. Nussbaum, 1990, 1995; Katz, 1997; Carr, 2005; Jollimore and Barrios, 2006). Imaginative fiction is, of course, not the only potentially fruitful avenue for this kind of investigation. The medium of film, for example, might serve equally well. But the novel is a form that lends itself particularly well to the exploration of key themes in Freire's philosophy and pedagogy.

One book with special promise in this area is Hermann Hesse's *The Glass Bead Game* (Hesse, 2000a). Education figures prominently in a number of Hesse's novels (e.g., Hesse, 1968, 1999, 2000b). Hesse also addressed educational questions in some of his short stories (see Hesse, 1974a) and nonfiction writings (Hesse, 1974b, 1978). It is in *The Glass Bead Game*, however, that his most comprehensive, complex, and probing examination of an educational setting occurs. *The Glass Bead Game* was Hesse's last and longest novel. Hesse agonized over the book, taking more than ten years to complete it (see Field, 1968; Mileck, 1970; Norton, 1973; Remys, 1983). It was first published (as *Das Glasperlenspiel*) in 1943 and appeared in English translation (originally under the title *Magister Ludi*) in 1949. Shortly after the publication of the book, Hesse was awarded the Nobel Prize for literature. The main part of *The Glass Bead Game* tells the story of Joseph Knecht, who spends most of his life in Castalia, a "pedagogical province" of the twenty-third century. Castalia places a premium on intellectual pursuits, at the center of which is the Glass Bead Game. The exact workings of the Glass Bead Game in its twenty-third century form remain uncertain, but the narrator informs us that the game is like a universal language: a way of connecting traditions and cultures from both the East and the West and of playing with all disciplines and values. Castalia is a hierarchical society, with students at different levels of schooling and masters of the various arts. At the summit of the Order of the Glass Bead Game is the Magister Ludi (Master of the Game). Knecht progresses through the school system in Castalia, studies the game deeply, and is eventually appointed Magister Ludi. He exercises his responsibilities in this position with distinction, but as time passes, he becomes increasingly critical of Castalia's rigidity, restrictiveness, and separation from the rest of the world. Doubts that have been present since his student days find their ultimate expression in his dramatic and difficult decision to resign his post as Magister Ludi. He seeks permission from the Board of Educators to leave the Order and dedicates himself to the task of tutoring Tito, the son of his old friend Plinio. This process barely begins, however, when Knecht dies suddenly while swimming with Tito in an icy mountain lake. The main part of the book is preceded by the narrator's general introduction to the history of the game, and is followed by thirteen poems and three fictional autobiographies (presented as the posthumous writings of Joseph Knecht).

At the center of *The Glass Bead Game* is the educational transformation of Joseph Knecht. But what kind of transformation occurs, and how does this come about? Freire's educational philosophy is helpful in addressing this question. Knecht's transformation, it will be argued here, can be seen as a process of conscientization, through which a dedicated scholar and loyal citizen of Castalia gradually develops an increasingly critical view of the pedagogical province. Dialogue plays a crucial role in shaping Knecht's reflective, questioning orientation toward the world. Freirean theory, I hope to show, allows us to reflect carefully on the nature of Castalian society, appreciate more deeply the experiences of Hesse's characters, and better understand the educational significance of the book. At the same time, Hesse's

The Concept of Conscientization

novel permits aspects of Freire's work to be considered in a fresh light and explored more fully.

The Concept of Conscientization

Conscientization is one of the best known but most frequently misunderstood aspects of Freire's work. In early publications (Freire, 1972b, 1976), Freire discusses conscientization—*conscientização* in the original Portuguese—in relation to different groups within Brazilian society. He describes three modes of consciousness, or ways of thinking and being: magical (semi-intransitive), naïve (transitive), and critical. Magical consciousness prevailed among rural peasant communities and was characterized by a fatalistic attitude, a lack of historical awareness, and a focus on survival. Naïve consciousness was predominant in the urban centers that emerged in Brazil following World War II. Its defining features included an emphasis on polemics rather than argument, the oversimplification of problems, and a lack of interest in investigation and dialogue. Critical consciousness was characteristic of "authentically democratic regimes" and included elements such as depth in the interpretation and addressing of problems, the testing of findings and openness to revision, a willingness to accept responsibility, sound argumentation, the practice of dialogue, and acceptance of "what is valid in both old and new" (Freire, 1976, p. 18). Conscientization consisted in the movement from either magical or naïve consciousness toward critical consciousness. Education, Freire believed, could play a key role in facilitating this process.

This early depiction of different modes of consciousness has been taken by some as an indication that Freire intended conscientization to be seen in terms of clear-cut, progressive levels or "stages." Removed from its original context, conscientization has sometimes been applied as a means for describing a process of individual development through fixed, sequential stages of consciousness (e.g., Smith, 1976). As has been argued elsewhere (Roberts, 1996c), the "stages" model of conscientization has some significant epistemological problems. The characterization of conscientization as a process of "consciousness raising" (e.g., Berger, 1974) leads to further difficulties. This suggests a hierarchy of consciousnesses, ignoring the cultural specificity of different modes of knowing and being. Some ways of understanding the world, it can be argued, are more helpful than others—but only in certain contexts and for particular purposes. The depictions of magical and naïve consciousness were Freire's attempt to capture prevailing patterns of thought and attitudes among different groups of Brazilians during specific periods of that country's history. Freire's focus was not on individuals, and he did not see magical consciousness, naïve consciousness, and critical consciousness as *predefined* levels or stages—that is, as universal categories, applicable to all people at all times and in all circumstances. With the enormous interest in Freire's work following the publication of *Pedagogy of the Oppressed* (Freire, 1972a), conscientization came to be seen as a kind of "magic bullet": a revolutionary pedagogical "method" capable of eliminating oppression where other approaches had failed. Freire disavowed such readings. He insisted that conscientization is not a panacea for social ills (Freire, 1998b, p. 55). He stressed that his philosophy and pedagogy could not be reduced to a "method" or even a set of methods (Freire, 1997b). He reinforced the view that conscientization was a complex, multifaceted, ongoing process, and that it could only be understood in relation to other key concepts in his work such as dialogue and praxis. He emphasized the limits as well as the possibilities in educational initiatives. In the end, frustrated with what he saw as persistent misunderstandings of his intentions, Freire largely abandoned the term. From the late 1970s to the mid-1980s, he seldom discussed conscientization in any detail. In later publications (e.g., Freire, 1996, 1997a, 1998b, 2004), he returned to the concept, this time integrating it with a wider body of theory generated through his dialogical encounters with other scholars such as Ira Shor (Freire and Shor, 1987), Myles Horton (Horton and Freire, 1990), and Antonio Faundez (Freire and Faundez, 1989).

Although the notion of conscientization has been subject to considerable controversy and confusion over the years, some of its key features have been clearly evident from Freire's earliest writings. Conscientization can be seen as the process of developing a critical consciousness, particularly but not exclusively in relation to social structures, practices, and prevailing ideas. The deepening of one's understanding of society through conscientization involves, among other things, learning to place social problems in their broader contexts, establishing relationships between different phenomena, and appreciating the historical nature of human existence. Conscientization does not take place through fixed, inevitable, irreversible stages;

rather, it occurs as "a process at any given moment" (Freire, 1985, p. 107). Freire does not portray conscientization in a linear fashion but instead stresses the fluid, dynamic nature of the process. It is not a matter of first developing a critical consciousness and then engaging in action, and through this bringing about social transformation. In the process of conscientization, reflection and action are necessarily intertwined. For Freire, all aspects of reality are in motion. There is a constant interaction between "consciousness" and "world" (Freire, 1972b). Given this process of incessant change, one can, at best, only come *closer* to understanding a given object of study (Freire and Shor, 1987). If the "object of study" in the process of conscientization is the social world, Freire recognizes that there is no *one* legitimate way of comprehending the problems in that world. What conscientization demands of us is that we strive to deepen and extend our current understanding. This requires the application of intellectual virtues, such as a willingness to question (without assuming that everything needs to be questioned all the time), a probing and inquiring stance when faced with a problem, open-mindedness, curiosity, and a certain humility (recognizing, among other things, that we cannot "know it all" and that there is always more to learn).

Conscientization has ontological, epistemological, ethical, and educational dimensions. Conscientization is, Freire argues, fundamental to our very being as humans. It is "a requirement of our human condition" (Freire, 1998b, p. 55). The form conscientization takes, however, will differ from one context to another. Developing a critical consciousness involves seeking to know oneself, others, and the world (cf. van Gorder, 2007). Knowing here, as Freire describes it, is more than mere surface comprehension. It is a process of striving to delve beneath surface appearances, of endeavoring to understand an object of study rigorously. This is not an abstract, purely cognitive process, separated from the rest of the world. Rather, knowing is an intensely practical process, intertwined with the messy realities of everyday life. Knowing, as Freire conceives of it, is something one engages in with one's whole being—with feeling, willing, and action as well as with reason (see Freire, 1997a, p. 30). Seeking to know in this manner demands ethical and political commitment. *Conscientization*, as the term suggests, involves the cultivation of not just a certain kind of critical awareness but of *conscience* (Freire, 2004, p. 78). The key to enacting this process in an educational setting, Freire argued, is critical dialogue. Freire argues that as humans we are beings of communication (see Freire, 1976, 1996, 1998b, 2004), and that dialogue is a crucial part of the process of becoming more fully human. Educational dialogue, as has been noted earlier in this book, is not mere idle conversation; rather, it is purposeful and rigorous, with a clear sense of structure and direction. Dialogical education focuses on posing and addressing problems rather than giving answers; it draws, and reflects critically, on the knowledge and experience of participants; and it assumes that knowledge is not static but ever evolving (Freire, 1972a). Critical dialogue fosters a better understanding of "self" and "society," enhances the appreciation of "otherness," and allows participants to develop a deeper awareness of themselves as unfinished beings.

Uncertainty, Critical Thought, and Social Life

Conscientization requires a willingness to live with, and indeed embrace, uncertainty. In his later works, as I noted in the previous chapter, Freire spoke often of the need not to become too certain of one's certainties. This does not mean that nothing can be taken as given for particular purposes. Freire acknowledged that we must take certain things for granted in order to make decisions and take action as human beings. Freire's point is that if reality is constantly changing, we, too, can never completely "stand still"; our understanding of the world must always be open to change. Freire explains:

> I have been always engaged with many thoughts concerning the challenges that draw me to this or that issue or to the doubts that make me unquiet. These doubts take me to uncertainties, the only place where it is possible to work toward the necessary provisional certainties. It is not the case that it is impossible to be certain about some things. What is impossible is to be absolutely certain, as if the certainty of today were the same as that of yesterday and will continue to be the same as that of tomorrow. (Freire, 1997a, pp. 30–31)

The Glass Bead Game, through the life of Joseph Knecht, demonstrates the importance of uncertainty and critical thought—not just for individuals, but for groups and indeed whole societies. Castalia, Hesse's novel shows, is in a state of decay as a society precisely because most of its citizens fail to question its structures, its system of education, and its superiority over other societies. The hierarchical nature of Castalian society encourages order and conformity. Castalians have little respect for history, and although they believe themselves to have gone beyond the follies of the Feuilleton Age (the first half of the twentieth century), they have not learned from some of the mistakes made in that period. They are, in Freirean terms, too certain of their certainties. They seek to uphold some traditions but abandon others too quickly. They do not have, as Freire puts it, either a willingness to consider the new or the good sense not to abandon the old just because it is old (Freire, 1976, p. 18). When faced with challenges, many Castalians withdraw further into the protective confines of the pedagogical province or respond with coldness and incomprehension. Those within the Order who do not conform lead a precarious existence (as is the case with Tegularius, Joseph's oversensitive but brilliant friend), and are sometimes treated with outright contempt and brutality (as occurs with Bertram, the deputy of the Magister Ludi in office just prior to Knecht's investiture: see Friedrichsmeyer, 1974).

In some important respects, Castalia provides largely unfriendly soil for the cultivation of a critical mode of being. There is, as Osman Durrani (1982) argues, a naïve quality to some of the analytical statements by even the most admirable characters. The Music Master is perhaps the most striking example:

> It is beyond doubt... that in the Magister Musicae Hesse has created a good, almost a saintly figure. In his serenity, his goodwill towards Knecht, and his unpretentious devotion to art, he appeals to the reader as an emblem of all that is best in the province. But although he may be above criticism as a human being, it is equally true that he is naïvely optimistic about the organization to which he belongs, and blind to its defects. (p. 660)

Knecht constitutes an exception to the rule in Castalia (Swales, 1978; Roberts, 2008c). This does not mean that the pedagogical province has played no role in the cultivation of his critical consciousness. Castalia plays a part in providing the culture of intellectual discipline necessary for carefully structured, in-depth reflection. Knecht learns through his involvement with the Glass Bead Game and his interactions with other Castalians the value of reasoning, deliberation, and contemplation. Reflective reasoning allows him to make the unprecedented decision to relinquish his role as Magister Ludi and to leave the Order of the Glass Bead Game. Knecht's Circular Letter to the Board of Educators, in which he requests permission to leave and outlines his reasons for doing so, is, in many respects, a model of thoughtful, carefully constructed argument. That said, Knecht's analysis of Castalia's limits also has its own limits. His critique of Castalian hierarchy lacks a theory—or at least a well-articulated theory—of power or politics. Little is said about the sexism inherent in the Castalian system. Castalia is not merely a hierarchy but a *male* hierarchy, and Knecht fails to render this problematic. Knecht wishes to bridge the two spheres—the hermetically sealed "inner" world of Castalia and the wider outside world—but he has only a vaguely formed and somewhat romantic idea of what life in the outside world entails.

Knecht, then, might remove himself from Castalia, but Castalia continues to "live through" him. He has, in Freirean terms, been conditioned but not *determined* by his context (Freire, 1998b, p. 26). The structures, practices, attitudes, and ideas that characterize the pedagogical province play their part in making Knecht the man that he becomes, but he cannot be reduced to merely the sum of these influences. Hesse placed supreme importance on the integrity of the individual (see Hesse, 1974b, 1978), and *The Glass Bead Game* is, among other things, a critique of the tendency in social systems to suppress individuality. At the same time, Hesse recognized that we are social and historical beings, and his portrait of Knecht is consistent with this (cf. Wilde, 1999). Knecht cannot shed the dominant influence of Castalia on his life—on his mode of thinking and being—and yet he is not *merely* Castalian. Knecht's conscientization involves, among other things, the gradual deepening of his understanding of the relationship between "self" and "society." Knecht's growing consciousness of himself is, as Hilde Cohn (1950) points out, a key theme in the novel. But this is a consciousness of himself *with others*. Castalia might have been the dominant influence on Knecht's life, but others who represent and carry with them the outside world—Plinio Designori and Father Jacobus—also play pivotal roles in making him the man that he becomes. The next section elaborates on how and why this is so.

The Role of Dialogue

Dialogue plays an important pedagogical role in the development of Knecht's critical consciousness and is one of the defining characteristics of his relationships with Plinio Designori and Father Jacobus. Joseph's first encounter with Plinio is at Waldzell. Only the brightest of the elite students in Castalia attend the school at Waldzell. Waldzell is the home of the Glass Bead Game, and it is here that the Magister Ludi resides. Plinio is a youth from a prominent family outside Castalia who is sent to Waldzell to experience the unique intellectual stimulation and learning provided by the pedagogical province. Not long after encountering Plinio, Joseph senses that "this other boy would mean something important to him, perhaps something fine, an enlargement of his horizon, insight or illumination, perhaps also temptation and danger" (Hesse, 2000a, p. 86). Plinio and Joseph begin what will become a lifelong friendship. They become the key protagonists in a series of vigorous debates over the strengths and weaknesses of the Castalian system. Plinio attacks the pedagogical province, and Knecht defends Castalian ideals. In their debates, Plinio and Joseph exhibit many of the qualities of Freirean dialogue. They enter into their exchanges with a searching, probing, questioning frame of mind; they demonstrate an ability to challenge as well as to be challenged; and they deepen and extend their views through interaction with each other. Their early exchanges are characterized by youthful exuberance and enthusiasm, but with time and the advancement of years, qualities such as humility and tolerance come more to the fore. There is at first a sort of battle of wills and ideas, but this later becomes, for some of the time at least, more a demonstration of profound respect and a willingness to listen to and learn from each other.

When the two protagonists meet again after being separated for many years, there is a certain weariness in both of them. Plinio is weighed down by his political and family responsibilities, and Knecht is burdened with his duties as Magister Ludi. Knecht appears to adopt a somewhat condescending air in his conversation with Plinio. Plinio seems to be reaching out to him, seeking to establish a stronger emotional connection with his friend, but the Magister Ludi responds in a disarmingly "cheerful" manner. He listens carefully to what Plinio has to say; yet he seems at this point to be still too much the representative of Castalia, rather than Joseph the human being. Listening, as Freire sees it, is an important part of genuine dialogue. It is "a permanent attitude on the part of the subject who is listening, of being open to the word of the other, to the gesture of the other, to the differences of the other" (Freire 1998b, p. 107). This is not merely a rational but also an emotional process. Plinio cannot understand Knecht's apparent amusement in the face of a heartfelt confession from an old friend. At first glance, it is almost as if the detachment typical of the Castalian hierarchy cannot avoid seeping into Knecht, despite his clear differences with other members of the Order. Plinio, as an outsider, experiences this more acutely than others who come into contact with Knecht. Knecht responds, however, by saying: "if I do not go along with your sadness ... , that does not mean I don't recognize it or take it seriously" (Hesse 2000a, p. 293). As the dialogue continues, the two friends consider their differences as well as similarities and reflect on their earlier encounters. Knecht is about to make the momentous decision to resign his position as Magister Ludi, and he, too, seeks to strengthen his emotional bond with Plinio—but in his own distinctive way, with "cheerful serenity ... even in unhappiness and suffering" (p. 300).

Knecht's relationship with Father Jacobus also plays a pivotal role in his subsequent development. Knecht is sent by the Castalian authorities on a mission to a Benedictine monastery in Mariafels. Father Jacobus is one of the monastery's most respected figures, and Knecht develops a strong intellectual admiration for him. During his stay at the monastery, Joseph learns that he and Jacobus share an interest in the work of a teacher, Johann Albrecht Bengel. They engage in a critical but cheerful dialogue about Bengel, "a fruitful conversation, out of which sprang mutual understanding and a kind of friendship" (Hesse, 2000a, p. 154). As Knecht's relationship with Father Jacobus grows and matures, the respect between the two men deepens: "Jacobus enjoyed the exchange of views with so well trained yet still so supple a young mind; this was a pleasure he did not often have. And Knecht found his association with the historian, and the education Jacobus provided, a new stage on the path of awakening—that path which he nowadays identified as his life" (p. 155).

What does Knecht learn from Father Jacobus? The narrator's answer is that "he learned history" (p. 155). "He learned the laws and contradictions of historical studies and historiography. And beyond that, in the following years he learned to see the present and his own life as historical realities" (p. 155). Arguably, however, Knecht learns much more than this from his relationship with Jacobus. He sharpens his awareness of some of the limits of Castalian society, laying the foundations of the argument that will later underpin his Circular Letter to the Board of Educators; he develops a more nuanced view of his own strengths and weaknesses; and, importantly, he learns the value of dialogue at both an individual and societal level. Knecht's dialogue with Father Jacobus provides the basis for a better relationship—one of greater trust, improved communication, and sounder understanding—between Castalia and the Catholic Church.

Joseph and Jacobus change as individuals through their dialogical encounters. Near the beginning of their relationship, Father Jacobus approaches their conversations with a certain aggressiveness. Indeed, there is a degree of close-mindedness in his stance. Jacobus adopts a reactionary posture, making belittling remarks about Castalia and responding to Knecht in at times thunderous tones (pp. 155–156). He has spells of "angry unfairness" (p. 158). He lacks, in Freirean terms, the humility and the open-mindedness necessary to engage fully in educational dialogue. At first, he sees virtually nothing of value in the pedagogical province: "Whenever he found something objectionable in Knecht's way of thinking, he blamed it on that 'modern' Castalian spirit with its abstruseness and its fondness for frivolous abstractions. And whenever Knecht surprised him by wholesome views and remarks akin to his own thought, he exulted because his young friend's sound nature had so well withstood the damage of Castalian education" (p. 155). Despite his youth, Joseph displays a calmness and an equanimity that is, in the earlier stages of their relationship, sometimes lacking in the older man. Yet, on a number of philosophical and historical matters, Knecht cannot deny the power of Jacobus's reasoning. He is encouraged, in part by the initial ferocity of Jacobus's attacks, to probe his own assumptions further and to ask more searching questions of the Castalian way of life than would have been possible on his own. Father Jacobus, although too quickly dismissive of Castalia in his early conversations with Knecht, remains modest about his own achievements. Knecht speaks with him simply as a fellow scholar, a colleague in the pursuit of truth. He is at first unaware of Father Jacobus's standing as a man of the highest reputation, constantly in demand for advice, "someone who was consciously participating in world history, and helping to shape it as the leading statesman of his Order" (p. 158). Father Jacobus, like Knecht, values dialogue for its own sake as well as for the learning it facilitates. Both Jacobus and Knecht love the very process of mutual inquiry, of exchanging views and testing one's ideas in the company of another. Over time, Father Jacobus comes to appreciate that Castalia and the Church are perhaps not so far apart as he had hitherto imagined.

Hesse's novel allows us to see more clearly how Freirean dialogue "works" in a wider educational context. It does not do so, however, in a didactic or mechanical fashion. The three key participants in the dialogues that play such an important role in Knecht's life—Plinio, Father Jacobus, and Knecht himself—are all complex, multilayered, sometimes contradictory human beings. They have character flaws as well as strengths, and these have a bearing on the nature of their exchanges. At times, their conversations have an *anti*dialogical character, with one or both of the participants lacking in the humility, openness, or willingness to listen and learn necessary for genuine Freirean dialogue. Importantly, the book shows how context and experience impact on the content, tone, and consequences of dialogue. Knecht, Jacobus, and Plinio have all enjoyed certain privileges. Knecht and Jacobus have been "protected" from some of the demands of the outside world by their respective Orders (Knecht more so than Jacobus), and Plinio has been fortunate enough to have come from a wealthy family. Their individual backgrounds, to varying degrees and in different ways, set limits on their thinking as they enter into their conversations with others. Yet, *through* dialogue, something more than the mere combination of their respective views emerges. Knecht, Jacobus, and Plinio *change* as their conversations progress. In all three cases, their view of Castalia deepens; all three, in distinctive ways given their different positions, come to view the pedagogical province in a more critical, balanced, and mature light.

Conscientization and the Nonneutrality of Education

The analysis to this point begs the question: What is the basis on which Knecht's views (and those of Plinio and Father Jacobus) might be said to be "more critical, balanced, and mature"? Against what criteria can such judgments be made? This is important not just in understanding Knecht's transformation in *The Glass Bead Game* but in addressing some of the epistemological assumptions underlying Freire's approach to dialogue and conscientization. Gert Biesta's work on the "impossibility of education" (Biesta, 1998, 2005) is helpful in addressing this point. The impossibility of education, Biesta argues, lies in its unpredictability. Education cannot be reduced to mere technique or to a process of teachers molding students. In thinking about education we must take into account the ways in which students "use" what is presented by the teacher. It is this "use" of what is presented that makes education possible—but also unpredictable (1998, pp. 503–504). This has implications for critical pedagogy:

> If it is the case that the very possibility of education is sustained by its impossibility, then it follows that the idea of critical pedagogy as a positive program and project is problematic for two different reason[s]. First, because such a program can only be successful if it is able to control the "use" of what it tries to achieve.... Second, because such a program would eventually imply an erasure of the political realm, of the realm where the risk of disclosure is a possibility. This is the main danger implied in the normalizing tendency of critical pedagogy. (p. 504)

For Biesta, the only way for critical pedagogy to proceed, if it is to maintain pedagogical and political consistency, is to perpetually challenge all claims to authority, including those made by critical pedagogy itself (p. 505). Such a challenge cannot be mounted in the name of "some superior knowledge or privileged vision" but can only proceed, Biesta suggests, on the basis of a "fundamental *ignorance*" (p. 505). Biesta elaborates:

> Such ignorance is neither naïveté nor skepticism. It just is an ignorance that does not claim to know how the future will be or will have to be. It is an ignorance that does not show the way, but only issues an invitation to set out on the journey. It is an ignorance that does not say what to think of it, but only asks, "What do you think about it?" In short, it is an ignorance that makes room for the possibility of disclosure. It is, therefore, an emancipatory ignorance. (p. 505)

Biesta notes that this seems to contradict a key tenet in the critical tradition, namely, the idea that "emancipation can be brought about when people have an adequate understanding of, if not simply the plain truth, about their own situation" (p. 505). Biesta's response is not to deny that change is possible or to see knowledge as futile. Instead, his approach "signifies the end of the 'innocence' of knowledge as a critical instrument, and thus the end of the possibility of demystification. It urges us to recognize that we are always operating in a field of power/knowledge *against* power/knowledge" (p. 506). Biesta advances a notion of "counterpractice," a form of transgression as "the experimental illumination of limits" (p. 507). He concludes:

A counterpractice should not be designed out of an arrogance that it will be better (or that one claims to know that it will be better; once again: ignorance) than what exists. A counterpractice is only different. The critical task of a counterpractice can therefore only be to show (to prove, Foucault says) that the way things were was only one (limited) possibility. But this step is crucial, as it opens up the possibility "of no longer being, doing, or thinking what we are, do, or think." (p.507)

This provides an intriguing standpoint from which to reconsider Freirean philosophical assumptions and Knecht's process of conscientization. Biesta's notion of "emancipatory ignorance" bears some resemblance to the Freirean idea of uncertainty. Uncertainty, from Freire's point of view, is ethically desirable, as is the kind of ignorance promoted by Biesta. Uncertainty provides the "motor," or impetus, for questioning and ongoing critical thought. Being prepared to not only live with but *embrace* uncertainty affirms our existence as curious, inquiring beings (cf. Curzon-Hobson, 2002). Uncertainty on its own does not constitute critical consciousness (in the Freirean sense), but it is essential for it. Biesta's suggestion that emancipatory ignorance "does not show the way, but only issues an invitation to set out on the journey" is also largely consistent with Freirean theory and Knecht's educational path in *The Glass Bead Game*. Freire states emphatically that it is not his job as an educator to *impose* his political views on students; rather, his role is to provide the conditions for students to investigate matters of political significance themselves (see Freire's comments in Escobar et al., 1994). Teachers, he insists, have a responsibility to not only allow but actively encourage the consideration of ethical and political alternatives. The educational imperative, if it might be stated in those terms, is to make such a journey *matter* for students. The point is not to prescribe (or proscribe) answers but to foster an educational environment where students will learn how to *ask questions*. This, from a Freirean perspective, is where an important element in the nonneutrality of education lies: the favoring of some pedagogical dispositions—for example, a willingness to question, to inquire, and to engage in dialogue—over others. These are the qualities Joseph Knecht develops in his process of conscientization, and they distinguish him from some of his colleagues in Castalia. Biesta, it seems to me, also presupposes a form of nonneutrality in his work, inasmuch as he favors (for instance) the possibility of disclosure, the value of interrogating our presuppositions about power/

knowledge, and the very idea of inviting students to set out on an educational journey.

Biesta claims that a counterpractice should be only different, not better. Freire seems to suggest, however, that conscientization involves the development of a mode of thinking and being that is preferable over some other ways of thinking and being. A searching, questioning, probing, investigative, dialogical, critical approach to understanding and living in the world, Freire implies, is better than, say, a passive, unquestioning, monological orientation. From this perspective, it might be said that Knecht, Plinio, and Jacobus all develop a "better"—more "critical, balanced, and mature"—understanding of the world through their dialogical relationships with each other. Freire argues against political prescriptiveness in educational settings, but he is, as we have seen in earlier chapters, not an epistemological or ethical relativist. Biesta cautions against the idea of believing we can or should "demystify" the world for others. Freire does not want teachers to assume they have a right or a responsibility to clear away clouds of student ignorance; on the other hand, he also does not want teachers to pretend they have nothing of value to offer students in assisting them to learn. Teachers have an important role to play in allowing students to see, in Biesta's terms, that the way things are is not the only way they could be. This is made more possible by some pedagogical approaches than others. For example, if teachers were to encourage students to adopt or investigate just one view on a contentious social issue, when they are aware of well-developed competing views, they would be at odds with the Freirean imperative to foster exploration of alternatives. The Castalian education system does not prohibit students from investigating alternatives, but neither does it actively encourage them to do so. Knecht, through his dialogues with Plinio and Father Jacobus, as well through his own studies and reflections, comes to believe that many of his fellow Castalians are too narrow and rigid in their view of themselves, their society, and the lives of others in the outside world. Knecht's conscientization does not, however, lead him to reject all he has learned in the pedagogical province. To the contrary, Knecht, by being prepared to ask questions, to probe further than most of his classmates and many of the Masters, and to enter into debates with Plinio and Jacobus, comes to appreciate more deeply the aesthetic richness and complexity of the Glass Bead Game. Knecht does not, by the time he is ready to leave his position as Magister Ludi, see himself as having "demystified"

Castalia. He has formed a more critical view of the pedagogical province, but he has also developed a greater awareness of his own limits and of the need for ongoing reflection, dialogue, and action. This idea is developed more fully in the next section.

Conscientization: An Ongoing Process

A key element in Knecht's conscientization is his growing awareness of himself as an unfinished human being. Knecht has a maturity beyond his years. He is an exemplary student and scholar, a fine administrator, a respected figure among his peers (at all stages of his life), a thoughtful and caring person, and a brilliant exponent of the Glass Bead Game. He reaches the very summit of the Castalian hierarchy with his appointment, at a comparatively young age, as Magister Ludi. He has honesty and integrity, and abhors nastiness when he observes this in others. In his magisterial duties, he carries himself with dignity and poise. In many ways, he lives the ideal Castalian life, fulfilling his calling to greatness within the pedagogical province. And yet, Knecht's decision to leave Castalia is made with a profound awareness that he has much more to achieve. In this respect, he exhibits one of the key characteristics of conscientization: an awareness of our unfinishedness as human beings and of the ethical implications arising from this (see Freire, 1998b, p. 55). In his tenure as Magister Ludi, Knecht had come to value, more and more, the process of teaching, finding his work with younger students especially rewarding. This, he comes to believe, is where his key contribution lies. He leaves Castalia with a renewed sense of freedom—an open embracing of uncertainty—and a new appreciation for the beauty of the day and the world. He has hope for the future and is filled with a quiet excitement about the challenges that lie ahead in his new role as a tutor for Tito, Plinio's son. He has come to realize that there is a whole new world outside Castalia, vibrant and complex, waiting to be explored:

> Life in the world, as the Castalian sees it, is something backward and inferior, a life of disorder and crudity, of passions and distractions, devoid of all that is beautiful or desirable. But the world and its life was in fact infinitely vaster and richer than the notions a Castalian has of it; it was full of change, history, struggles, and eternally new

beginnings. It might be chaotic, but it was the home and native soil of all destinies, all exaltations, all arts, all humanity; it had produced languages, peoples, governments, cultures; it has also produced us and our Castalia and would see all these things perish again, and yet survive. My teacher Jacobus had kindled in me a love for this world which was forever growing and seeking nourishment. But in Castalia there was nothing to nourish it. Here we were outside of the world; we ourselves were a small, perfect world, but one no longer changing, no longer growing. (Hesse, 2000a, pp. 378–379)

Knecht, then, by his own assessment, remains incomplete and is eager to continue his growth as a human being. This focus on incompleteness was arguably both a deliberate decision on the part of Hesse as author and a reflection of Hesse the man on his own path of spiritual and intellectual development. There was a certain unity in Hesse's life, as there was in Knecht's, and the same themes find expression, in different ways, again and again in his writing. But although *The Glass Bead Game* was Hesse's last novel, and in this limited sense brought his work to a close, he continued to read, write, and reflect until his death at the age of eighty-five. Hesse, like Knecht, could only ever find relative and temporary stability. He was always, as Freire would have put it, a restless being, constantly curious, always striving to know more (cf. Freire, 1985). Hesse felt from an early age that for him it was to be "a poet or nothing at all" (Helt, 1996), just as it seemed for Joseph Knecht to be Castalian or nothing at all. Hesse might have gone through more overt trials in his school days and experienced greater difficulty in dealing with an authoritarian system of education than appeared to be the case with Joseph. And although Hesse's relationship with his parents was to leave its imprint on a number of his writings, Joseph's parents might have died while he was still very young (the narrator leaves some uncertainty on this point). But the seeds of change—of not simply accepting what tradition and authority had decreed—were planted for both Hesse and Knecht before they had emerged into full adulthood, and these were to grow and take more robust form in the decades that followed. Hesse experienced periods of serious depression and even despair throughout his life (see Mileck, 1978). He turned to the spiritual teachings of the East (while also not ignoring the religious traditions of the West), aestheticism, and psychoanalysis for answers to the questions being posed in his restless mind. And although the last third of his long life was in many ways more settled than his earlier years, there was never a point at which he declared or seemed to feel that he could be fully content, fully at rest, completed. This, I believe, is what he wanted to convey in the book (and this view was very much shared by Freire): All of us remain incomplete; we go to our graves never having realized all we might have achieved, sometimes with a mixture of pride and regret, but always with further questions and more work to do.

Concluding Comments

It is clear from Freire's later publications (e.g., Freire, 1994, 1997b, 1998a, 1998b, 1998c, 2004, 2007) that he wanted his readers to keep "reinventing" his work. This process demands that we not forget the circumstances under which Freire's books were authored, and that we attempt to come as close as possible to understanding the deeper meaning behind his texts, while also accepting that other contexts and situations require new readings, different methods, and fresh applications of his ideas. This chapter has been completed in this spirit of "reinventing" Freire by applying key elements of his theoretical framework to Hermann Hesse's *The Glass Bead Game*. The central character in Hesse's novel, Joseph Knecht, undergoes a gradual but profound process of educational transformation. Knecht's conscientization mirrors many of the features of Freire's educational ideal. He develops a critical, questioning frame of mind, becoming "less certain of his certainties" as he grows older, and this leads to his eventual decision to resign his post as Magister Ludi. Knecht's dialogical relationships with other key characters play an important role in this process. He feels an increasingly strong need to teach— to play a role in shaping and guiding young people, not just within but beyond the pedagogical province. This distinguishes him from most of his fellow Castalians, who see themselves as separate from and superior to the rest of world. Castalia remains a closed, inward-looking, rigid hierarchy, and Knecht struggles against this. At the end of the main part of the novel, Knecht remains an incomplete being and is aware of himself as such. His sudden death brings his personal quest to a premature close, but it is clear that the educational process he has started will continue with Tito and others.

It should be noted, in closing, that this is only one of the books by Hermann Hesse that lends itself readily to Freirean analysis. Several of Hesse's other novels—particularly, but not exclusively, *Beneath the Wheel* (1968) and *Siddhartha* (2000b)—could also be examined fruitfully from a Freirean point of view. There are, moreover, strong connections that can be drawn between Freire and other literary figures. As I argued in the previous chapter, Dostoevsky, with his searching exploration of philosophical themes in works such as *The Brothers Karamazov*, is one writer who stands out here, but there are many others who offer rich possibilities for analysis. For educational philosophers (and not just those concerned with Freire), the list of novelists who might prove helpful is extensive. Leo Tolstoy, George Eliot, Virginia Woolf, Franz Kafka, Albert Camus, Simone de Beauvoir, Jean Paul Sartre, Iris Murdoch, Milan Kundera, Umberto Eco, Ben Okri, and Margaret Atwood, to name a few, have all, in different ways, addressed complex ethical, epistemological, and ontological dilemmas—with important implications for education—in their novels. By putting educational theorists into conversation with novelists—or the characters they create—light can be shed on both genres of written work. Academic books permit the systematic, reasoned, coherent development of educational ideas; novels, or at least *some* novels, allow us to see how these ideas can be "lived out" in the thoughts, feelings, actions, relationships, and experiences of characters. This chapter has made only a modest beginning in this area, and there is considerable scope for further work of this kind.

Chapter 8

Bridging East and West

Freire and the *Tao Te Ching*

Just over a decade ago I received a review copy of *Mentoring the Mentor* (Freire et al., 1997b), a collection of critical essays on the work of Paulo Freire. Among other items of interest, I discovered a chapter by James Fraser (1997) on the themes of love and history in Freire's thought. One aspect of this chapter in particular caught my eye. In addressing a number of ideas in Freire's approach to liberating education, Fraser cited passages from the *Tao Te Ching*. The comparison intrigued me, and I made a mental note to one day return to it. I had at that time read the *Tao Te Ching* only once, and my initial reaction in seeing the link Fraser made between Lao Tzu and Freire was one of mild skepticism. The two bodies of work—Taoist philosophy and Freirean pedagogy—seemed somewhat remote from each other, separated not merely by geography and the passage of time but by fundamental differences in ontological, ethical, and political orientation.

With the passing of years and several rereadings of the *Tao Te Ching*, in a number of translations, I now believe the gulf between Freirean and Taoist thought is not as great as I had originally supposed. The comparative analysis undertaken in this chapter will show that there are some significant differences between Freire and Lao Tzu on matters of epistemology, politics, and education, but these are, potentially at least, *productive* tensions worthy of careful reflection. There are, moreover, some surprising similarities that can be identified, and these, too, warrant continuing exploration.

CHAPTER 8

The *Tao Te Ching* is one of the classic works of ancient Eastern philosophy and is the best known of the Taoist texts. It has been translated into English numerous times, and there has been much debate over the merits of different versions. Different spellings of the key terms in Taoist philosophy are also used. *Tao* is sometimes written in English as *Dao,* and in such cases the book becomes the *Dao De Jing.* The book is also sometimes known as the *Lao Tzu.* Fraser's point of reference in discussing Freire and Taoist ideas is Stephen Mitchell's version of the text (Mitchell, 1991). For the passages quoted by Fraser, I shall use the Mitchell text; elsewhere, preference will sometimes be given to the translations by Ellen Chen (Chen, 1989) and D. C. Lau (Lao Tzu, 1963). In adopting any English version, one must always be mindful that no translation can quite do justice to the original text.

The chapter is structured in three parts. The first section provides an overview of the origins, structure, and content of the *Tao Te Ching.* The second part summarizes Fraser's application of ideas from the *Tao Te Ching* to Freirean theory. This is followed, in the final section, by a more detailed discussion of several key themes in Freirean and Taoist thought: the relationship between action and nonaction, the nature and role of knowing and knowledge, and the relationship between ignorance, happiness, and education.

Reading the *Tao Te Ching*

The *Tao Te Ching* (pronounced "Dow Deh Jing," Mitchell, 1991, p. vii) is attributed to Lao Tzu, an older contemporary of Confucius (551–479 B.C.) (Lau, 1963, p. viii). Lao Tzu is reported to have met with Confucius and, at the latter's request, given him concise advice on the art of living. The earliest general history of China, the *Shih chi* (*Record of the Historian*), was composed by Ssu-ma Ch'ien at the beginning of the first century B.C. (p. viii). In that work, it is noted:

> Lao Tzu cultivated the way and virtue, and his teachings aimed at self-effacement. He lived in Chou for a long time, but seeing its decline he departed; when he reached the Pass, the Keeper there was pleased and said to him, "As you are about to leave the world behind, could you write a book for my sake?" As a result, Lao Tzu wrote a work in two books, setting out the meaning of the way and virtue in some five thousand characters, and then departed. None knew where he went to in the end. (cited in Lau, 1963, pp. viii–ix)

It has been claimed by some that as a result of the "way" he created, Lao Tzu lived to 160 or even 200 years of age (Lau, 1963, p. ix). There is, however, considerable uncertainty over Lao Tzu's biography and the authorship of the *Tao Te Ching*. Indeed, according to Lau, Lao Tzu was probably not a historical figure at all. The *Tao Te Ching* is one of several Chinese works from the second half of the fourth and first half of the third centuries B.C., with titles meaning "elder" or "old man of mature wisdom." "Lao Tzu" can be interpreted as "old man," and the *Tao Te Ching* falls into a genre of Chinese literature consisting of sayings embodying the kind of wisdom associated with old age. Lau elaborates:

> There is no reason to suppose that the titles imply that these works were written by individuals. They are best looked upon as anthologies which were compiled from short passages by an editor or a series of editors. Most of these short passages reflect the doctrines of the time but some represent sayings of considerable antiquity. [...] It is probably because "Lao Tzu" happened to be the name of one of the hermits in the Confucian stories and also figured as the title of one of these anthologies of wise sayings that the *Lao tzu* alone has survived and is attributed to a man who instructed Confucius in the rites. (pp. xi–xii)

Regardless of the accuracy of legends associated with Lao Tzu as a historical figure, it is clear that the period during which the *Tao Te Ching* was produced was a "golden age of Chinese thought" (p. xii). A number of different schools of thought emerged, including those of Mo Tzu and Yang Chu, both founded by Confucius, as well as Taoism. "Taoism" comes from *tao chia*: the school of the way (p. xiv). While the *Tao Te Ching* is the best known work in Taoism, texts such as the *Chuang-tzu* and *Lieh-tzu* are also important and differ somewhat from the *Tao Te Ching* on a number of points of ethics and political philosophy (see Wong, 1997). Other works in the Taoist canon include the *T'ai Shang Ch'ing-ching Ching* ("Cultivating Stillness") (Wong, 1992), the *Tao-hsüan p'ien* ("The Mysteries of the Tao"), the *Wu-hsüan p'ien* ("Understanding the Mysteries") and the *T'ai-hsüan pao-tien* ("The Sacred Treatise on the Great Mystery") (Wong, 2004).

The *Tao Te Ching* comprises eighty-one short "chapters," ranging in length from a few lines to several paragraphs. The chapters are verse-like expressions of ideas, often in the form of opposites. Taoists live happily with apparent contradictions, letting them exist "without replying or favoring one solution over the other" (Slater, 2004, p. 152). Opposites in Taoism are complementary rather than irreconcilable; they work together to form a unity (Glanz, 1997, p. 196). The classic representation of this idea is the yin/yang symbol, now so well known in the Western world. The content of the *Tao Te Ching* is both abstract and concrete. The discussion of the unnamable Tao in Chapter 1 might seem mysterious and evocative, but the *Tao Te Ching* is also, as some read it, a manual on the art of living (Mitchell, 1991, p. vii): Its purpose is practical rather than theoretical, and the Tao can be seen as "an inward guide of good and bad, precious and vile, noble and vulgar" (Slater, 2004, p. 150).

The themes traversed in the *Tao Te Ching* are wide-ranging. The text addresses questions of metaphysics, ontology, epistemology, ethics, politics, and aesthetics. The central concept of Taoism, "the way," is notoriously difficult to define. In fact, a key idea in Taoism, and in the *Tao Te Ching* specifically, is that the way cannot be defined. We can at best come to an approximation in our understanding of the concept, as the opening words of the *Tao Te Ching* make clear:

> The way that can be spoken of
> Is not the constant way;
> The name that can be named
> Is not the constant name. (Lao Tzu, 1963, ch. 1)

In Mitchell's version of the text, these words become: "The tao that can be told / is not the eternal Tao / The name that can be named / is not the eternal Name" (Mitchell, 1991, ch. 1). Chen's translation is slightly different again: "Tao that can be spoken of, / is not the Everlasting (*ch'ang*) Tao. / Name that can be named, / Is not the Everlasting (*ch'ang*) name" (Chen, 1989, ch. 1).

Ram-Prasad (2005) argues that the question "What is *dao*?" rests on a mistake. The question "presupposes that there is a reality that has to be sought out, whose structure, now hidden from us, has to be revealed" (p. 46). The Taoist sees this in a different way: "[T]here is a world that we live in, and how we behave is different from how nature is, to our detriment. The question then is "How is the *dao* to be followed?" (p. 46). Lao Tzu allows some understanding of the Tao to develop by inviting readers to consider what it is *not*. Comparisons with God, the Absolute, brahman, and the like are, in Ram-Prasad's view, inadequate. Tao is not a metaphysical entity, or a single specific "way." The sum of all particular ways is not itself a tao or way. The key question about a tao or way is "what it does (that is, how it is followed)" (p. 49). Ram-Prasad continues: "The totality is there, but it is nameless, because what can be named is only a *dao*/way that can be followed—and we have seen that the sum of *dao*/ways is not what is or can be followed. The only constant is the fact that ... there are *dao*/ways to be followed" (p. 49). Glanz (1997) provides further helpful comments:

> The Tao, according to ancient Chinese texts, is the unifying, unseen, yet ever present force that governs the universe. With no beginning or end, the Tao in its essence represents the universal undifferentiated state beyond the laws of duality that control our physical existence. The Tao embodies a perfect harmonious state of the universe before and after creation—balanced and centred. According to Taoist thought, the Tao, independent of human existence, represents the structural idea that unifies creation. In other words, the Tao is the fundamental harmony or oneness that pervades the universe. (p. 195)

Other key elements of the *Tao Te Ching* include the concepts of non-action, self-transformation, tranquility, and self-equilibrium (Chen, 1989, p. 18). Taoism emphasizes submissiveness and yielding (Lai, 2008). It shows that there is strength in weakness and that by not forcing things, much can often be achieved. Taoism seeks to promote peacefulness among people, harmony with nature, and respect for all things. The *Tao Te Ching* warns against activities that encourage people to desire more than they currently have; this, it is suggested, will lead to unhappiness and disharmony. If we seek happiness and good health, we should, from a Taoist point of view, avoid "attachment to material things, and activities that excite the mind, rouse the emotions, tire the body, and stimulate the senses" (Wong, 1997, p. 25). The Taoist sage, as a leader, aims not to increase knowledge and learning among those governed but to maintain a certain innocence and ignorance. The sage does not seek power, or fame, or success. He or she does what needs to be done and then quietly withdraws. The sage does not preach morals or compliance with convention but demonstrates by example and lives in accordance with eternal Tao. These ideas and other central tenets of Taoism will be discussed in more detail in the sections that follow.

CHAPTER 8

Fraser on Freire and Lao Tzu

Fraser argues that in earlier times and in other traditions Freire would have been seen as "not only a great teacher but also a spiritual guide" (Fraser, 1997, p. 175). There is, Fraser claims, a strong sense of "love, humility, and rootedness in life" (p. 175) in Freire's work. Fraser wishes to enter into a conversation with Freire on matters of faith and spirituality, love and history, but he does not want to impose a religious framework on Freire's writings that Freire himself would not accept. He cautions against the dangers of sentimentality and of treating Freire as a kind of saint, in undertaking this task. Fraser maintains that at the heart of Freire's revolutionary pedagogy lies the concept of love and, with this, a profound respect for the divine in every human being. A liberating approach to education with the principle of love at its center demands democratic, purposeful dialogue. Fraser sees in Freirean theory a rejection of the intellectual vanguardism found in some Eastern European and communist regimes. He also draws attention to another common problem in interpreting and applying Freire's ideas: "the focus on liberating method at the expense of liberating content" (p. 186). Teachers, Fraser reminds us, cannot be neutral as far as pedagogical content is concerned. To focus on dialogue as a mere method, ignoring the need for social action and change, is to miss the point of Freirean pedagogy. Teachers have a potentially significant role to play in bringing about the kind of social change Freire has in mind (including a more equitable distribution of wealth and resources), but the positions they occupy are by no means unproblematic. Teachers can join with others in a struggle against oppression, in its multitude of different forms, but in doing so they can sometimes carry with them what Freire referred to in earlier work as the "oppressor within" (cf. Freire, 1972a). Fraser reinforces Freire's point that educational efforts are always located in a particular moment in history, in the lived "flesh and blood" struggles of human beings. Freirean pedagogy is, in many respects, the antithesis of escapist spirituality. Freire encourages teachers and students to learn from the past and to consider possible futures, but his pedagogy is also rooted in the present and the concrete.

Fraser makes three references to the *Tao Te Ching* in his chapter. The first is in relation to the point that liberation cannot be imposed from above. Each person, Fraser suggests, "must be the maker of her or his own liberation" (p. 177). Fraser quotes the following lines from the *Tao Te Ching*:

> Can you love people and lead them
> without imposing your will?
> Can you deal with the most vital matters
> by letting events take their course?
> Can you step back from your own mind and thus understand all things?
>
> Giving birth and nourishing,
> having without possessing,
> acting with no expectations,
> leading and not trying to control:
> this is the supreme virtue. (Mitchell, 1991, ch. 10)

These words, Fraser claims, capture "a very Freirian approach to life, and to education" (Fraser, 1997, p. 178).

Fraser goes on to stress the importance of seeing those with whom educators work as whole people. In elaborating on this point, he refers to a portion of Chapter 17 of the *Tao Te Ching*:

> If you don't trust the people,
> you make them untrustworthy.
>
> The Master doesn't talk, he acts.
> When his work is done,
> the people say, "Amazing:
> we did it, all by ourselves!" (Mitchell, 1991, ch. 17)

Fraser argues that the last part of this chapter ("Amazing: we did it, all by ourselves") is consistent with the Freirean idea of teachers and students, or political leaders and the people, engaging in a common struggle, thereby becoming one. The common victory, "achieved by all for the benefit of all" (Fraser, 1997, p. 192), becomes something to celebrate. Fraser refers to Freire's shift from the language of "I" ("I am," "I know," "I free myself," and so on) to the language of "we" ("we are," "we know," "we save ourselves"), and suggests that once this point has been reached, "distinctions and roles, teachers and learners, have disappeared in a mutual quest for liberation" (p. 192).

CHAPTER 8

Fraser's final reference to the *Tao Te Ching* is in relation to his point about hope, opportunity, and action being located in the present—in the immediate historical moment. This, Fraser says, is part of what makes Freire's work both utopian and practical. Here, Lao Tzu's notion that "[t]he Master gives himself up to whatever the moment brings" (Mitchell, 1991, ch. 50) is quoted. In linking this point to Freire's work, Fraser continues:

> It is this very base in affirming agency in the midst of concrete conditions where human beings live that Freire finds the condition for hopefulness. Because he has such deep trust in the people, Freire sees hope and possibility in the midst of oppressive situations that would lead others only to despair. His hope is not based on an easy optimism but on a deeply held confidence in the link of the concrete and the possible. (Fraser, 1997, p. 195)

Bridging East and West—Or, a Bridge too Far?

Fraser's essay makes an important contribution to Freirean scholarship. This would be the case without the references to Taoist thought, but this dimension of the essay gives added significance to some of the claims Fraser makes about Freire's philosophy, pedagogy, and politics. Fraser is not the first to apply Taoist ideas to education (see, for example, Glanz, 1997; MacKinnon, 1996; San, 2006; Slater, 2004; Zigler, 2007). Nor is Taoism the only Eastern philosophical tradition to have been explored in education journals in the West. Others have used the terminology of Taoism in discussing Freire's work (Ramdas, 1997) and have compared Confucian and Freirean pedagogical principles (Ng, 2000; Shim, 2007). Several authors have considered the educational implications of Buddhist ideas (e.g., Vokey, 1999; Johnson, 2002; Jagodzinski, 2002). Fraser's chapter is helpful, however, in stimulating further reflection on Freire and Taoism. This section makes a start in this direction with a discussion of differences and similarities between Freire and Lao Tzu on several key epistemological, ethical, and educational themes.

Action and Nonaction

The passages quoted by Fraser warrant closer examination. In each case, Fraser has quoted only part of the relevant chapter from the

Tao Te Ching, and in some instances the missing words, together with some of the words included in the passages quoted, prompt some questions about the similarities between Freirean and Taoist ideas. For example, the *Tao Te Ching* refers to "letting events take their course" when dealing with most vital matters, and to "acting with no expectations" (Mitchell, 1991, ch. 10). Fraser refers to Chapter 50 but does not quote these words: "[The Master] doesn't think about his actions; they flow from the core of his being." Elsewhere in the *Tao Te Ching*, the question is posed: "Do you want to improve the world?" The answer given is: "I don't think it can be done / The world is sacred. / It cannot be improved" (ch. 29). Chapter 29 concludes by noting that the Master "sees things as they are, / without trying to control them. / She lets them go their own way, / and resides at the center of the circle." This idea of centering oneself in the Tao and letting "all things take their course" finds expression earlier in the text (ch. 19). From near the beginning of the *Tao Te Ching* we are advised: "Practice not-doing, / and everything will fall into place" (ch. 3).

These passages and others in the *Tao Te Ching* lend weight to the view that Taoism promotes a certain passivity in human affairs. On the face of it, this is in tension with the Freirean commitment to reflective, transformative action. Freire does not advocate "not-doing," at least not as the default response to social problems. He does not simply let events take their course, and he does not accept that the world cannot be improved. He *does* want teachers and students to think about their actions, and he might argue that in many situations it would be impossible to act without expectations. His espousal of ideals such as critical thought, hope, and political commitment seems to be very much at odds with a Taoist orientation to human affairs.

Yet, care needs to be taken here in the way words from the *Tao Te Ching* are interpreted. Sometimes "not-doing" constitutes a form of action. In an educational dialogue, for example, a teacher must (as Freire would have it) learn the art of patient listening—of sometimes not speaking, in order to allow contrary positions to be expressed, reflected upon, and discussed by others. The Master, according to the *Tao Te Ching*, "acts without doing anything / and teaches without saying anything." *Silence* (which may or may not emerge when a teacher practices the art of listening) can play an important pedagogical role, opening up a space for contemplation that would otherwise be compromised by the clutter of too much talk. We can, of course, teach without saying anything in a variety of other ways—through our gestures and movements, the decisions we make, the priorities we set, the commitments we demonstrate, the relationships we build, and so on.

Mitchell (1991) argues that the *Tao Te Ching* does not support a position of passivity. Instead, it offers a paradigm for nonaction where this is the "purest and most effective form of action" (p. viii). Mitchell compares the Taoist notion of "doing nothing" to the state reached by a good athlete, where "the right stroke or the right movement happens by itself, effortlessly, without any interference of the conscious will" (p. viii). Nothing is done under such circumstances because the "doer has wholeheartedly vanished into the deed" (p. viii). This is not altogether dissimilar to the process Freire describes in explaining the act of study. Freire speaks of a form of knowing where the scholar becomes immersed in the act of seeking to understand the object of study as deeply as possible. It might be said here that the knower and the known become one. The knower remains an active, reflective subject, and in this sense retains a kind of distance from the known. But the very act of distancing—of "stepping back" in order to know—becomes also a means for coming closer to (and integrating more fully with) the object of study. Freire himself would often become utterly absorbed in his studies, reading or writing with such intense concentration that he would lose track of time and awareness of his immediate surroundings. This utter absorption can be seen as *both* "action" and "nonaction." It is precisely the "nonaction" part of the particular form of action that gives it its distinctive character.

Knowledge and Knowing

Even if we acknowledge this connection, there are still important differences. For the *Tao Te Ching* warns against the very idea of pursuing knowledge. Freire tends to place greater epistemological value on the process of knowing than the accumulation of knowledge, and in this sense, he is not completely at odds with Lao Tzu. The last chapter of the *Tao Te Ching* (ch. 81) states: "One who knows (*chih*) does not accumulate knowledge, / [o]ne who accumulates knowledge (*po*) does not know" (Chen, 1989, p. 231). Lau (1963) translates this passage as "One who knows has no wide learning; he who has wide learning does not know" (p. 88). It might be suggested that this is, in large part, a problem of balancing breadth and depth in understanding—as addressed in Chapter 5 of this book. By emphasizing "wide learning," as Lau puts it, we inhibit depth in understanding—including our understanding of ourselves. This, however, would be an inadequate response, for at the heart of the *Tao Te Ching* is a more fundamental distinction between different approaches to knowledge.

In Chapter 65 of the *Tao Te Ching* the following words are found: "Those in the past who were good at practicing Tao, / Did not want to enlighten (*ming*) the people, / But to keep them in ignorance (*yü*)" (Chen, 1989, p. 204). The text continues: "People are hard to rule, / Because they know (*chih*) too much. / Therefore, to rule a nation by knowledge, / Is to be the nation's thief. / Not to rule a nation by knowledge, / Is to be the nation's blessing." (pp. 204–205). These ideas rest on a distinction between two different modes of knowing: the verbal (spoken) and the nonverbal (unspoken). According to Chen, the former "describes consciousness coming out from nature without return while the latter belongs to a reversive consciousness in dynamic union with the unconscious" (p. 206). The sage needs to understand this distinction and keep the people away from the knowledge that departs from nature. Chen observes: "Knowledge or consciousness as a movement away from nature leads to externalization, discord, and, finally, death. The sage ruler, by keeping his people in ignorance, preserves the peace and harmony of nature in society."

This approach to knowledge and politics raises important questions not just for Freireans but for all educationists. For if Lao Tzu is taken seriously here, it is not clear what remains of the project of education per se—that is, of *any* process of deliberate, purposeful teaching and learning. Freire would not support a position of keeping people in ignorance. He would accept that it is not possible to know all things and that difficult decisions must often be made by teachers and learners in prioritizing different forms of knowledge. But a political philosophy based on the deliberate cultivation of ignorance would have been repugnant to him. Freire recognized the practical limits to the pursuit of knowledge (time is one of those limits, as discussed in Chapter 5), but he did not want to close off areas of prospective inquiry to learners or set up pedagogical conditions conducive to the maximization of ignorance. Nor did he want to impede the process of reflection—and this seems to be ruled out, or at least discouraged, by the *Tao Te Ching*.

It might be argued that what is being advocated in the *Tao Te Ching* is not the dissolution of all learning but merely the return to a particular type of learning that can sometimes be lost. What we need, a Taoist might say, is to relearn the process of connecting with nature. There is an ambiguity in the *Tao Te Ching* over the meaning of *nature*. It seems reasonably clear that what is being referred to in the text is something more than, or perhaps other than, "the natural environment." Exactly what that is, however, remains uncertain. Perhaps it is that which is "natural" to us as human beings. We might want to employ a term such as *human nature* to try to capture this. There is at best only an implied and vaguely expressed view of human nature in Lao Tzu's text, but even if it were possible to pin this down in more precise detail, it is not obvious that the knowledge advocated in the *Tao Te Ching* should be regarded as a return to this. A better way to understand this, I think, is to see the *Tao Te Ching* as advocating alignment of all we do with the natural harmony of the universe—with the way things "naturally" are, always have been, and always will be.

Although Taoism stresses nonverbal knowing over verbal knowing, this does not mean there should be an emphasis on "doing" over "merely talking," or verbalism, as Freire called it in *Pedagogy of the Oppressed* (1972a). For, as we have already seen, the *Tao Te Ching* promotes an ideal of *not*-doing. If we accept Mitchell's argument that Taoist not-doing is analogous to the total immersion in an activity characteristic of elite athletes, there is still a form of reflective knowledge required here that, prima facie, seems to be ruled out by Lao Tzu's text. The complete integration of oneself with an activity does not emerge from "nowhere"; it is *learned*. Indeed, it is often the case that the more one devotes oneself to the deliberate practicing of one's sport or art, year after year, reflecting on and learning from mistakes, the more likely one is to be able to reach the state Mitchell describes: that is, one where "the right stroke or the right movement happens by itself, effortlessly, without any interference of the conscious will" (Mitchell, 1991, p. viii). Coaches, mentors, and teachers play crucial roles in the development of such abilities, and their work, at least in part, involves talking and direct instruction—the promotion of conscious, verbal knowing. Verbal knowing is thus not necessarily at odds with nonverbal knowing. The latter may depend on the former, and the former always involves an element of the latter.

"Nonverbal" knowing, as Chen describes it, bridges the conscious and the unconscious, whereas "verbal" knowing does not. Yet, this seems to set up a false dichotomy, not only between two different forms of knowing but between two different modes of being. Chen's account recognizes that the knowing Subject can come to understand or experience the unconscious, and this, for Chen, means to be in accord with "nature." Conscious activity of a certain kind, then, can allow us to know the unconscious. But Taoism, as interpreted by Chen, does not allow for the identification of a conscious element in the unconscious. The unconscious is simply "there": It is not in any way constructed; it does not change or evolve over time. From a Freirean perspective, this can be seen as a peculiarly antidialectical approach to the relationship between conscious knowing and unconscious knowing. Although Freire does not have a well-developed theory of the unconscious, his references in early writings (e.g., Freire, 1972a) to "the oppressor within" give some indication of the general direction of his thought in this domain. Oppression, in its myriad forms, cannot be explained merely in terms of social structures or practices; rather, it becomes "embedded" in the minds of those who are oppressed, giving unconscious shape to worldviews and decisions that reinforce the very oppression being experienced (cf. van Gorder, 2007). Importantly, for Freire, the unconscious is not *fixed* but is rather subject to the influence of reflective, active, knowing human beings.

Ignorance, Happiness, and Education

The *Tao Te Ching* suggests that people will be happier if they are kept in a state of ignorance. Surprisingly, Freire might not argue against this. He would agree that rulers who wish to maintain stability and govern with relative ease might, at least for the short term, benefit from an unreflective population of political Subjects. Freire might have some reservations about using the term *Subject,* with a capital S, if people are, in effect, encouraged to become more like *objects.* He might concede that those denied knowledge can feel they are happy ("Eliminate ... learning so as to have no worries," says the *Tao Te Ching*: ch. 20, Chen, 1989, p. 102) and that developing a critical consciousness is a sure road to a certain kind of discomfort and even suffering. None of this, however, justifies a political strategy of maintaining and promoting ignorance. This for Freire, would go to the heart of our thinking about the purposes of education. Education, from a Freirean point of view, is *meant* to make people uncomfortable. An educated life is a life filled with questions and uncertainties. It is, in some senses, a restless life; one in which we can never declare the end has been reached and nothing more needs to be done. For some, these characteristics are conducive to happiness; for others, unhappiness.

If it is true that from a Freirean perspective, one can never permanently "sit still," this does not mean that moments of stillness are ruled out by Freire's epistemological and ethical orientation. To the contrary: Freirean reflection positively demands this. If we think of a "moment" in this context not as the passing of a few seconds of time but as any identifiable period characterized by particular forms of thought, feeling, or action, reflection in the Freirean sense needs both stillness and restlessness. We need passion and commitment, for example, but these qualities must, from a Freirean point of view, be coupled with humility, care, and respect for others. Freirean reflection, grounded in an ethic of love, is active but not aggressive. Although some commentators have stressed the differences between Freirean pedagogy and meditative practice in education (e.g., Robinson, 2004), there is, to my way of thinking, no need to see it this way. Much depends, of course, on the meditative tradition with which one is dealing, but many approaches to meditation will include concentration and/or contemplation as key elements. Many will involve some form of focused, but not "forced," attention on an object or idea or ideal. Most will form part of a wider ethic of care for others and for the world of which they are a part (as well as care for the self). Seen in this light, Freirean pedagogy is highly compatible with attempts to integrate contemplation or meditation into educational environments (e.g., Kesson, 2002; Hart, 2004; Altobello, 2007). From a Freirean perspective "sitting still" is necessary for the concentrated, reflective attention required in addressing an object of study. "Sitting still" is also needed in an educational dialogue, where the ability to listen quietly and carefully to others is vital. But "sitting still" is not *sufficient* in bringing the Freirean ideal to life: There is a need also, at times, for considered action and for personal and social change.

Freire has little to say, directly, about happiness. Happiness, from a Freirean perspective, is not in itself the goal of life. A happy life is not the same as a *good* life. A good life, as far as Freire is concerned, is one lived with love, hope, dialogue, curiosity, tolerance, and political commitment, among other things. It involves seeking to *know* and to *transform*; it integrates reflection with action. These characteristics have been discussed in greater detail in preceding chapters and in other work (e.g., Roberts, 2000, 2008a, 2008b). Freire does not articulate a conception of "the good life" as an individual ideal. Rather, we must construct a picture of what a good life might mean by considering Freire's wider ethical, political, and educational ideas. It does not make sense, from a Freirean standpoint, to discuss the pursuit of individual ideals without also investigating the social and economic structures, policies, and practices that impede or enable the realization of those ideals. A Freirean interest in "the good life" is thus more properly conceived as an inquiry about the conditions (inner and external) conducive to good *lives*. Freire would want those lives to be "happy" ones, but not if the price to be paid for this is the maintenance of mass ignorance.

Freire might have said, moreover, that unhappiness in the form of distress is a reasonable and desirable quality to cultivate at certain times in a human life, in response, for example, to problems of starvation, exploitation, mass slaughter, the spread of preventable diseases, environmental destruction, and the persecution of animals or children. Keeping those not affected by such problems free of the burden of knowing about them might grant them more peaceful, comfortable, happier lives, but such an approach, Freire would have argued, cannot be justified from either an ethical or an educational point of view. As the title of one of Freire's latest books indicates, there is value, at times, in developing what might be called "a pedagogy of indignation" (2004), where distress and anger, when coupled with love, hope, dialogue, critical reflection, and political commitment, can have a potentially productive role to play in education and wider social life.

The *Tao Te Ching* is helpful in prompting a reexamination of some of our most deeply held views about the role of education. We tend to believe education is fundamentally worthwhile. There is, to be sure, an extensive literature on the harm that can be done by educational institutions. Freire himself was one of the key figures in highlighting the potentially oppressive nature of schooling, as were deschoolers such as Ivan Illich (1971) and Everett Reimer (1971). And numerous sociologists of education, including many of a Marxist or feminist persuasion, have demonstrated convincingly that schooling can play a significant role in perpetuating inequities across class, gender, and other lines. For the most part, however, this substantial body of critical work does not question the underlying notion that education, understood in a certain way, is ethically desirable.

Education, many theorists have pointed out, must not be equated with "schooling" or "training" or "indoctrination." The idea that "education" implies something worthwhile—an idea articulated and defended most famously, though not unproblematically, by R. S. Peters (1970, 1973)—is taken for granted by many, even if the question of what counts as worthwhile is often subject to vigorous debate. The *Tao Te Ching* challenges this assumption. As Lau (1963) observes: "If the Taoist philosopher could have visited our society, there is no doubt that he would have considered popular education and mass advertising the twin banes of modern life. The one causes the people to fall from their original state of innocent ignorance; the other creates new desires for objects no one would have missed if they had not been invented" (p. xxxi). The aim of the sage, Lau says, "is to keep the people in a childlike state where there is no knowledge and so no desire beyond the immediate objects of the senses" (p. xxxii).

It is instructive to contemplate not only whether the Taoist position can be justified (from an ethical point of view), but whether it is *possible*. For to interact with others and the world in almost any way is to establish the potential for learning and the development of knowledge. Unless there is a deliberate attempt to maintain "innocent ignorance" via, say, drugs or a sophisticated and sustained process of indoctrination, it is difficult to imagine how a ruler might keep adults in a childlike state. To grow into and through adulthood involves some form of change, not merely in the physical sense but intellectually and emotionally. To attempt to educate, whether through formal institutions (such as schools) or informally (e.g., by "learning on the job" or the passing on of traditional lore and custom), is merely to build in a more systematic way on what would already be occurring through the activities of everyday life.

Chapter 48 of the *Tao Te Ching* suggests that "[t]o pursue (*wei*) learning one increases daily," whereas "[t]o pursue ... Tao one decreases daily" (Chen, 1989, p. 168). Moving closer to the Tao, according to Chen, involves progressively dropping our human projects, decreasing our stock of human knowledge, until there is nothing for us to do (p. 170). From a Freirean point of view, this is neither desirable nor possible. Knowledge grows as human beings interact with the world. Over time, we might "forget" certain forms of knowledge, and there are limits to what can be known at any given time, but the potential for relearning is always present. Freire would support the notion of seeking spaces within the hustle and bustle of everyday activity for calm, peaceful reflection, but not with a goal of curtailing the development of knowledge and learning or of reaching a point where human beings will have nothing to do. As far as Freire was concerned, there will *always* be something to do. This need not be "doing" in the sense of moving about in the world, or of talking or writing or listening. But "doing nothing," while we remain alive as human beings, is impossible.

As noted earlier, Freire would also find a political strategy of deliberately cultivating a state of ignorance objectionable from an ethical point of view. The Taoist sage "empties the minds (*hsin*) of his people, / Fills their bellies, / Weakens their wills" (ch. 3, Chen, 1989, p. 58). Such an approach, Freire would argue, ignores a fundamental feature of our ontology—we are curious, inquiring, *learning* beings— and dehumanizes both those denied the possibility of seeking knowledge and those responsible for this denial. He would concede that there are always *risks* in fostering educational development and the growth of knowledge, but this, too, is a distinguishing feature of human existence. To be human is to be open to the possibility of change. If the Freirean position on the potential value of education is accepted, teachers and others who seek to educate must bear a heavy burden of responsibility, for if they do their jobs well, those with whom they work will change forever. There is, as it were, "no going back" in Freirean education. The same would be true, however, for the Taoist sage seeking to maintain a state of ignorance among those ruled. Once a commitment has been made to decreasing knowledge, any deviation from this path risks the possibility that learning will resume again.

Concluding Comments

In comparing Freirean and Taoist ideas, it is possible to identify both similarities and differences. As Fraser (1997) points out, both Freire and Lao Tzu are against the imposition of one's will (as a leader, a teacher, or anyone else in a position of authority) on others. There must, from both a Taoist and a Freirean point of view, be considerable trust in the capacity of human beings to lead themselves. Gentleness and humility are valued highly in both the *Tao Te Ching* and Freire's educational philosophy. In Taoism, as in Freirean thought, there is an acceptance that human beings are, or ought to be, integrated with wider world. For a Taoist, this means reconnecting with "nature," with the natural order of things; for a Freirean, the process of integration also involves seeing ourselves as part of a wider *social* world. In both Freire's work and the *Tao Te Ching* there is a recognition of the need to center ourselves in the present. Both Freire and Lao Tzu stress the importance of *being* rather than *having*. They believe a materialistic attitude is destructive and want to encourage us to love the simple things in life. Both thinkers see limits in a concept of knowledge based too heavily on intellectual mastery. Finally, both Freire and Lao Tzu are concerned with transformation, even if they differ in their views of what this entails.

On some fundamental questions of epistemology, ethics, and education, however, key differences emerge. The *Tao Te Ching* advocates the cultivation of a state of ignorance; Freire stands opposed to this. Lao Tzu wants to inhibit the development of knowledge and learning; Freire, although recognizing that not all forms of learning are worthwhile, sees the potential for educational initiatives to play an important role in the wider process of liberation. A Taoist is concerned that education will lead to the creation of new desires and to unhappiness; a Freirean accepts a certain restlessness as part of a good human life and does not see happiness as the ultimate ethical end to which we should strive. Education, for a Freirean, is meant to "trouble" us; the Taoist, by contrast, wants to encourage people to accept things as they are, and education is not always conducive to this. Although Taoists in the later "warring states" period believed "political involvement and longevity were inherently incompatible" and urged the separation of the sage from the rest of the world, the *Tao Te Ching* sees a role for the sage in the process of government (Wong, 1997, p. 27). In the *Tao Te Ching*, the sage "minimized his desires, lived simply, and attained longevity, while functioning as the head of the state" (p. 27). The *Tao Te Ching* promotes neither complete noninvolvement nor total passivity. Nonetheless, Taoism, even as represented by the *Tao Te Ching*, suggests a more passive ethical and political philosophy than is evident in Freire's work. Nonaction might also be action, as discussed previously, but in Freirean theory there is greater emphasis on active social change.

The differences between Taoist and Freirean thought need not be regarded as insurmountable barriers to further inquiry and productive dialogue. Indeed, it is perhaps precisely because there are such clear contrasts on some key points that much of value can come from such comparisons. Putting such apparently different bodies of work into conversation with each other can foster deep reflection on the ontological, epistemological, and ethical assumptions that underpin our efforts as educators. More than this, Taoism allows us to contemplate the very idea of *wanting* to educate. For many in the educational world, this is akin to examining afresh our very reason for being. That process is worth undertaking, despite the risks such an enterprise holds. Freire provides some answers for those who seek to consider how and why education might be worthwhile, but he should not read on his own. Taoists, together with thinkers from a wide variety of other scholarly, religious, and cultural traditions, have much to contribute to the ongoing discussion of Freire's work.

References

Allman, P. 1999. *Revolutionary Social Transformation: Democratic Hopes, Political Possibilities and Critical Education*. Westport, CT: Bergin and Garvey.
Alter, R. 1993. "The Persistence of Reading." *Partisan Review* 60 (4): 510–516.
Altobello, R. 2007. "Concentration and Contemplation." *Journal of Transformative Education* 5 (4): 354–371.
Andreola, B. A. 2004. "Letter to Paulo Freire," in P. Freire, *Pedagogy of Indignation*. Boulder, CO: Paradigm.
Apple, M. 1979. *Ideology and the Curriculum*. London: Routledge and Kegan Paul.
———. 1985. *Education and Power*. London: Routledge and Kegan Paul.
———. 1999. "Freire, Neo-Liberalism and Education." *Discourse: Studies in the Cultural Politics of Education* 20 (1): 5–20.
Aristotle. 1976. *Ethics*. The Nicomachean Ethics, rev. ed., trans. J. A. K. Thomson. Harmondsworth: Penguin.
Armstrong, K. B. 2005. "Autophotography in Adult Education: Building Creative Communities for Social Justice and Democratic Education." *New Directions for Adult and Continuing Education* 107: 33–44.
Aronowitz, S. 1993. "Paulo Freire's Radical Democratic Humanism," in P. McLaren and P. Leonard, eds., *Paulo Freire: A Critical Encounter*. London: Routledge.
Aronowitz, S., and H. A. Giroux. 1986. *Education under Siege*. London: Routledge.
Baird, I. C. 1999. "The Examined Life: Women's Liberatory Learning within a Locked-in Society." *International Journal of Lifelong Education* 18 (2): 103–109.
Bakhtin, M. 1984. *Problems of Dostoevsky's Poetics*, ed. and trans. C. Emerson. Manchester, UK: Manchester University Press.

Bartlett, L. 2005. "Dialogue, Knowledge, and Teacher-Student Relations: Freirean Pedagogy in Theory and Practice." *Comparative Education Review* 49 (3): 344–364.

Bartolome, L. I. 1994. "Beyond the Methods Fetish: Towards a Humanizing Pedagogy." *Harvard Educational Review* 64 (2): 173–194.

Bauman, Z. 1988. "Is There a Postmodern Sociology?" *Theory, Culture, and Society* 5: 217–237.

———. 1993. "The Fall of the Legislator," in T. Docherty, ed., *Postmodernism: A Reader*, 128–140. London: Harvester Wheatsheaf.

Beck, C., and C. M. Kosnik. 1995. "Caring for the Emotions: Towards More Balanced Schooling." *Philosophy of Education Society Yearbook: 1999*. Urbana-Champaign, IL: Philosophy of Education Society.

Berger, B. 1993. "Multiculturalism and the Modern University." *Partisan Review* 60 (4): 516–526.

Berger, P. 1974. "'Consciousness Raising' and the Vicissitudes of Policy," in *Pyramids of Sacrifice: Political Ethics and Social Change*, 111–132. New York: Basic Books.

Biesta, G. 1998. "Say You Want a Revolution ... Suggestions for the Impossible Future of Critical Pedagogy." *Educational Theory* 48: 499–510.

———. 2005. "What Can Critical Pedagogy Learn from Postmodernism? Further Reflections on the Impossible Future of Critical Pedagogy," in I. Gur-Ze'ev, ed., *Critical Theory and Critical Pedagogy Today: Toward a New Critical Language in Education*, 143–159. Haifa: Studies in Education, University of Haifa.

Bloom, A. 1988. *The Closing of the American Mind*. New York: Simon and Schuster.

———. 1991. *Giants and Dwarfs*. New York: Touchstone.

Blumenfeld-Jones, D. 2004. "The Hope of a Critical Ethics: Teachers and Learners." *Educational Theory* 54 (3): 263–279.

Boler, M. 1997. "Disciplined Emotions: Philosophies of Educated Feelings." *Educational Theory* 47 (2): 203–227.

———. 1999a. *Feeling Power: Emotions and Education*. New York: Routledge.

———. 1999b. "Posing Some Feminist Queries to Freire," in P. Roberts, ed., *Paulo Freire, Politics and Pedagogy: Reflections from Aotearoa-New Zealand*, 61–69. Palmerston North: Dunmore Press.

Borg, C., and P. Mayo. 2000. "Reflections from a 'Third Age' Marriage: Paulo Freire's Pedagogy of Reason, Hope and Passion—An Interview with Ana Maria (Nita) Freire." *McGill Journal of Education* 35 (2): 105–120.

Boshier, R. 1999. "Freire at the Beach: Remembering Paulo in the Bright Days of Summer." *Studies in Continuing Education* 21 (1): 113–125.

———. 2002. "Farm-Gate Intellectuals, Excellence and the University Problem in Aotearoa/New Zealand." *Studies in Continuing Education* 24 (1): 5–24.

REFERENCES

Bowers, C. A. 1983. "Linguistic Roots of Cultural Invasion in Paulo Freire's Pedagogy." *Teachers College Record* 84 (4): 935–953.

Bowers, C. A., and F. Appfel-Marglin, eds. 2005. *Rethinking Freire: Globalization and the Environmental Crisis.* Mahwah, NJ: Lawrence Erlbaum.

Bruss, N., and D. P. Macedo. 1984. "A Conversation with Paulo Freire at the University of Massachusetts in Boston." *Journal of Education* 166 (3): 215–225.

———. 1985. "Toward a Pedagogy of the Question: Conversations with Paulo Freire." *Journal of Education* 167 (2): 7–21.

Brustein, R. 1993. "Dumbocracy in America." *Partisan Review* 60 (4): 526–534.

Burch, K. 1999. "Eros as the Educational Principle of Democracy." *Studies in Philosophy and Education* 18 (3): 123–142.

Burton, M., and C. Kagan. 2005. "Liberation Social Psychology: Learning from Latin America." *Journal of Community and Applied Social Psychology* 15: 63–78.

Campos, M. D. 1990. "Interview with Paulo Freire." *UNESCO Courier* (December): 4–10.

Carey, J. W. 1992. "Political Correctness and Cultural Studies." *Journal of Communication* 42 (2): 56–72.

Carr, D. 2005. "On the Contribution of Literature and the Arts to the Educational Cultivation of Moral Virtue, Feeling and Emotion." *Journal of Moral Education* 34: 137–151.

Castells, M., R. Flecha, P. Freire, H. A. Giroux, D. Macedo, and P. Willis. 1999. *Critical Education in the New Information Age.* Lanham, MD: Rowman and Littlefield.

Chambers, E. 1992. "Work-Load and the Quality of Student Learning." *Studies in Higher Education* 17 (2): 141–153.

Chen, E. M. 1989. *The Tao Te Ching: A New Translation with Commentary.* St. Paul, MN: Paragon House.

Coben, D. 1998. *Radical Heroes: Gramsci, Freire, and the Politics of Adult Education.* New York: Garland.

Cohn, H. D. 1950. "The Symbolic End of Hermann Hesse's *Glasperlenspiel.*" *Modern Language Quarterly* 11: 347–357.

Convergence. 1998. Special issue: A Tribute to Paulo Freire: 31.

Cunningham, A. 2001. *The Heart of What Matters: The Role for Literature in Moral Philosophy.* Berkeley: University of California Press.

Curzon-Hobson, A. 2002. "Higher Education in a World of Radical Unknowability: An Extension of the Challenge of Ronald Barnett." *Teaching in Higher Education* 7 (2): 179–191.

Dallaire, M. 2001. *Contemplation in Liberation—A Method for Spiritual Education in the Schools.* Lewiston, NY: Edwin Mellen.

Darder, A. 2002. *Reinventing Paulo Freire: A Pedagogy of Love*. Boulder, CO: Westview.

———. 2003. "Teaching as an Act of Love: Reflections on Paulo Freire and His Contributions to Our Lives and Our Work," in A. Darder, M. Baltondano, and R. D. Torres, eds., *The Critical Pedagogy Reader*, 497–509. London: RoutledgeFalmer.

Delbanco, A. 1993. "The Politics of Separatism." *Partisan Review* 60 (4): 534–542.

Dickstein, M. 1993. "Correcting PC." *Partisan Review* 60 (4): 542–549.

Dillon, D. 1985. "Reading the World and Reading the Word: An Interview with Paulo Freire." *Language Arts* 62 (1): 15–21.

dos Santos, W. L. P. 2008. "Scientific Literacy: A Freirean Perspective as a Radical View of Humanistic Science Education." *Science Education* 93: 361–382.

Dostoevsky, F. 1981. *The Gambler*, trans. A. R. MacAndrew. New York: Norton.

———. 1983. *Memoirs from the House of the Dead*, trans. J. Coulson, ed. R. Hingley. Oxford: Oxford University Press.

———. 1991. *The Brothers Karamazov*, trans. R. Pevear and L. Volokhonsky. New York: Vintage.

———. 1993. *Crime and Punishment*, trans. R. Pevear and L. Volokhonsky. New York: Vintage.

———. 1994. *Demons*, trans. R. Pevear and L. Volokhonsky. New York: Vintage.

———. 2001. *The Idiot*, trans. R. Pevear and L. Volokhonsky. London: Granta.

———. 2003. *The Adolescent*, trans. R. Pevear and L. Volokhonsky. New York: Everyman's.

———. 2004. *Notes from Underground*, trans. R. Pevear and L. Volokhonsky. New York: Everyman's.

———. 2009. *A Writer's Diary*, trans. K. Lantz, ed. G. S. Morson. Evanston, IL: Northwestern University Press.

Dowbor, L. 1997. "Preface," in P. Freire, *Pedagogy of the Heart*, 21–28. New York: Continuum.

D'Souza, D. 1991. *Illiberal Education: The Politics of Race and Sex on Campus*. New York: Free Press.

Duarte, E. 2006. "Critical Pedagogy and the *Praxis* of Worldly Philosophy." *Journal of Philosophy of Education* 40 (1): 105–114.

Dunn, L. L. 1998. "Freire's Lessons for Liberating Women Workers." *Convergence* 31 (1–2), 50–60.

Durrani, O. 1982. "Hermann Hesse's Castalia: Republic of Scholars or Police State?" *Modern Language Review* 77: 655–669.

Ellsworth, E. 1989. "Why Doesn't This Feel Empowering? Working Through the Repressive Myths of Critical Pedagogy." *Harvard Educational Review* 59 (3): 297–324.

Endres, B. 2001. "A Critical Read on Critical Literacy: From Critique to Dialogue as an Ideal for Literacy Education." *Educational Theory* 51 (4): 401–413.

Escobar, M., A. L. Fernandez, G. Guevara-Niebla, and P. Freire. 1994. *Paulo Freire on Higher Education: A Dialogue at the National University of Mexico*. Albany: State University of New York Press.

Field, G. W. 1968. "On the Genesis of the *Glasperlenspiel*." *German Quarterly* 41: 673–688.

Findsen, B. 2007. "Freirean Philosophy and Pedagogy in the Adult Education Context: The Case of Older Adults' Learning." *Studies in Philosophy and Education* 26: 545–559.

Foucault, M. 1980. *Power/Knowledge: Selected Interviews and Other Writings, 1972–1977*, trans. C. Gordon, L. Marshall, J. Mepham, and K. Soper; ed. C. Gordon. London: Harvester.

Foucault, M., and G. Deleuze. 1977. "Intellectuals and Power," in M. Foucault, *Language, Counter-Memory, Practice: Selected Essays and Interviews*, trans. D. F. Bouchard and S. Simon; ed. D. F. Bouchard, 205–217. Ithaca, NY: Cornell University Press.

Frank, J. 2003. Review of J. P. Scanlan, *Dostoevsky the Thinker*. Ithaca, NY: Cornell University Press, 2002. *Common Knowledge* 9 (2): 345.

Fraser, J. W. 1997. Love and History in the Work of Paulo Freire," in P. Freire, J. W. Fraser, D. Macedo, T. McKinnon, and W. T. Stokes, eds., *Mentoring the Mentor: A Critical Dialogue with Paulo Freire*, 175–199. New York: Peter Lang.

Freedman, E. B. 2007. "Is Teaching for Social Justice Undemocratic?" *Harvard Educational Review* 77 (4): 442–473.

Freire, A. M. A. 2001. *Chronicles of Love: My Life with Paulo Freire*. New York: Peter Lang.

Freire, A. M. A., and D. Macedo, eds. 1998. *The Paulo Freire Reader*. New York: Continuum.

Freire, P. 1972a. *Pedagogy of the Oppressed*. Harmondsworth, UK: Penguin.

———. 1972b. *Cultural Action for Freedom*. Harmondsworth, UK: Penguin.

———. 1973. *Education for Critical Consciousness*. New York: Continuum.

———. 1976. *Education: The Practice of Freedom*. London: Writers and Readers.

———. 1978. *Pedagogy in Process: The Letters to Guinea-Bissau*. London: Writers and Readers.

———. 1983. "The Importance of the Act of Reading." *Journal of Education* 165 (1): 5–11.

———. 1985. *The Politics of Education*. London: MacMillan.

———. 1987. "Letter to North American Teachers," in I. Shor, ed., *Freire for the Classroom: A Sourcebook for Liberatory Teaching*, 211–214. Portsmouth, NH: Boynton/Cook.

———. 1993. *Pedagogy of the City*. New York: Continuum.

———. 1994. *Pedagogy of Hope*. New York: Continuum.

———. 1995. "The Progressive Teacher," in M. de Figueiredo-Cowen and D. Gastaldo, eds., *Paulo Freire at the Institute*, 17–24. London: University of London, Institute of Education.

———. 1996. *Letters to Cristina: Reflections on My Life and Work*. London: Routledge.

———. 1997a. *Pedagogy of the Heart*. New York: Continuum.

———. 1997b. "A Response," in P. Freire, J. W. Fraser, D. Macedo, T. McKinnon, and W. T. Stokes, eds., *Mentoring the Mentor: A Critical Dialogue with Paulo Freire*, 303–329. New York: Peter Lang.

———. 1998a. *Teachers as Cultural Workers: Letters to Those Who Dare Teach*. Boulder, CO: Westview.

———. 1998b. *Pedagogy of Freedom: Ethics, Democracy, and Civic Courage*. Lanham, MD: Rowman and Littlefield.

———. 1998c. *Politics and Education*. Los Angeles: UCLA Latin American Center Publications.

———. 2004. *Pedagogy of Indignation*. Boulder, CO: Paradigm.

———. 2007. *Daring to Dream: Toward a Pedagogy of the Unfinished*. Boulder, CO: Paradigm.

Freire, P., and A. Faundez. 1989. *Learning to Question: A Pedagogy of Liberation*. Geneva: World Council of Churches.

Freire, P., and D. Macedo. 1987. *Literacy: Reading the Word and the World*. London: Routledge.

———. 1993. "A Dialogue with Paulo Freire," in P. McLaren and P. Leonard, eds., *Paulo Freire: A Critical Encounter*, 169–176. London: Routledge.

———. 1995. "A Dialogue: Culture, Language, and Race." *Harvard Educational Review* 65 (3): 377–402.

Freire, P., and C. Rossatto. 2005. "An Interview with Paulo Freire," in C. Rossatto, *Engaging Paulo Freire's Pedagogy of Possibility: From Blind to Transformative Optimism*, 13–19. Lanham, MD: Rowman and Littlefield.

Freire, P., and I. Shor. 1987. *A Pedagogy for Liberation*. London: MacMillan.

Friedrichsmeyer, E. 1974. "The Bertram Episode in Hesse's *Glass Bead Game*." *Germanic Review* 49: 284–297.

Gee, J. P. 1988. "The Legacies of Literacy: From Plato to Freire through Harvey Graff." *Harvard Educational Review* 58 (2): 195–212.

Gilligan, C. 1982. *In a Different Voice: Psychological Theories and Women's Development*. Cambridge, MA: Harvard University Press.

Giroux, H. A. 1983. *Theory and Resistance: A Pedagogy for the Opposition*. London: Heinemann.

———. 1988. *Teachers as Intellectuals*. Westport, CT: Bergin and Garvey.

———. 1993. "Paulo Freire and the Politics of Postcolonialism," in P. McLaren and P. Leonard, eds., *Paulo Freire: A Critical Encounter*, 177–188. London: Routledge.

Glanz, J. 1997. "The Tao of Supervision: Taoist Insights into the Theory and Practice of Educational Supervision" *Journal of Curriculum and Supervision* 12 (3): 193–211.

Glass, R. D. 2001. "On Paulo Freire's Philosophy of Praxis and the Foundations of Liberation Education." *Educational Researcher* 30 (2): 15–25.

Graff, G. 1992. *Beyond the Culture Wars: How Teaching the Conflicts Can Revitalize American Education.* New York: Norton.

Gramsci, A. 1971. *Selections from the Prison Notebooks of Antonio Gramsci,* trans. Q. Hoare and G. Nowell Smith. London: Lawrence and Wishart.

Gribble, J. 1983. "Literature and the Education of the Emotions," in *Literary Education: A Revaluation,* 95–113. Cambridge: Cambridge University Press.

Grof, S. 2000. *Psychology of the Future: Lessons from Modern Consciousness Research.* Albany: State University of New York Press.

Gruenewald, D. A. 2003. "The Best of Both Worlds: A Critical Pedagogy of Place." *Educational Researcher* 32 (4): 3–12.

Guishard, M. 2009. "The False Paths, the Endless Labors, the Turns Now This Way and Now That: Participatory Action Research, Mutual Vulnerability, and the Politics of Inquiry." *Urban Review* 41: 85–105.

Hadot, P. 1995. *Philosophy as a Way of Life.* Cambridge, MA: Blackwell.

Hall, S. 1994. "Some 'Politically Incorrect' Pathways through PC," in S. Dunant, ed., *The War of the Words: The Political Correctness Debate,* 164–183. London: Virago.

Hargreaves, A. 1998. "The Emotional Practice of Teaching." *Teaching and Teacher Education* 14: 835–854.

Harris, K. 1990. "Empowering Teachers: Towards a Justification for Intervention." *Journal of Philosophy of Education* 24 (2): 171–183.

Hart, T. 2004. "Opening the Contemplative Mind in the Classroom." *Journal of Transformative Education* 2 (1): 28–46.

Helt, R. C. 1996. *'A Poet or Nothing at All': The Tübingen and Basel Years of Hermann Hesse.* Providence, RI: Berghahn.

Hepburn, R. W. 1972. "The Arts and the Education of Feeling and Emotion," in R. F. Dearden, P. H. Hirst, and R. S. Peters, eds., *Education and Reason (Part 3 of Education and the Development of Reason),* 94–110. London: Routledge and Kegan Paul.

Hesse, H. 1968 [1906]. *Beneath the Wheel,* trans. M. Roloff. New York: Picador.

———. 1974a. *Stories of Five Decades,* trans. R. Manheim, with two stories trans. D. Lindley, ed. T. Ziolkowski. London: Triad/Panther.

———. 1974b. *Reflections,* selected from his books and letters by V. Michels, trans. R. Manheim. New York: Farrar, Straus, and Giroux.

———. 1978. *My Belief: Essays on Life and Art,* trans. D. Lindley, with two essays translated by R. Manheim, ed. T. Ziolkowski. London: Triad/Panther.

———. 1999 [1919]. *Demian*, trans. M. Roloff and M. Lebeck. New York: Harper Perennial.

———. 2000a [1943]. *The Glass Bead Game*, trans. R. Winston and C. Winston. London: Vintage.

———. 2000b [1922]. *Siddhartha*, trans. S. C. Kohn. Boston: Shambhala.

Holst, J. D. 2006. "Paulo Freire in Chile, 1964–1969: *Pedagogy of the Oppressed* in Its Sociopolitical Economic Context." *Harvard Educational Review* 76 (2): 243–270.

Horton, M., and P. Freire. 1990. *We Make the Road by Walking: Conversations on Education and Social Change*, eds. B. Bell, J. Gaventa, and J. Peters. Philadelphia, PA: Temple University Press.

Hughes, K. P. 1998. "Liberation? Domestication? Freire and Feminism in the University." *Convergence* 31 (1–2): 137–145.

Illich, I. 1971. *Deschooling Society*. Harmondsworth, UK: Penguin.

Jackson, S. 1997. "Crossing Borders and Changing Pedagogies: From Giroux and Freire to Feminist Theories of Education." *Gender and Education* 9 (4): 457–467.

Jagodzinski, J. 2002. "The Ethics of the 'Real' in Levinas, Lacan, and Buddhism: Pedagogical Implications." *Educational Theory* 52 (1): 81–96.

Jardine, L. 1994. "Canon to the Left of Them, Canon to the Right of Them," in S. Dunant, ed., *The War of the Words: The Political Correctness Debate*, 97–115. London: Virago.

Johnson, I. 2002. "The Application of Buddhist Principles to Lifelong Learning." *International Journal of Lifelong Education* 21 (2): 99–114.

Jollimore, T., and S. Barrios. 2006. "Creating Cosmopolitans: The Case for Literature." *Studies in Philosophy and Education* 25: 263–283.

Kahn, R. 2006a. "Paulo Freire and Eco-Justice: Updating *Pedagogy of the Oppressed* for the Age of Ecological Calamity." *Paulo Freire Institute Online Journal* 1 (1): 1–11.

———. 2006b. Review of C. A. Bowers and F. Appfel-Marglin, eds., *Rethinking Freire: Globalization and the Environmental Crisis*, Mahwah, NJ: Lawrence Erlbaum, 2005. *Teachers College Record* 108 (1): 63–67.

Kahn, R., and D. Kellner. 2007. "Paulo Freire and Ivan Illich: Technology, Politics and the Reconstruction of Education." *Policy Futures in Education* 5 (4): 431–448.

Katz, M. 1997. "On Becoming a Teacher: May Sarton's *The Small Room*." *Philosophy of Education 1997*. Urbana-Champaign, IL: Philosophy of Education Society.

Kelly, A. 1988. "Dostoevskii and the Divided Conscience." *Slavic Review* 47 (2): 239–260.

Kesson, K. 2002. "Contemplative Spirituality, Currere, and Social Transformation: Finding Our 'Way,'" in T. Oldenski and D. Carlson, eds., *Educational Yearning: The Journey of the Spirit and Democratic Education*, 46–70. New York: Peter Lang.

REFERENCES

Kimball, R. 1991. *Tenured Radicals: How Politics Has Corrupted Our Higher Education*. New York: Harper Perennial.

———. 1993. "From Farce to Tragedy." *Partisan Review* 60 (4).

Kramer, H. 1993. "Confronting the Monolith." *Partisan Review* 60 (4): 569–573.

Kristeva, J. 1986. "A New Type of Intellectual: The Dissident," in T. Moi, ed., *The Kristeva Reader*, 292–300. Oxford: Blackwell.

Lai, K. L. 2008. *An Introduction to Chinese Philosophy*. Cambridge: Cambridge University Press.

Lange, E. 1998. "Fragmented Ethics of Justice: Freire, Liberation Theology, and Pedagogies for the Non-Poor." *Convergence* 31 (1–2): 81–93.

Lankshear, C. 1993. "Functional Literacy from a Freirean Point of View," in P. McLaren and P. Leonard, eds., *Paulo Freire: A Critical Encounter*, 90–118. London: Routledge.

Lankshear, C. (with J. P. Gee, M. Knobel, and C. Searle) 1997. *Changing Literacies*. Buckingham, UK: Open University Press.

Lankshear, C., with M. Lawler. 1987. *Literacy, Schooling, and Revolution*. London: Falmer.

Lao Tzu. 1963. *Tao Te Ching*, trans. D. C. Lau. London: Penguin.

Lau, D. C. 1963. "Introduction," in Lao Tzu, *Tao Te Ching*, trans. D. C. Lau, vii–xlv. London: Penguin.

Ledwith, M. 2001. "Community Work as Critical Pedagogy: Re-Envisioning Freire and Gramsci." *Community Development Journal* 36 (3): 171–182.

Lehman, D. 1993. "The Reign of Intolerance." *Partisan Review* 60 (4): 598–603.

Leistyna, P. 1999. *Presence of Mind: Education and the Politics of Deception*. Boulder, CO: Westview.

Lensmire, T. J. 1997. "The Teacher as Dostoevskian Novelist." *Research in the Teaching of English* 31 (3): 367–392.

Lewis, T. E. 2009. "Education in the Realm of the Senses: Understanding Paulo Freire's Aesthetic Unconscious through Jacques Rancière." *Journal of Philosophy of Education* 43 (2): 285–299.

Loury, G. C. 1993. "Self-Censorship." *Partisan Review* 60 (4): 608–620.

Lownds, P. 2005. Review of P. Mayo, *Liberating Praxis: Paulo Freire's Legacy for Radical Education and Politics*. New York: Praeger, 2004. *Journal of Transformative Education* 3 (2): 177–184.

Luke, A. 1991. "The Political Economy of Reading Instruction," in C. D. Baker and A. Luke, eds., *Towards a Critical Sociology of Reading Pedagogy*, 3–25. Philadelphia: John Benjamins.

Luke, C., and J. Gore. 1992. *Feminisms and Critical Pedagogy*. London: Routledge.

Lyotard, J.-F. 1993. "Tomb of the Intellectual," in J.-F. Lyotard, *Political Writings*, trans. B. Readings and K. P. Geiman, 3–7. Minneapolis: University of Minnesota Press.

Macedo, D. 1997. "An Anti-Method Pedagogy: A Freirian Perspective," in P. Freire, J. W. Fraser, D. Macedo, T. McKinnon, and W. T. Stokes, eds., *Mentoring the Mentor: A Critical Dialogue with Paulo Freire*, 1–9. New York: Peter Lang.

———. 2001. "Introduction," in A. M. A. Freire, *Chronicles of Love: My Life with Paulo Freire*, 1–9. New York: Peter Lang.

Mackie, R. 1980. "Contributions to the Thought of Paulo Freire," in R. Mackie, ed., *Literacy and Revolution: The Pedagogy of Paulo Freire*, 93–119. London: Pluto.

MacKinnon, A. 1996. "Learning to Teach at the Elbows: The Tao of Teaching." *Teaching and Teacher Education* 12 (6): 653–664.

Malcolm, L. 1999. "Mortimer Adler, Paulo Freire, and Teaching Theology in a Democracy." *Teaching Theology and Religion* 2 (2): 77–88.

Mao Tse-Tung. 1968. *Four Essays on Philosophy*. Peking: Foreign Languages Press.

Marcus, S. 1993. "Self-Totalitarianism." *Partisan Review* 60 (4): 630–638.

Margonis, F. 2003. "Paulo Freire and Post-Colonial Dilemmas." *Studies in Philosophy and Education* 22 (2): 145–156.

Martin, J. 1993. "The Postmodern Argument Considered." *Partisan Review* 60 (4): 638–654.

Mayo, P. 1993. "When Does It Work? Freire's Pedagogy in Context." *Studies in the Education of Adults* 25 (1): 11–30.

———. 1994. "Gramsci, Freire, and Radical Adult Education: A Few 'Blind Spots.'" *Humanity and Society* 18 (3): 82–98.

———. 1996. "Transformative Adult Education in an Age of Globalization: A Gramscian-Freirean Synthesis and Beyond." *Alberta Journal of Educational Research* (June): 148–160.

———. 1997. "Tribute to Paulo Freire (1921–1997)." *International Journal of Lifelong Education* 16 (5): 365–370.

———. 1999. *Gramsci, Freire, and Adult Education: Possibilities for Transformative Action*. London: Zed.

———. 2001. "Remaining on the Same Side of the River: A Critical Commentary on Paulo Freire's Later Work." *Review of Education/Pedagogy/Cultural Studies* 22 (4): 369–397.

———. 2002. Review of P. Roberts, *Education, Literacy, and Humanization: Exploring the Work of Paulo Freire*. Westport, CT: Bergin and Garvey, 2000. *International Journal of Lifelong Education* 21 (4): 392–396.

———. 2004. *Liberating Praxis: Paulo Freire's Legacy for Radical Education and Politics*. New York: Praeger.

———. 2007. "Critical Approaches to Education in the Work of Lorenzo Milani and Paulo Freire." *Studies in Philosophy and Education* 26: 525–544.

McLaren, P. 1989. *Life in Schools: An Introduction to Critical Pedagogy in the Foundations of Education*. London: Longman.

———. 1997. "Freirian Pedagogy: The Challenge of Postmodernism and the Politics of Race," in P. Freire, J. W. Fraser, D. Macedo, T. McKinnon, and W. T. Stokes, eds., *Mentoring the Mentor: A Critical Dialogue with Paulo Freire*, 99–125. New York: Peter Lang.

———. 1999. "A Pedagogy of Possibility: Reflecting upon Paulo Freire's Politics of Education." *Educational Researcher* 28: 49–56.

———. 2000. *Che Guevara, Paulo Freire, and the Pedagogy of Revolution*. Lanham, MD: Rowman and Littlefield.

McLaren, P., and C. Lankshear. 1993. "Critical Literacy and the Postmodern Turn," in C. Lankshear and P. McLaren, eds., *Critical Literacy: Politics, Praxis, and the Postmodern*, 379–419. Albany: State University of New York Press.

McLaren, P., and C. Lankshear, eds. 1994. *Politics of Liberation: Paths from Freire*. London: Routledge.

McLaren, P., and P. Leonard, eds. 1993. *Paulo Freire: A Critical Encounter*. London: Routledge.

Mejía, A. 2004. "The Problem of Knowledge Imposition: Paulo Freire and Critical Systems Thinking." *Systems Research and Behavioral Science* 21: 63–82.

Mejía, A., and A. Espinosa. 2007. "Team Syntegrity as a Learning Tool: Some Considerations about Its Capacity to Promote Critical Learning." *Systems Research and Behavioral Science* 24: 27–35.

Merkin, D. 1993. "Notes of a Lonely White Woman." *Partisan Review* 60 (4): 654–660.

Messer-Davidow, E. 1993. "Manufacturing the Attack on Higher Education." *Social Text* 36: 40–80.

Mileck, J. 1970. "*Das Glasperlenspiel*: Genesis, Manuscripts, and History of Publication." *German Quarterly* 43: 55–83.

———. 1978. *Hermann Hesse: Life and Art*. Berkeley: University of California Press.

Mitchell, S. 1991. *Tao Te Ching*. New York: Harper Perennial.

Morgan, J. 1994. "Learning to Live with Emotion." *Educational Philosophy and Theory* 26 (2): 67–81.

Morrow, R. A. and C. A. Torres. 2002. *Reading Freire and Habermas: Critical Pedagogy and Transformative Social Change*. New York: Teachers College Press.

Murrell, P. C., Jr. 1997. "Digging Again the Family Wells: A Freirian Literacy Framework as Emancipatory Pedagogy for African-American Children," in P. Freire, J. W. Fraser, D. Macedo, T. McKinnon, and W. T. Stokes, eds., *Mentoring the Mentor: A Critical Dialogue with Paulo Freire*, 19–58. New York: Peter Lang.

Neiman, A. M. 2000. "Self Examination, Philosophical Education and Spirituality." *Journal of Philosophy of Education* 34 (4): 571–590.

Neuhaus, R. J. 2003. "Dostoevsky and the Fiery Word." Review of J. Frank, *Dostoevsky: The Mantle of the Prophet*, Princeton, NJ: Princeton University Press, 2002. *First Things: A Monthly Journal of Religion and Public Life* (March): 74–81.

New English Bible: New Testament. 1961. Oxford: Oxford University Press.

Ng, G. A. Wenh-In. 2000. "From Confucian Master Teacher to Freirian Mutual Learner: Challenges in Pedagogical Practice and Religious Education." *Religious Education* 95 (3): 308–319.

Nias, J. 1996. "Thinking about Feeling: The Emotions in Teaching." *Cambridge Journal of Education* 26: 293–306.

Noddings, N. 1984. *Caring*. Berkeley: University of California Press.

Norton, R. C. 1973. *Hermann Hesse's Futuristic Idealism:* The Glass Bead Game *and Its Predecessors*. Bern, Switzerland/Frankfurt, West-Germany: Herbert Lang/Peter Lang.

Nussbaum, M. 1990. *Love's Knowledge: Essays on Philosophy and Literature*. New York: Oxford University Press.

———. 1995. *Poetic Justice: The Literary Imagination and Public Life*. Boston: Beacon.

Oates, J. C. 1968. "The Double Vision of *The Brothers Karamazov*." *Journal of Aesthetics and Art Criticism* 27 (2): 203–213.

O'Cadiz, M. D. P., L. Wong, and C. A. Torres. 1998. *Education and Democracy: Paulo Freire, Social Movements, and Educational Reform in São Paulo*. Boulder, CO: Westview.

O'Keefe, B. J. 1992. "Sense and Sensitivity." *Journal of Communication* 42 (2): 123–130.

Oldenski, T. 2002. "The Critical Discourses of Liberation Theology and Critical Pedagogy," in T. Oldenski and D. Carlson, eds., *Educational Yearning: The Journey of the Spirit and Democratic Education*, 133–162. New York: Peter Lang.

O'Neil, W. 1970. "Properly Literate." *Harvard Educational Review* 40 (2).

Peters, M. 1999. "Freire and Postmodernism," in P. Roberts, ed., *Paulo Freire, Politics and Pedagogy: Reflections from Aotearoa-New Zealand*, 113–122. Palmerston North: Dunmore Press.

Peters, M., and C. Lankshear. 1996. "Critical Literacy and Digital Texts." *Educational Theory* 46 (1): 51–70.

Peters, R. S. 1970. *Ethics and Education*. London: Allen and Unwin.

———. 1973. *Authority, Responsibility and Education*, rev. ed. London: Allen and Unwin.

Petras, J., and H. Veltmeyer. 2003. "Whither Lula's Brazil? Neoliberalism and 'Third Way' Ideology." *Journal of Peasant Society* 31 (1): 1–44.

Pevear, R. 1991. "Introduction," in F. Dostoevsky, *The Brothers Karamazov*, trans. R. Pevear and L. Volokhonsky. New York: Vintage.

———. 2002. "To Find the Man in Dostoevsky." *Hudson Review* 55 (3): 495–503.

Phillips, M. 1994. "Illiberal Liberalism," in S. Dunant, ed., *The War of the Words: The Political Correctness Debate,* 35–54. London: Virago.

Phillips, W. 1993. "Against Political Correctness: Eleven Points." *Partisan Review* 60 (4): 670–676.

Pratt, M. L. 1992. "Humanities for the Future: Reflections on the Western Culture Debate at Stanford," in D. J. Gless and B. H. Smith, eds., *The Politics of Liberal Education* 13–31. Durham, NC: Duke University Press.

Radosh, R. 1993. "McCarthyism of the Left." *Partisan Review* 60 (4): 677–684.

Ramdas, L. 1997. "The *Tao* of Mangoes, Adult Education, and Freire: The Continuing Challenges and Dilemmas." *Convergence* 30 (2–3).

Ram-Prasad, C. 2005. *Eastern Philosophy.* London: Weidenfeld and Nicolson.

Reimer, E. 1971. *School Is Dead.* Harmondsworth, UK: Penguin.

Remys, E. 1983. *Hermann Hesse's* Das Glasperlenspiel: *A Concealed Defense of the Mother World.* New York: Peter Lang.

Rindner, E. C. 2004. "Using Freirean Empowerment for Health Education with Adolescents in Primary, Secondary, and Tertiary Psychiatric Settings." *Journal of Child and Adolescent Psychiatric Nursing* 17 (2): 78–84.

Roberts, P. 1993. "Philosophy, Education and Literacy: Some Comments on Bloom." *New Zealand Journal of Educational Studies* 28 (2): 165–180.

———. 1996a. "The Danger of Domestication: A Case-Study." *International Journal of Lifelong Education* 15 (2): 94–106.

———. 1996b. "Defending Freirean Intervention." *Educational Theory* 46 (3): 335–352.

———. 1996c. "Rethinking Conscientisation." *Journal of Philosophy of Education* 30 (2): 179–196.

———. 1996d. "Structure, Direction and Rigour in Liberating Education." *Oxford Review of Education* 22 (3): 295–316.

———. 1997. "Political Correctness, Great Books and the University Curriculum," in M. Peters, ed., *Cultural Politics and the University,* 103–134. Palmerston North: Dunmore Press.

———. 1998. "Knowledge, Dialogue and Humanization: The Moral Philosophy of Paulo Freire." *Journal of Educational Thought* 32 (2): 95–117.

———. 1999a. "A Dilemma for Critical Educators?" *Journal of Moral Education* 28 (1): 19–30.

———, ed. 1999b. *Paulo Freire, Politics and Pedagogy: Reflections from Aotearoa-New Zealand.* Palmerston North: Dunmore Press.

———. 2000. *Education, Literacy, and Humanization: Exploring the Work of Paulo Freire.* Westport, CT: Bergin and Garvey.

———. 2003a. "Epistemology, Ethics and Education: Addressing Dilemmas of Difference in the Work of Paulo Freire." *Studies in Philosophy and Education* 22 (2): 157–173.

———. 2003b. "Pedagogy, Neoliberalism and Postmodernity: Reflections on Freire's Later Work." *Educational Philosophy and Theory* 35 (4): 467–481.

———. 2008a. "Teaching as an Ethical and Political Process: A Freirean Perspective," in V. Carpenter, J. Jesson, P. Roberts, and M. Stephenson, eds., *Ng Kaupapa Here: Connections and Contradictions in Education*, 99–108. Melbourne, Australia: Cengage.

———. 2008b. "Liberation, Oppression, and Education: Extending Freirean Ideas." *Journal of Educational Thought* 42 (1): 83–97.

———. 2008c. "Life, Death, and Transformation: Education and Incompleteness in Hermann Hesse's *The Glass Bead Game*." *Canadian Journal of Education* 31 (3): 667–696.

———. 2008d. "From West to East and Back Again: Faith, Doubt and Education in Hermann Hesse's Later Work." *Journal of Philosophy of Education* 42 (2): 249–268.

———. 2008e. "Teaching, Learning and Ethical Dilemmas: Lessons from Albert Camus." *Cambridge Journal of Education* 38 (4): 529–542.

———. 2008f. "Bridging Literary and Philosophical Genres: Judgment, Reflection and Education in Camus' *The Fall*." *Educational Philosophy and Theory* 40 (7): 873–887.

———. 2009a. "Education, Death, and Awakening: Hesse, Freire and the Process of Transformation." *International Journal of Lifelong Education* 28 (1): 57–69.

———. 2009b. "Technology, Utopia and Scholarly Life." *Policy Futures in Education* 7 (1): 65–74.

Roberts, P., and M. A. Peters. 2008. *Neoliberalism, Higher Education and Research*. Rotterdam: Sense Publishers.

Robinson, P. 2004. "Meditation: Its Role in Transformative Learning and in the Fostering of an Integrative Vision for Higher Education." *Journal of Transformative Education* 2 (2): 107–119.

Rossatto, C. 2005. *Engaging Paulo Freire's Pedagogy of Possibility: From Blind to Transformative Optimism*. Lanham, MD: Rowman and Littlefield.

Rozas, C. 2007. "The Possibility of Justice: The Work of Paulo Freire and Difference." *Studies in Philosophy and Education* 26: 561–570.

Ruitenberg, C. 2004. "Don't Fence Me in: The Liberation of Undomesticated Critique." *Journal of Philosophy of Education* 38 (3): 341–350.

San, S. K. 2006. "Action Learning Guided by Tao for Lifelong Learning." *Action Learning: Research and Practice* 3 (1): 97–105.

Sartre, J. P. 1973. "Revolution and the Intellectual (an Interview with Jean-Claude Garot)," in *Politics and Literature*, trans. J. A. Underwood and J. Calder, 13–35. London: Calder and Boyars.

Scanlan, J. P. 1999. "The Case against Rational Egoism in Dostoevsky's *Notes from Underground*." *Journal of the History of Ideas* 60 (3): 549–567.

———. 2002. *Dostoevsky the Thinker*. Ithaca, NY: Cornell University Press.

Scheffler, I. 1960. *The Language of Education.* Springfield, IL: Charles C. Thomas.

Schugurensky, D. 1998. "The Legacy of Paulo Freire: A Critical Review of His Contributions." *Convergence* 31 (1–2): 17–28.

Sherman, A. 1980. "Two Views of Emotion in the Writings of Paulo Freire." *Educational Theory* 30 (3): 35–38.

Shim, S. H. 2007. "A Philosophical Investigation of the Role of Teachers: A Synthesis of Plato, Confucius, Buber, and Freire." *Teaching and Teacher Education* 24: 515–535.

Shor, I. 1980. *Critical Teaching and Everyday Life.* Boston: South End.

———, ed. 1987. *Freire for the Classroom.* Portsmouth, NH: Boynton/Cook.

———. 1992. *Empowering Education: Critical Teaching and Social Change.* Chicago, IL: Chicago University Press.

———. 1993. "Education Is Politics," in P. McLaren and P. Leonard, eds., *Paulo Freire: A Critical Encounter,* 25–35. London: Routledge.

———. 1996. *When Students Have Power: Negotiating Authority in a Critical Pedagogy.* Chicago, IL: Chicago University Press.

———. 1998. "The Centrality of Beans: Remembering Paulo." *Convergence* 31 (1–2): 75–80.

Sidorsky, D. 1993. "Multiculturalism and the University," *Partisan Review,* 60 (4), 709–722.

Siegel, H. 1997. "Teaching, Reasoning, and Dostoevsky's *The Brothers Karamazov,*" in *Rationality Redeemed? Further Dialogues on an Educational Ideal,* 39–54. New York: Routledge.

Slater, J. J. 2004. "The Tao of Caring: The Prisoner's Dilemma in Education Resolved." *Curriculum and Teaching Dialogue* 6 (2): 145–157.

Slater, J. J., S. M. Fain, and C. A. Rossatto, eds. 2002. *The Freirean Legacy: Educating for Social Justice.* New York: Peter Lang.

Smith, G. 1999. "Paulo Freire: Lessons in Transformative Praxis," in P. Roberts, ed., *Paulo Freire, Politics and Pedagogy: Reflections from Aotearoa-New Zealand.* Palmerston North: Dunmore Press.

Smith, W. 1976. *The Meaning of Conscientizacao: The Goal of Paulo Freire's Pedagogy.* Amherst, MA: Center for International Education.

Solomon, R. C. 1986. "Literacy and the Education of the Emotions," in S. de Castell, A. Luke, and K. Egan, eds., *Literacy, Society, and Schooling: A Reader,* 37–58. Cambridge: Cambridge University Press.

Soltis, J. F. 1978. *An Introduction to the Analysis of Educational Concepts,* 2nd ed. Boston: Addison-Wesley.

Spring, J. 1994. *Wheels in the Head: Educational Philosophies of Authority, Freedom, and Culture from Socrates to Paulo Freire.* New York: McGraw-Hill.

Stefanos, A. 1997. "African Women and Revolutionary Change: A Freirian and Feminist Perspective," in P. Freire, J. W. Fraser, D. Macedo, T. McKinnon, and W. T. Stokes, eds., *Mentoring the Mentor: A Critical Dialogue with Paulo Freire,* 243–271. New York: Peter Lang.

Steiner, R. 1995. *Intuitive Thinking as a Spiritual Path: A Philosophy of Freedom*, trans. M. Lipson. Hudson, NY: Anthroposophic Press.

Street, B. 1984. *Literacy in Theory and Practice*. Cambridge: Cambridge University Press.

Swales, M. 1978. *The German Bildungsroman from Wieland to Hesse*. Princeton, NJ: Princeton University Press.

Taboo: The Journal of Culture and Education. 1997. Special issue on Paulo Freire 2 (Fall): 1–188.

Taylor, P. V. 1993. *The Texts of Paulo Freire*. Buckingham: Open University Press.

Torres, C. A. 1994a. "Paulo Freire as Secretary of Education in the Municipality of São Paulo." *Comparative Education Review* 38 (2): 181–214.

———. 1994b. "Education and the Archeology of Consciousness: Freire and Hegel." *Educational Theory* 44 (4): 429–445.

———. 1994c. "Introduction," in M. Escobar, A. L. Fernandez, G. Guevara-Niebla, and P. Freire, *Paulo Freire on Higher Education: A Dialogue at the National University of Mexico*. Albany: State University of New York Press.

Torres, C. A., and P. Noguera, eds. 2008. *Social Justice Education for Teachers: Paulo Freire and the Possible Dream*. Rotterdam: Sense Publishers.

van Gorder, A. C. 2007. "Pedagogy for the Children of the Oppressors: Liberative Education for Social Justice among the World's Privileged." *Journal of Transformative Education* 5 (1): 8–32.

Vokey, D. 1999. "Macintrye, Moral Value, and Mahayana Buddhism: Embracing the Unthinkable in Moral Education." *Educational Theory* 49 (1): 91–106.

Walker, J. 1980. "The End of Dialogue: Paulo Freire on Politics and Education," in R. Mackie, ed., *Literacy and Revolution: The Pedagogy of Paulo Freire*, 120–150. London: Pluto.

Weiler, K. 1991. "Paulo Freire and a Feminist Pedagogy of Difference." *Harvard Educational Review* 61 (4): 449–474.

Weiner, E. J. 2003. "Secretary Paulo Freire and the Democratization of Power: Toward a Theory of Transformative Leadership." *Educational Philosophy and Theory* 35 (1): 89–106.

Wilde, L. 1999. "The Radical Appeal of Hermann Hesse's Alternative Community." *Utopian Studies* 10: 86–97.

Wong, E. 1992, *Cultivating Stillness: A Taoist Manual for Transforming Body and Mind*. Boston: Shambhala.

———. 1997. *The Shambhala Guide to Taoism*. Boston: Shambhala.

———. 2004. *Nourishing the Essence of Life: The Outer, Inner, and Secret Teachings of Taoism*. Boston: Shambhala.

Zembylas, M. 2002. "'Structures of Feeling' in Curriculum and Teaching: Theorizing the Emotional Rules." *Educational Theory* 52 (2): 187–208.

Zigler, R. L. 1994. "Reason and Emotion Revisited: Achilles, Arjuna, and Moral Conduct." *Educational Theory* 44 (1): 63–79.

———. 2007. "The Tao of Dewey." *Encounter: Education for Meaning and Social Justice* 20 (1): 37–42.

Index

Abstract nature of Freire's work, 36, 118, 121, 122
Action and nonaction, 148–150
The Adolescent (Dostoevsky), 116
Aesthetics, 45–46, 47, 89
Alternatives, denial of, 10
Andreola, Balduino A., 14, 15
Anger, political, 16–17
Antidialogical stance, 71
Araújo Freire, Ana Maria, 14, 16–17, 34, 36–37, 114
Aristotle, 45
Association of Nicaraguan Women, 61
Authoritarianism: dogmatic and reactionary stances, 21, 74–76

Bachelor of arts degree, 95–96
Bakhtin, Mikhail, 111
Banking education, 58, 87
Bauman, Zygmunt, 23, 28
Beauty, 46, 89
Beneath the Wheel (Hesse), 140
Berger, Brigitte, 78–79
Biesta, Gert, 134–136
Biographical information, Freire's, 2–7
Bloom, Allan, 65
Boler, Megan, 113
Book banning, 77
Books, Freire's love of, 43

Breadth in reading, 90–101, 94, 95, 96, 97, 100–101, 150–151
The Brothers Karamazov (Dostoevsky), 48–49, 107, 110–113, 115–117

Capitalism. *See* Neoliberalism
Castalia (fictional pedagogical province), 11, 123, 127, 129, 131–132, 136–138
Catholicism, radical, 40–41, 107
Chambers, Ellie, 90
Chen, Ellen, 151, 152–153
Childhood experience, 85–86
Chile: Freire's criticism of Left and Right intolerance, 73–74; Freire's radicalization, 3; shaping Freire's view of liberation, 43–44, 58
Christianity: Dostoevsky's tension between humanism and, 110, 112, 115; Gospels as a call for social action, 41; radical Catholicism, 40–41, 107
Class analysis, 79, 80–81
Classic texts, 95–96
Class suicide, 25
The Closing of the American Mind (Bloom), 65
Coercion to a position, 73
Community, loss of sense of, 39–40
Comparative methodology, 7

Conformity: dogmatic and reactionary stances, 74–76; political correctness and, 10, 69–70
Confucius, 142
Conscience, 126–127
Conscientization, 124–127; in Hesse's *Glass Bead Game*, 11; movement toward critical consciousness, 72; nonneutrality of education, 133–137; as ongoing process, 137–139; uncertainty and, 127–129
Consciousness: characterizing critical consciousness, 72–73; conscientization, 124–127; consciousness raising, 124–125; constant searching, 36–37; Dostoevsky's plurality of, 111; Hesse's *Glass Bead Game*, 128–129; importance of dialogue in developing Hesse's Joseph Knecht's, 129–133; political correctness and, 77; Taoist knowing and not-knowing, 153; world and, 5
Conservative view, political correctness and, 66–69, 77, 78–79
Contradictions, Taoism and, 143–144
Cooking, 80
Core curricula: balancing breadth and depth, 10, 90–101; oppositional groups advocating, 83; political correctness, 77; quality and quantity in critical reading, 93–96; time constraint, 91–93
Course planning, 90–91
Crime and Punishment (Dostoevsky), 116, 117
Critical consciousness. *See* Consciousness
Critical dialogue. *See* Dialogue
Critical educational ideal, 43–49, 46. *See also* Education
Critical intellectual. *See* Intellectual, critical

Critical literacy. *See* Literacy
Critical pedagogy: nonneutrality of, 133–135; transformationist view of education, 68
Critical reading. *See* Reading
Critical thought, 16, 73–74
Criticism, impeding, 10
Cultural Action for Freedom (Freire), 3
Cultural pluralism, 79–80
Culture: understanding emotions, reason, and language through, 37
Curiosity, importance of: aesthetic curiosity, 46; reading childhood environment, 86; role of the intellectual, 19–20; theory and practice of critical literacy, 89
Curricula. *See* Core curricula

Daring to Dream (Freire), 13–14
Debate, stifling, 10
Decency, 46
Dehumanization, 5–6, 35, 60–61
Deleuze, Gilles, 23
Democracy, 16, 124
Demons (Dostoevsky), 107, 110
Depth in reading, 90–101, 150–151
Descriptive definition, 53, 54, 55
Dialogue: antidialogical stance, 71; complexity of Freire's concept of, 8–9; conscientization, 126–127; Dostoevsky's and Freire's works, 110–113; emotions exerting undue influence, 38–39; humility in, 42; importance to the development of Hesse's Joseph Knecht, 129–133; intolerance, conformity, and suppression of, 74–76; love as foundation of, 20–21, 41–42; multiculturalism and, 80; *Pedagogy of Indignation*, 16; as revolutionary virtue, 23, 24
Diversity, political correctness and, 78
Doctoral degree, 95–96
Dogmatism, 71, 73–74
Domestication, literacy as, 60

INDEX

Dostoevsky, Fyodor, 140; commonalities with Freire's work, 11; dialogue in the works of, 110–113; education as struggle, 105–106; reason and emotion, 48–49, 113–116; study and debate of the works of, 106; transformation, 116–118; uncertainty, 109–110; weaknesses in the works of, 118–119
Dowbor, Ladislau, 39–40
D'Souza, Dinesh, 65

Eastern philosophy, 15–16. *See also* *Tao Te Ching*
Ecological issues, 15, 45
Economic models. *See* Neoliberalism
Education: Freire's, 2; as permanent process of formation, 25; political nature of, 4–5; structured, purposeful, and rigorous dialogue characterizing, 71–72; Taoist view of, 155–156; as transformation, 116–118
Education, Literacy, and Humanization (Roberts), 7
Education: The Practice of Freedom (Freire), 72
Educational theory, origins of, 4
Effortlessness, 150
Elitism, Freirian pedagogy as, 22
Emancipatory ignorance, 134–136
Emotion: critical reading, writing, and investigation, 44; engaging with the text, 48–49; ethical and educational significance of, 113–116; Freire's prioritizing of reason and rational processes over, 31–32; *Pedagogy of Indignation*, 14, 18–19; political dimension of education, 44; reason and emotion in Freire's life and work, 33–39; solidarity and, 39–40; as uncritical force, 46
Emotionality, 32, 38, 49
Engagement with ideas and texts: critical reading as an act of knowing, 87; Dostoevsky and Freire, 112–113; entering into the text, 89; Freire's educational thought and, 8; reason and emotion driving, 38, 47; time constraints, 91–93
Epistemology. *See* Ontology, epistemology, and ethic
Essentialist definition of literacy, 10, 55–56, 59, 61
Ethical universalism, 26, 36
Ethics: defining literacy, 57; Dostoevsky's moral philosophy, 107; Dostoevsky's tension between humanism and Christian ethics, 110; in Dostoevsky's works, 112; respecting political difference, 76; Taoist view of ignorance and happiness, 154, 155–156; virtue ethics, 45
Ethnic minorities: class and, 80–81; political correctness in education, 65; unity in diversity, 79
Evil, 115
Exile, 3
Experience: Dostoevsky and Freire's works drawing on, 107–108; integrating literacy learning with, 109; reading the word and the world, 85–86

Faith, 107
Families, 14–15
Farm-gate intellectuals, 26
Faundez, Antonio, 3
Feelings. *See* Emotion
Felt reasons, 115
Feminist pedagogies, 23, 24
Fiction. *See* Dostoevsky, Fyodor; *The Glass Bead Game*; Hesse, Hermann
Foucault, Michel, 9, 23, 25
Frank, Joseph, 114
Fraser, James, 11–12, 141, 146, 147, 148–149
Free trade agreements, 27

181

INDEX

Freire, Ana Maria. *See* Araújo Freire, Ana Maria
Freire, Elza, 107, 109

The Gambler (Dostoevsky), 107
General definitions of education, 52
Glanz, J., 145
The Glass Bead Game (Hesse): conscientization and dialogue, 11; conscientization as ongoing process, 137–139; emancipatory ignorance, 135–136; nonneutrality in education, 136–137; premise of, 121–122; role of dialogue in critical consciousness, 129–133; uncertainty and critical thought, 127–128
Globalization, 27
Gospels, 41, 107
Gramsci, Antonio, 23
Great Books program, 83
Guevara, Che, 40

Habermas, Jürgen, 44
Happiness, Taoist view of, 153–157
Hegel, G.W.F., 5
Hesse, Hermann, 11. *See also The Glass Bead Game*
Hillary, Edmund, 26
Holistic reading of Freire's work, 35
Hope, feeling and action, 40
Horton, Myles, 3
Human ideals, 98–99
Humanism, 110
Humanization: dogmatic stances, 73–74; as incomplete process, 5–6; literacy as domestication and literacy for liberation, 60–61; love as defining characteristic of, 40–41; political correctness and, 70–71; reason and, 35
Human nature, Taoist view of, 152
Humility: courage and, 29; Dostoevsky and Freire valuing, 118–119; in Hesse's *Glass Bead Game*, 132, 133; love and, 42; questioning texts, 46–47

Ideals, human, individual, and social, 98–99
Ideas in formation, 108
Ideology, political correctness and, 68–69, 75–76, 77. *See also* Neoliberalism
The Idiot (Dostoevsky), 107
Ignorance: emancipatory, 134–136; Taoist, 153–157
Illiberal Education (D'Souza), 65
Imperative, educational, 135
"The Importance of the Act of Reading" (Freire), 85
Improper literacy, 61–62
Incompetence, 24
Indignation, 16–17
Individual ideals, 98–99
Individuality, 129
Innocent knowing, 24
Intellectual, critical: critical educational ideal, 9–10; importance of humility, 28–29; roles and responsibilities of the critical intellectual, 19–28; universal and specific intellectuals, 25–26
Intolerance: dogmatic and reactionary stances, 74–76; Freire's criticism of Left and Right intolerance, 73–74; political correctness and, 10, 69–70, 71
Intuition, 37–38
Irrationalism, Dostoevsky's, 114–115

Kimball, Roger, 65, 66–67
Knowing, process of: conscientization, 126–127; critical reading as an act of knowing, 60, 84, 86–87; joy and rigor of study, 43; Taoist knowledge and knowing, 150–153; Taoist not-doing and, 150; unfinishedness of humans and, 36–38

Kramer, Hilton, 78
Kristeva, Julia, 23

Language: aesthetic dimension of, 46; expressing love of knowledge and humanity, 37; Freire's passion for, 43; Glass Bead Game as universal language, 123
The Language of Education (Scheffler), 52
Lao Tzu, 141–145, 148, 150
Lau, D.C., 142, 143
Learning to Question (Freire), 75
Legitimation, crisis of, 28
Lensmire, Timothy, 111–112
Letters, Freire's, 17
Letters to Cristina (Freire), 43
Liberation: Fraser's view of self-liberation, 146–147; Freire's failure to address connections between reason, emotion, and spirituality, 45; Gospels as a call for social action, 41, 107; human ideals, 98–99; literacy as domestication and literacy for liberation, 60–62; political correctness and, 70–71; as process of struggle against oppression, 35–36, 43–44
Life and work, 2–7
Listening: as act of love, 41–42; in Hesse's *Glass Bead Game*, 130–131; in the works of Dostoevsky and Freire, 112–113
Literacies, 56–58, 60
Literacy: critical reading as an act of knowing, 86–87; descriptive definition, 53, 54, 55; essentialist definition, 55–56; ethical questions in defining education, 54–55; Freire's success with programs for, 2, 3; Freirian view of critical literacy, 84–89; integrating literacy learning with experience, 109; linking "word" with "world," 72–73, 109; multiple definitions, 10, 51; normative view of, 59–60; particularist definition, 56–57; political correctness, 66; political nature of education, 4–5; process of liberation from oppression, 58–59; programmatic definition, 53–54; reading and, 58–60; reading the word and the world, 84–86; stipulative definition, 52, 54, 55; theory and practice, 88–90. *See also* Reading
Literary qualities of Freire's work, 121
Literary works and educational philosophy, 11
Literature, value of, 11
Living, manual on the art of, 144
Love: Dostoevsky's belief in the importance of, 115–116; as foundation for Freire's pedagogy, 40–41; Fraser on Freire's concept of, 146; importance in education, 8; intellectual disposition, 20; listening as, 41–42; struggling with the text with love, 47–49
Love, humanistic, 17
Lydiard, Arthur, 26
Lyotard, Jean-François, 23

Macedo, Donaldo, 13–14, 34
Magical consciousness, 124, 125
Magister Ludi (Hesse). *See The Glass Bead Game*
Major subject, 95
Maoism, 9
Mao Tse-Tung, 23
Marketization policies, 16, 27
Martin, Jerry, 67–68
Marx, Karl/Marxist thought: depth and breadth in reading, 94; Freire's educational ideal, 5, 9; gulf between theory and practice, 88; love as defining characteristic of humanization, 40–41; role and responsibility of the intellectual, 23; transformationist view of education, 68

Master's degree, 95–96
Masters of humanity, 15
Meditative practice, 154
Memoirs from the House of the Dead (Dostoevsky), 107, 116, 117
Mentoring the Mentor (Freire), 141
Messer-Davidow, Ellen, 68
Mistakes, learning from, 109
Mitchell, S, 150
Modernity: universal human ethic, 36; view of the critical intellectual, 18
Morality, 54, 114
Multiculturalism, 78–81

Naïve consciousness, 124, 125
Nature, Taoist view of, 152, 157–158
Neoliberalism: deproblematizing the future, 27; ethics of, 26–27; importance of solidarity in the struggle against, 39–40; *Pedagogy of Indignation*, 14, 16; political correctness and, 67; resistance to, 21–22; role of the intellectual in examining, 22
Neutrality of education, 133–137, 146
Nicaragua, 61
Nichomachean Ethics (Aristotle), 45
Nobel Prize, 123
Nonaction, 148–150
Nonneutrality of education, 133–137, 146
Nonverbal knowing, 152–153
Normative view of literacy, 59–60
Not-doing, Taoist, 149, 150, 152
Notes from Underground (Dostoevsky), 107, 110, 114–115

Ontology, epistemology, and ethic: Freire's educational theory and, 5, 36; humanization, 35; Marxian influence, 23; role of the critical intellectual and, 19–20; Taoism and, 144
Opposites, Taoist, 143–144
Oppression: conscientization, 72; conscious knowing and unconscious knowing, 153; dehumanizing lack of love characterizing, 40–41; dehumanizing oppressors and oppressed, 71; engagement with the text, 47–48; human ideals, 99; liberation as a process of struggle against, 35–36, 43–44, 60–62; literacy as domestication and literacy for liberation, 60–62; as manifestation of dehumanization, 5–6; multiculturality as social and dialogical struggle, 79–80; proper and improper literacies, 61–62

Particularist definition, 56–57, 58
Passivity, Taoist, 149
Paternalism, 23, 24
A Pedagogy for Liberation (Freire and Shor), 47, 58–59, 93
Pedagogy in Process (Freire), 3, 23
Pedagogy of Freedom (Freire), 36, 46
Pedagogy of the Heart (Freire), 36
Pedagogy of Hope (Freire), 76, 79
Pedagogy of Indignation (Freire), 9, 13–19, 19–20
Pedagogy of the Oppressed (Freire), 3, 34, 40–41, 121, 152
Pejorative concept, political correctness as, 70–71
Perspectives on reading, 96–97
Petrashevsky Circle, 106, 110
Phillips, William, 67, 79
Philosophy as a way of life, 34
Pluralism, 76
"Poem of the Grand Inquisitor" (Dostoevsky), 110
Poetry, Freire's, 121
Political commitment: acknowledging, 76, 78; critical consciousness and, 73; Dostoevsky and Freire, 106–107, 110–111; literacy and the process of liberation from oppression,

58–59; reason, emotion, and, 31–32
Political correctness: characteristics of, 10; conservative view, 66–69, 77, 78–79; Freire's opposition to policies and practices, 65–66; implications of a Freirian view, 77–81; intolerance, conformity, and suppression of criticism, 74–76; many faces of, 66–71
Political nature and dimension of education: conservative view of, 77; critical literacy in theory and practice, 88–90; origins of Freire's educational theory, 4–5; *Pedagogy of Indignation,* 14; reason and emotion in study, 44; role and responsibility of the intellectual, 22. *See also* Political correctness
Polyphonic novels, Dostoevsky's, 111
Postmodernism: Freire's account of oppression and liberation, 35–36; transformationist view of education, 67–68; view of the critical intellectual, 18
Postmodernist turn in social theory, 17–18
Praxis, 71
Prescriptive literacy, 10, 56, 58, 59, 61
Programmatic definition, 53–54, 56
Proper literacy, 61–62
Publications, 3

Quality and quantity in critical reading, 93–96
Questioning: characterizing critical consciousness, 72–73; dogmatic and reactionary stances prohibiting, 74–76; Dostoevsky's commitment to, 110–111; the educational imperative, 135; in Hesse's *Glass Bead Game,* 130; importance of how, why, when, and where to ask, 102; narrowing the focus of questioning, 97–100; political correctness and, 69–70; role of the critical intellectual, 20

Racism, 79
Radicalism: political correctness and, 67, 68; radical Catholicism, 40–41, 107
Ram-Prasad, C., 144–145
Rationalism. *See* Reason
Reactionary stance, 74
Reading: aesthetics and, 45–46, 47; breadth and depth in, 90–101, 100–101; engaging with the text, 47; essentialist definition, 55–56; linking word and world, 42; literacy and, 58–59, 58–60; multiple perspectives, 96–97; narrowing the focus of questioning, 97–100; oppositional groups defining core curriculum, 83; quality and quantity, 93–96; rationalism and emotions, 44; struggling with the text with love, 47–49; time constraints, 91–92, 91–93. *See also* Literacy
Reason: critical educational ideal, 9–10; emotion, political commitment, and, 31–32; emotion and reason in Dostoevsky's works, 114–116; emotion and reason in Freire's life and work, 18–19, 33–39; engaging with the text, 48–49; political dimension of education, 44; solidarity and, 39–40
Reformist view of core curriculum, 83, 90
Research methodology, 17–18
Revolutionary stance: love as a revolutionary value, 20, 40–41; revolutionary nature of Freire's text, 25
Risk-taking, 76, 89
Roles and responsibilities of the critical intellectual, 9, 19–28
Rural community: liberating literacy, 62

Sartre, Jean-Paul, 23
Scheffler, Israel, 10, 51–54, 55
Schnackenberg, Tom, 26
Scientific definitions of education, 52
Searching, process of, 36
Self-annihilation, 42
Sherman, Ann, 31–33, 49
Shih chi (Record of the Historian), 142
Shor, Ira, 7
Siddhartha (Hesse), 140
Siegel, Harvey, 115
Silence, Taoist, 149–150
Social action: Gospels as a call for, 41, 107; love and, 20; political dimension of critical education, 44–45; proper and improper literacies, 61–62
Social change: the "oppressor within" teachers, 146; relationship between emotion, education and, 32
Social criticism: critical literacy and, 84
Social ideals, 98–99
Social inequality: critical educational ideal, 43–44
Socialism, 22
Social theory: postmodern turn in, 17–18
Solidarity, 21–22, 39
Soltis, Jonas, 53–55
Specific intellectuals, 25–26
Spiritual emergency, 117
Spirituality: Freire as spiritual guide, 146; Freire's failure to address connections between reason, emotion, and, 45; *Pedagogy of Indignation*, 14, 15–16
Stages model of conscientization, 124
Steiner, Rudolf, 34
Stillness, moments of, 154
Stipulative definition of literacy, 10, 52, 54, 55, 57

Structure: importance in educational dialogue, 38
Struggle: education as common struggle, common victory, 147; education as transformation through, 105–106, 117; multiculturality, 79–80
Struggle, liberation as process of, 35, 39, 43–44
Study: love of, 42–43
Submissiveness and yielding, 145

Talking books, 33, 108
Tao Te Ching: action and nonaction, 148–150; embodying wisdom of old age, 143; Freire-Lao Tzu connection, 146–148; Freirian thought and, 11–12, 141, 157–159; hiddenness of the way, 144–145; ignorance, happiness, and education, 153–157; knowledge and knowing, 150–153; translations, 142
Teachers: as learners, 26
Teachers As Cultural Workers (Freire), 38
Teacher-student relations, 6
Teaching: as act of love, 42; love for, 41–42; stipulative definition, 52
Technology and education, 14, 39–40
te Kanawa, Kiri, 26
Tenured Radicals (Kimball), 65
Text: contexts and, 72–73; love of, 42; reading the word and the world, 85. *See also* Reading; Writing
Theology of liberation: Gospels as a call for social action, 41
Theory-practice link in critical literacy, 84, 88–90
Third Way approaches, 27
Time constraints in curriculum planning, 90–93, 101–102
Tolerance: intellectual disposition, 20; love and, 21; *Pedagogy of Indignation*, 16; political correctness and, 74–75, 78

INDEX

Traditionalism: core curriculum, 83, 90; critical intellectual, 18
Transformationist view of education, 67–68, 116–118, 123–124

Uncertainty, 108–110, 118–119, 127, 134–135, 139, 153–154
Unconscious: Taoist knowing and not-knowing, 153. *See also* Consciousness
Unfinished beings, humans as, 35, 36
Unity in diversity, 21–22, 79, 80–81
Universal human ethic, 36
Universal intellectuals, 25
Universalism, 9, 23, 25, 26, 36
Urban community: liberating literacy, 62

Vanguardism, 9, 23, 146
Verbal knowing, 152–153
Violence, 15
Virtue ethics, 45
Voices, interplay of, 111–112. *See also* Dialogue

Way, the (Taoist thought), 144
Way of life, emotion and reason as, 33–34
We Make the Road by Walking (Freire), 80
Western Civilization courses, 83, 90
Wide learning, 150–151
Will, role in pedagogical goals, 14
Women: cultural burdens on men and women, 80; political correctness in education, 65; proper literacy, 61–62
Word and the world, reading, 10, 84–86, 85–88, 99, 103
World: consciousness and, 5
World, reading the, 85–86, 88
Writer's Diary, A (Dostoevsky), 110
Writing: essentialist definition, 55–56; reading the word and the world, 85–86; theory and practice of critical literacy, 89
Writing reality, 86

Yin/yang symbol, 144

Credits

The author and publisher gratefully acknowledge permission to reproduce material from the following sources.

Roberts, P., 1996. "Critical Literacy, Breadth of Perspective, and Universities: Applying Insights from Freire." *Studies in Higher Education* 21 (2): 149–163. Reprinted by permission of the publisher (Taylor & Francis Ltd, www.tandf.co.uk/journals).

Roberts, P. 1997. "Paulo Freire and Political Correctness." *Educational Philosophy and Theory* 29 (2): 83–101. Reprinted by permission of the editor and Wiley-Blackwell Publishers.

Roberts, P. 2005. "A Framework for Analysing Definitions of Literacy." *Educational Studies* 31 (1): 29–38. Reprinted by permission of the publisher (Taylor & Francis Ltd, www.tandf.co.uk/journals).

Roberts, P. 2005. "Freire and Dostoevsky: Uncertainty, Dialogue, and Transformation." The final, definitive version of this paper has been published in the *Journal of Transformative Education* 3 (1): 126–139, by SAGE Publications Ltd. All rights reserved. © 2005 Sage Publications. online. sagepub.com.

Roberts, P. 2005. "Pedagogy, Politics and Intellectual Life: Freire in the Age of the Market." *Policy Futures in Education* 3 (4): 446–458. Reprinted by permission of the editor.

Roberts, P. 2007. "Conscientisation in Castalia: A Freirean Reading of Hermann Hesse's *The Glass Bead Game*." *Studies in Philosophy and Education* 26 (6): 509–523. © Springer Science+Business Media B.V. 2007. Repinted with kind permission from Springer Science+Business Media.

Roberts, P. 2008. "Reason, Emotion, and Politics in the Work of Paulo Freire," in C. A. Torres and P. Noguera, eds., *Social Justice Education for Teachers: Paulo Freire and the Possible Dream*, 101–118. Rotterdam: Sense Publishers. Reprinted by permission of Sense Publishers.

About the Author

Peter Roberts is Professor of Education at the University of Canterbury in New Zealand. Prior to taking up his current appointment, he served for thirteen years at the University of Auckland and seven years at the University of Waikato. His primary areas of scholarship are philosophy of education and educational policy studies. His research interests include the ethics and politics of education, literature and education, the work of Paulo Freire, and tertiary education policy.

Professor Roberts has published widely in international journals. His work has appeared in the *British Journal of Educational Studies*, the *Oxford Review of Education*, the *Cambridge Journal of Education*, *Educational Theory*, the *Journal of Philosophy of Education*, *Studies in Philosophy and Education*, *Educational Philosophy and Theory*, the *Journal of Moral Education*, the *Journal of Transformative Education*, *Studies in Higher Education*, the *International Review of Education*, the *International Journal of Lifelong Education*, and many other journals. His books include *Education, Literacy, and Humanization* (Westport, CT: Bergin and Garvey, 2000), *Digital Developments in Higher Education* (edited with Mark Chambers, Cambridge, UK: Taylor Graham Publishing, 2001), and *Neoliberalism, Higher Education and Research* (with Michael Peters, Rotterdam: Sense Publishers, 2008), among others.

Professor Roberts is an associate editor, consulting editor, or member of an editorial board or advisory panel for ten international journals, and reviews for many others. In the past, he has served on the executive board of the Philosophy of Education Society of Australasia (PESA) and the Council of the Humanities Society of New Zealand. In 2008 he was made a Fellow of PESA in recognition of his "outstanding service to the Society and to the discipline of Philosophy of Education."